THE AMERICAN IDEA

THE AMERICAN IDEA

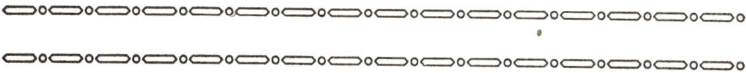

EUGENE T. ADAMS

CHARLES R. WILSON   ALFRED KRAKUSIN
ALBERT H. GARRETSON   JOHN B. HOBEN
THOMAS H. ROBINSON   GEORGE E. SCHLESSER
SIDNEY J. FRENCH   HOWARD B. JEFFERSON

Essay Index Reprint Series

BOOKS FOR LIBRARIES PRESS
FREEPORT, NEW YORK

College Library, Wayne, Nebr.

Copyright © 1942 by Harper & Brothers
All rights reserved

Reprinted 1970 by arrangement with
Harper & Row, Publishers, Inc.

INTERNATIONAL STANDARD BOOK NUMBER:
0-8369-1820-7

LIBRARY OF CONGRESS CATALOG CARD NUMBER:
73-117747

PRINTED IN THE UNITED STATES OF AMERICA

CONTENTS

Introduction, by Eugene T. Adams 1
1. The Historical Background of American Political Democracy, by Charles R. Wilson 8
2. American Democracy and American Government, by Albert H. Garretson 46
3. Democracy in the American Economy, by Thomas H. Robinson 64
4. The Spirit of American Science, by Sidney J. French 94
5. The Spirit of American Art, by Alfred Krakusin . 120
6. The Spirit of Modern American Literature, by John B. Hoben 153
7. Education in American Democracy, by George E. Schlesser 181
8. The Spirit of American Religion, by Howard B. Jefferson 204
9. The Spirit of American Philosophy, by Eugene T. Adams 233
Postscript: On Some Enemies of Democracy, by Eugene T. Adams 262
Bibliography 267
Index 271

THE AMERICAN IDEA

INTRODUCTION

What is the trouble with most of us? Year after year the majority of young men go out into the world without a very deep faith and conviction in the democratic way of life. It is time for us to catch the spirit of America, yes, the spirit of its past, of its destiny, together with the spirit of its culture, its psychology and its philosophy. . . . We can renew faith only by going beyond the transitory trappings of the American epic to the very heart and soul of our country. . . . Our way of life, with all its shortcomings, seems pretty sound to me, and I believe it is time for all of us to begin to get selfconscious about its positive values.[1]

In the beginning we, as a nation, set up housekeeping with borrowed furniture. Our philosophy, our literature and art, our economic outlook, were borrowed along with our citizenry. Slowly, more slowly in the cultural realm than one might imagine, we came of age and learned to stand on our own feet. We learned to sing our own songs, to search our own soul in literature and art, and to recognize our own geniuses.

The story of how America achieved the self-reliance that Emerson and others sought for her is one of the main themes of the present volume. We are especially concerned to show how these achievements are related to the democratic background from which they sprang. It is an unfinished story, for we are still coming of age in many respects, but native characteristics have emerged. "What so proudly we hail" is not merely a flag, but the achievements for which it stands, and the future which those achievements portend. To get a

[1] From a letter by William Travers Jerome III.

healthy appreciation of our native achievements is not to become narrowly nationalistic in our outlook. It is merely the first step toward self-understanding, and this is a necessary step toward understanding our role in the history of civilization.

The trouble with most of us is that we take our American citizenship for granted as much as we do our health. Its full meaning is seldom brought home to us. Let disease run epidemic around us or let us suffer enough from some acute illness, and we begin to sense what good health really means. Similarly, we become self-conscious American citizens chiefly when the threat of foreign "isms" has reached the epidemic stage or when we have been exposed to the inconveniences of other ways of living. Anyone who has spent some time abroad and felt the comforting strength of an American passport has doubtless experienced a heightened sense of the value of his citizenship. The face-on view of the Statue of Liberty is the best view.

One of the most widely heralded aspects of our life is its essential democracy, and surely this is one of our greatest achievements. Yet we are far from perfect in our handling of it. Too often we pay our respects to it with praise rather than practice. The trouble is that, as a word, it evokes a favorable emotional response (it's what might be called a "good" word) and so is often used to cloak all sorts of undemocratic behavior. If we really care about understanding democracy, instead of simply bragging about it, we must look for its *specific* expression in the different avenues of our daily life. Are science, art, philosophy, literature, education, and religion different in this country because they spring from a democratic background? Have we carried democracy into our economic processes? Have we achieved true political democracy? These are questions worth considering because it is only in terms of specific consequences that we can measure the value of those general terms which we dwell on with so much satisfaction — and with so little understanding.

Introduction

National characters develop in much the same way as personal ones. Both are the result of the interplay of many forces, and dominant traits slowly emerge which differentiate one character from another. Our national selfhood cannot be understood apart from our national history any more than an individual self can be understood apart from the background which produced it. Consequently, the first chapter in the present volume is given over to a historical sketch of the development of our political democracy. It indicates that history is not merely a series of epitaphs for departed things but that it is continuous with the present, and entirely dynamic in its unfolding.

The one certain lesson of history is that people must adapt themselves to change, or die. The ultra-conservative is simply a person with too much past in him; paradoxically enough, for all the past that he has in him, he fails to understand the dynamic character of the past itself. The ultra-radical, on the other hand, is simply a person whose Utopian dreams show too great a disdain of the past. He wants to get "there" without ever having been "here," and so jumps into the future with utter disregard of things that went before. To develop a historical sense is to develop a sense of perspective. Hence the value of an introductory chapter on American history.

But things are a little like Irishmen — they can be understood in more than one way. Besides knowing their history it is important to consider the developed structure of the institutions that any culture has produced. Consequently, the second chapter provides an account of our governmental structure as it actually works today. Federalism is an American achievement, and our chief contribution to the science of government. How it works, what modifications it has required, and the difficulties which it encounters are important topics of consideration for those who would catch the spirit of our country in the political realm.

The third chapter concerns itself with the working of our

economic system as contrasted with those in non-democratic countries. An interesting parallel between political and economic democracy emerges in the course of this discussion. Let unrestrained monopoly appear in either realm, and democracy ceases to function. Here is another reminder that it is only in terms of the specific application of the democratic principle that the real values of democracy can be found. We can talk about it all we want to, but if we don't apply it in particular instances we might as well use any other label. This chapter congratulates us, too, on our foresight in arranging to be born in a country so richly endowed with natural resources. The economic system which can exploit these resources to the greatest advantage to the greatest number of our citizens is destined to prevail in the long run. A good argument is presented for the case that a really free form of exchange of goods is most likely to serve this end.

Both governments and economic systems are merely means to furthering people's welfare, but this welfare itself is expressed in other than political or economic ways. A nation is rich in terms of its science, art, literature, education, religion and philosophy, as well as in terms of its material goods. The remaining chapters discuss the contributions which America has made in each of these several fields.

Science and democracy may not be mutually dependent, but they are not unrelated, for freedom of inquiry is the presupposition of successful science any time or any place; and democracy provides that freedom. A science dictated by political necessities is likely to be practical only in a shortsighted way. We have all witnessed the degradation of learning in Germany because of political interference. America has become the new home of many able German scholars who were forced to leave their country for purely political reasons. Science is essentially non-nationalistic but it requires the air of freedom in order to live.

In the realm of painting, the typical American outlook has been what is usually described as "realistic," an attitude that

Introduction 5

was prompted more by reason of frontier developments than by any political influence. Yet it is not hard to see that genuine art can thrive only in a background of freedom, where it need not be prostituted to propaganda purposes. This chapter illustrates very nicely our contention that culturally we came of age rather slowly. Conscious imitation of Old World art forms has prevailed in many quarters; however, the chapter deals with those Americans who have declared their intellectual independence and made sincerity their motto.

In literature we have made great strides in utilizing our native subject matter. Emerson could declare that we had not yet produced a single authentic voice. This deficiency has been amply overcome since then. American poets, novelists, and dramatists have produced a body of literature which is likely to endure as long as people read. If our literature must ever cease being realistic and critical because of political considerations we shall have entered the twilight zone of civilization. The chapter on this subject is a well-documented piece of evidence that literature must not necessarily be alien in order to assume classic proportions.

The next chapter has to do with our American educational system and its relation to the democracy which produced it. Perhaps in no other realm has our country taken so commanding a lead in cultural attainment. Universal education is a prime requirement if democracy is to work well. When everyone votes, it is important that everyone have enough knowledge to vote as wisely as possible. The story of how we progressed from relatively undemocratic educational procedures to more and more democratic ones is not only an interesting piece of history but a reality, the social significance of which is beyond conception. Abuses that thrive on ignorance can be dispelled only by knowledge, a knowledge whose source and guardian is a school system that reaches out to everyone able and willing to learn.

Art, literature, and education are essentially creations of

the spirit, but the highest aspirations of the human spirit are doubtless expressed in the various religious forms which human beings have developed. Characteristically enough, democratic America, with a jealous regard for individual liberties expressed in the Bill of Rights, has proved herself hospitable to innumerable manifestations of the religious impulse. Liberty for all has necessarily meant the development of a spirit of tolerance toward the right of others to disagree with us. The chapter which deals with the growth of religious institutions in America provides a clear analysis of the dependence of this principle of tolerance upon the democratic background in which it grew. It also provides further illustrations of the idea that we have learned to stand on our own feet, for originally an Old World intolerance dominated the religious outlook.

The final chapter shows that, after many years of living in the intellectual atmosphere of other lands, America has produced a native philosophy. Pragmatism — for that is the name most commonly applied to this philosophy — is essentially democratic. It insists that truth is subject to no monopolies and is best achieved in the open market of ideas, where free criticism and continuous experimentation become the criteria for determining which beliefs are best. It renounces all absolutes. If any one man were infallible and altogether good, as well as all-powerful, democracy might well give way to autocracy. Until such a person is found, democracy offers not only the most flexible political philosophy but the one most likely to be right in the long run.

This introduction does not attempt to summarize the content of the various chapters. They are largely interpretative and represent the best opinions of the men who specialize in the fields considered. One cannot even claim that, taken together, they are completely unified or that they provide anything like an exhaustive account of the spirit of American democracy. They should, however, invite attention to some

Introduction 7

of the more outstanding manifestations of it. Appreciative and critical attention to the values we have achieved is our only guarantee against indifference, the paralyzing indifference which can result from a lack of self-reliance on the one hand, or a smug complacency on the other.

CHAPTER 1

THE HISTORICAL BACKGROUND OF AMERICAN POLITICAL DEMOCRACY

by Charles R. Wilson

Some years ago a disillusioned armchair philosopher blurted out that a fool is a person who believes in democracy, sound business methods, and romance. Today there are those who would agree with him. But millions of others, whatever their frustration in love and business, will deny vehemently that democracy is nothing but a will-o'-the-wisp. Significantly enough, these are the plain people who have lived under a system of genuine self-government and who have horse sense enough to know when they are well off.

This is not to deny that in practice democracy has never lived up completely to the ideals from which it sprang. It has creaked and groaned in operation. It has revealed a seamy side and shabby spots. It has sometimes seemed too weak to protect itself from the iron-fisted attacks of ideologies which cannot exist in the same clime. But its very nature supplies it with a virtually inexhaustible source of latent power that has enabled it to cope with the almost overwhelming odds its own defects have occasionally turned against it. With all its shortcomings, it has offered the average man a larger amount of personal freedom, and greater opportunities to make the most of his talents, than any other system of government in the entire sweep of history. The man in the street, on whose shoulders, in the final analysis, all the institutions of civilization rest, has had a stake in it too valuable to

Historical Background of American Political Democracy

surrender. Possessed as he is of a persistent and almost divine determination to live his life as he himself sees fit, he has turned history into the obituary column of despotisms, with a new edition ever ready to go to press.

Even despairing liberals who point out that the war for human freedom has never been won must admit that crucial battles have been. Subjugated peoples have fought for generations and even centuries to free themselves from the self-assumed superiority of a conquering horde. With independence achieved, they have continued the struggle against attacks from within for a decent chance to rise above the level of animals. It is futile to deny that there has been progress. Whatever eddies there may have been, this is the main current in history, and there is nothing in present world conditions to indicate that the stream will be permanently forced out of its banks.

Analysts can easily collect "evidence" which seems to demonstrate that totalitarianism is the "wave of the future." But unless man has changed in his essential nature and the principle of historical continuity is a myth, such a judgment is more nearly a wave of intellectual bilge water. Far from being the wave of the future, totalitarianism is the contaminating seepage of the past. The true wave of the future is the revision and readjustment of democratic processes, so as to preclude the possibility of a plunge into the murky waters of medievalism by rabble-rousing paranoiacs who use the maladjustments of democracy as a springboard. Fortunately, democracy, like the Constitution of the United States, is general enough in its implications to permit adjustments of various kinds without destruction of its essential fabric. And in this fact lies the great hope for civilization as we know it.

Because democracy has meant different things to different people at different times, the American brand today not only differs in some respects from what it was in the past, but is unique in many ways compared with that in other nations.

Nevertheless, it is fundamentally similar to both. The basic assumption of American democracy has always been that the equality of man and the dignity of the individual are sacred. As Jefferson expressed it, "We hold these truths to be self-evident, that all men are created equal, [and] that they are endowed by their Creator with certain unalienable Rights."

Stemming from this fundamental assumption are the principles that have constituted the essential framework of political democracy in America. The first is that, with reasonable exceptions, all who submit to government have an equal right to share in its exercise. This is, of course, the "consent of the governed" principle which was laid down in the Declaration of Independence and which is accepted today as a truism. In 1776, however, it was only a pious hope. Actually it embodied the crux of a protracted struggle over the extension of the franchise which had begun long before the Declaration was penned and which was to continue long after the Jeffersonian sentiments had become the crescendo point in Fourth of July orations. Fought on many fronts — property qualifications, religious tests, "race, color, and previous condition of servitude" — the battle was not won, even as to the letter of the law, until 1920, when woman suffrage was written into the federal Constitution.

The second principle underlying American democracy is that the ultimate objective of government is to secure the greatest good for the greatest number of people. As expressed in the Declaration of Independence, this consisted of a guarantee of equal opportunity for life, liberty, and the pursuit of happiness. But this principle dragged into the open a seemingly irreconcilable conflict between human rights and property rights. Like the argument over the franchise, it had preceded the Declaration and was to continue far into the future. The Constitution of the United States, which in some respects represented a reaction from the idealism of the Declaration, threw it into bold relief. Changing the Jeffersonian phraseology back into the words of John Locke from

Historical Background of American Political Democracy 11

whom it was borrowed, the Constitution bespoke the protection of life, liberty, and property, with no indication of whether the emphasis was to be ascending or descending. Consequently, much of the constitutional theory in subsequent years was to consist of hair-splitting legalisms aimed at support of one or the other of the conflicting interests. As a matter of fact, political processes from the seventeenth to the twentieth century were dominated by the struggle.

The third principle in American democracy is the right of revolution. This embraces something of a contradiction, for the right of revolution clashes with the generally acknowledged right of an established government to protect itself against violence. The difficulty is resolved, however, by the faith that in a democratic system the government itself can never oppress. Only a particular administration may attempt to destroy the rights of the people. Consequently, every individual has an equal right of revolution against an administration so long as he does not aim at the subversion of the essential governmental system. Periodic epidemics of broken heads and bloody noses are averted by the common-sense recognition that revolution against an administration is better expressed by ballots than by bullets — through regular constitutional channels rather than through armed force. But if the administration will not recognize constitutional principles and all other avenues are blocked, the right of the people to use force without committing treason is an integral part of the American democratic theory.

So far, the general outlines of democracy in America square with those in other democratic nations. Actually, they represent a part of the "borrowed furniture" with which America set up housekeeping. Influenced by the peculiarities of their own history, however, the Americans developed special methods for putting their democracy into operation. Some of these were unique. Others are distinguished for the singular faith placed in them by America. But all of them, together with the "borrowed furniture" which they upholster, represent "What so proudly we hail" in American political democracy.

Inasmuch as these special methods were worked out the hard way and because, on the whole, they have given satisfactory results, Americans have tended to make fetishes of them. In what has sometimes approximated unreasoning devotion, we have frequently assumed that our methods are not only the best, but perhaps even the only way of securing real democracy. The truth is, however, that democracy is a principle and not a form. Seemingly valid forms may, on occasion, hamper it. On the other hand, it may express itself in spite of forms. Its vehicles are numerous and diverse. No nation has a monopoly on them. To analyze in this light the special methods the Americans have utilized is not to criticize them. It is rather to illuminate the processes of democracy in America.

Republicanism of the president-congress type is one of the special methods to which Americans are particularly attached. Their abiding faith in the essential democracy of the presidential system is a product of the fact that their independence was wrested from a monarchical England. But the truth is, of course, that democracy is determined not by who reigns but by who rules, and that by such a test monarchies may be even more democratic than presidential-republics. The government of England might be cited as a case in point. But from their birth as a nation, Americans have insisted upon making democracy and presidential-republicanism synonymous in their thinking. Frequently their inability to distinguish between the substance and the form of democracy has been extremely costly to them.

Written constitutions are another American attachment. The belief that they are the only iron-clad guarantee of self-government finds its origin in the fact that the constitutional argument against England prior to the Revolution was based in part upon written charters. It has culminated in forty-nine written constitutions in current American political life. Despite the common-sense principle that good faith is never injured by being reduced to writing, the experience of England has demonstrated that democratic processes may sometimes be even more fully safeguarded under an unwritten than under a written constitution. No one can deny that a written constitution has advantages. But it is not foolproof. Until it is amended, which is ordinarily a long and involved process, it may easily thwart rather than advance the public welfare. The crimes that have been committed against American democracy in the name of "constitutionality" are legion.

Place representation is still another American fetish. There is general agreement that if representation is to be truly democratic, representatives must be residents of the districts for which they speak. Like the others, this is a product of the revolutionary struggle against England. British statesmen argued that the colonies needed no American representation as such in Parliament inasmuch as they were "virtually" represented, as commoners, by the commoners of England. But "virtual" representation, in this particular instance, permitted the commoners of England to pass laws binding in America but not applicable to themselves. This patent injustice blinded the Americans to any possible validity of such representation under a governmental structure in which all persons would be equally subject to the laws. The net result was to obscure the fact that if a representative is directly responsible to his constituency, residence has little real relationship to democracy. A good representative living outside his district is infinitely preferable to a bad one living within it.

Fixed and regular elections are likewise considered indispensable to the American democratic process. Largely a reaction to English experience in the seventeenth century, this attitude has caused Americans to become oblivious of the fact that there are disadvantages as well as advantages to such a system. The advisability of a legally imposed election within some reasonable period of time cannot be doubted. But calendar regularity in elections has no necessary connection with either their need or their significance. Consequently, the formal, mathematical nature of the American system creates a situation in which there are frequently elections without issues, and, just as frequently, issues going stale for the want of an election. On the basis of issues, which are the food democracy feeds upon, there are times when many elections should be held during a given biennium, and others when a calendar-dictated canvass is totally superfluous.

The separation of powers within the government, between the legislative, executive, and judicial branches, is also highly regarded by Americans as a democratic device. Its roots run back to colonial experience, when it was used to hamstring royal and proprietary governors in the interests of autonomy. The fact is, however, that in any showdown the separation of powers is largely a fiction. Someone must have the final say in every government. In England, it is frankly a majority in the House of Commons. In the United States, it is potentially a two-thirds majority of Congress, against which, properly directed, no one in the government can prevail. In practice, however, that branch of the American government which at any given time has the strongest will is likely to be ascendant. There have been instances in which strong-minded Presidents have browbeaten both Court and Congress. There have been instances in which the Court has defied both President and Congress. There have been other instances in which Congress has cracked its whip over both President and Court. If by chance the ascendant branch happens to be the one farthest removed from the people, democracy suffers rather than benefits from what has proved to be the shifting rather than the partition of authority in government.

The division of power between the central and the state governments is another fundamental feature in American democratic practice. Its origin is to be found in the particularistic spirit which was the spearhead of the revolutionary movement against England. It was written into the Constitu-

Historical Background of American Political Democracy 15

tion as a result of the determination of the thirteen states not to submit to any "outside" interference with their internal affairs. But like the other peculiarly American modes of action, it is not the only satisfactory formula, and it is not an absolute guarantee of democracy. It is based, of course, upon the belief that division of power enables the people of a state to protect themselves against the excesses of an unwise or corrupt national government. But it largely ignores the fact that such a division likewise prevents the people of the United States from protecting themselves against the corruption or folly of a state in matters which technically are local but which frequently have national repercussions. In England there is no division between the local and the central governments. Even in the American states there is no division between the state and the county governments. Yet there is no indication (except, perhaps, in the grievances of such cities as New York and Chicago against the remainder of their states) that democracy has been seriously imperiled.

But what has been the story of political democracy in America? How did the American democracy come to be what it is today? What are the great milestones which mark its progress? Broadly speaking, the American story is merely one phase of the general evolution of democracy from ancient times to the present. It can, however, be isolated without too much distortion, and with some practical advantage.

The development of American democracy has consisted essentially of four major steps. The first, coming in the colonial period, was to secure for the settlers on the ground an actual share in their own government. The second, representing the crux of the revolutionary and constitutional periods, was to institutionalize self-government in America. The third, which was a protracted matter, was to extend political privilege to include not merely the few who originally secured it, but the many who made autonomy worth while. The fourth was to set in operation governmental techniques by which democracy, which fell short of Utopia even after the franchise had been extended, could be made significant. These are the warp and woof of American political history from the earliest time to the present day. They overlap from time to time, but on the whole they represent successive steps in the march of democracy.

Generally speaking, the British colonies in America were founded under a charter system in which an individual, a group, or a corporation was given an extensive grant of land and authority by the crown. All the colonies, except New Hampshire, had charters at one time or another. As the result of a trend which increased in tempo during the eighteenth century, however, all but five had become royal by 1776. In any case, throughout the colonial period the proprietor, the corporation, or the crown, as the case might be, had endeavored to protect its interests through the power of choosing a governor and a governor's council to rule in America. In the two-house legislative system that eventually developed, the governor's council became the senate, or upper house.

The first step in the development of American democracy was taken when the colonists secured the right to share in their government by sending representatives to what was to become the lower house of the colonial legislatures. This was the entering wedge to the autonomy which in turn seemed to be the prerequisite to an even fuller democracy. The process by which representation was secured differed from colony to colony. In Virginia, where it made its initial appearance, it came to the settlers as the gift of the Virginia Company of London. Prior to 1619, no colonial people — whether Spanish, French, or British — had any say on the way they were governed. But in that year a group of liberals, headed by Sir Edwin Sandys, were in temporary control of the Virginia Company. On their orders, two "burgesses" representing each of the eleven settlements in the colony were invited to meet with the governor and his council to participate in making local regulations with the effect of law.

Historical Background of American Political Democracy 17

In this fashion the first representative assembly on American soil came into being.

It was in Massachusetts, however, that the true outline of the American system of self-government — a governor, a lieutenant governor, a senate, and a house of representatives — first emerged. This came about when the charter of the Massachusetts Bay Company was transferred (1629–1630) to America and made the constitution of the colony. In this fashion the organization of a business corporation became the government of a colony.

According to the charter, control of the company was to rest in the hands of the "freemen" of the company (stockholders), who were to meet four times a year in general court (quarterly meetings of the stockholders), and pass by-laws governing the activities of the company. Annually they were to elect from their own number a governor (president of the corporation), deputy governor (vice-president), and eighteen "assistants" (board of directors). As time went on, the number of "freemen" increased, making for a larger enfranchised group within the colony. But the enfranchised group found it inconvenient to attend the general court meetings, and began to send representatives from the various towns to act for them. In this way they converted the general court into a representative assembly which was to become the lower house in a two-house legislature. The freemen, however, retained the right to elect the governor and legislators in both houses of the assembly, and in consequence had considerably more control over their government than did the Virginians.

In the other colonies, representative government came about through the creative initiative of the settlers (later recognized in charters), as in Connecticut and Rhode Island; by original charter provisions, as in Maryland, the Carolinas, and Pennsylvania; and by special dispensation of the individual proprietors and even the king as they realized the necessity of falling in line with the trend of the times if their colonies were to compete for settlers on equal terms with the others.

As was perhaps to be expected, the boon of representation started the colonies along the path which led to virtual autonomy within the empire. Gradually the colonial legislatures succeeded in establishing their authority over all those matters — internal, domestic, and local — which might be lumped together as intra-colonial affairs. The struggle was a long one in which the colonies used their control over appropriations, together with the legal technicalities possible under the British system, against both royal and proprietary agents. At the same time, however, they conceded that for reasons of expediency and convenience, if nothing else, the external, general, and intercolonial affairs — those which were common rather than peculiar to the individual colonies — were the province of the English government. Such matters as education, religion, internal improvements, marriage, and divorce were best left to the colonies to handle as they saw fit. But war and peace, regulation of trade, administration of the postal system, negotiation of treaties, supervision of the Indians, and control of the public lands were more logically administered by the mother country.

Without plan on anyone's part, therefore, and without much appreciation of its significance, a loose federal system had developed within the empire by 1763. Providing a relatively clear-cut division of power between the central authority represented by Parliament and the local authority represented by the colonial legislatures, it was neither institutionalized nor perfected. But it was essentially workable if left alone. British statesmen of the period, however, were more concerned with the theoretical nature of the empire than with the actual practical aspects. They seemed never to doubt that Parliament was supreme over the colonial legislatures in all matters whatsoever. Local authority, in their opinion, was a matter of sufferance and not of right; at any moment Parliament could intervene with legislation on any

Historical Background of American Political Democracy 19

matter under the sun, and this would be quite as binding on the colonists as on the inhabitants of Britain.

To the colonists, however, their connection with the empire was a personal union through the crown. While they were willing to recognize the supremacy of the king, they conceded nothing by way of right to Parliament. Viewing each legislature as a little Parliament in its particular colony, they insisted that it was on a par, so far as authority was concerned, with the Parliament of England. Except for the general legislation the colonies had permitted Parliament as a matter of convenience, the chief difference between the Parliament at Westminster and the Virginia legislature, for example, was that their respective laws were binding upon people of two entirely different localities. It would be quite as preposterous for Parliament to legislate upon matters peculiar to Virginia as it would be for the Virginia assembly to legislate on domestic matters in England. On this theoretical divergence, with the actual fact of a working federalism vainly crying for recognition, the British Empire was disrupted.

But autonomy within the empire was only one step toward democracy. In spite of the fact that the colonies had achieved a large degree of self-rule, they did not boast much real democracy. In all of them there were distinct class gradations. The upper classes, consisting of wealthy merchants in the north, large planters in the south, the royal and proprietary officials, the ministry of the established churches, and those who by one means or another had achieved financial independence, had the political situation under rigid control. Religious restrictions, property qualifications, and other limitations excluded the rank and file of the seaboard settlements from both voting and officeholding. Other discriminatory measures made for an even greater degree of aristocracy. Thus in many colonies primogeniture and entail, twin relics of feudalism, perpetuated medieval practices in America and prevented the break-up of the large estates which nurtured aristocracy. Even slavery existed from Massachusetts to Georgia when Jefferson was asserting that all men are created equal.

The closest approach to democracy in colonial America was to be found in the back country of the colonies — the frontier — that region which, north to south, had more in common, regardless of colonial lines, than did the frontier and the seaboard of the same colony. On the frontier, wherever it was to be found, wealth, family, and religion meant little. Every man stood on his own merits and had an equal opportunity to rise to a position of importance by demonstrating his worth to the community. But the frontier, representing a secondary stage of settlement, found itself discriminated against by the seaboard, which even in a short time had become a sectional vested interest.

Fearing that the developing strength of the back country would overturn the special privilege which was the foundation of the dominant aristocracy in the more settled regions, the eastern leaders resorted to the worst type of political skullduggery to keep it in leash. Frontier representation in the colonial legislatures was kept at a minimum by giving equal weight, regardless of population, to extremely small counties in the east and excessively large ones in the west. The tax system was also stacked against the back country. In some colonies, frontiersmen were required to support an established church in which they had no interest. Tax moneys were often squandered in the east instead of being allocated to provide the defense against the Indians and the internal improvements which the border settlements desired. Even a fair opportunity for justice was denied the back-country folk. Because of the size of the counties in the West, they frequently deemed it preferable to submit to injustice rather than spend the time and energy necessary for a long trip to the county seat where grievances had to be submitted to unsympathetic judges at fees payable by the plaintiff. The friction between the frontier and the seaboard over this type of practice had become a striking characteristic of American life long before the American Revolution.

With the democracy inherent in autonomy resting rather comfortably on a practical, working, relatively satisfactory federalistic system, it would have been quite possible to make the inevitable adjustment between the upper and lower crusts of American society within the British empire. But when the British government embarked upon a policy which seemed to threaten the carefully nurtured autonomy which even the conservatives of the colonies had come to cherish, the result was the revolt of America from the empire. Even more important, a frontal attack was made by the masses on the special privilege which had made the colonies High Tory outposts of the mother land. The American revolutionary struggle, then, embraced a revolution within a revolution. It was a two-edged sword aimed not merely at independence from England, but at the destruction of aristocracy in America. As Professor Carl Becker has expressed it, it was a struggle not merely for home rule, but for rule at home.

The military struggle between the Redcoats and the Patriots — the so-called Revolutionary War — was but a small, although extremely important, part of the American Revolution. While fighting continued from 1775 to 1781, the real revolution embraced the period from approximately the advent of the Grenville ministry in 1763 to at least the ratification of the Constitution in 1789. In the course of this greater American revolution, the independence which was achieved and the gains which were made for personal democracy told only part of the story. An American colonial policy fundamentally different from that of England was worked out, and the federal principle of government, which had slipped through the fingers of British statesmen, was formally institutionalized in the American Constitution.

The privileged class in America never wanted independence in the first place. They saw too clearly the domestic implications of the independence movement and understood that their dominant position would be threatened if the proponents of home rule were successful. Nevertheless, one important element of them, the merchant class, contributed materially, although entirely unwittingly, to the break-up of the empire.

In 1763, the British government concluded that the freedom of action enjoyed by the colonies did not contribute to the best interests of the empire. Consequently, it moved to tighten up its colonial administration. Among its intentions was the strict enforcement of Parliament-imposed regulations governing trade and navigation which, in accordance with accepted procedure, had been on the law books for decades but had become largely dead statutes through colonial disregard and British apathy. There was also the intention to tax the colonies for revenue; this not only had never previously been attempted, but also infringed upon what the colonial legislatures regarded as their own exclusive right.

The wealthy merchants, who had prospered during the period in which the Acts of Trade were not enforced, resented the new enforcement of old laws, and, aided by newspaper editors and lawyers who smarted under the imposition of a stamp tax, joined hands with the rank and file of the people in resisting the new policy. "No taxation without representation" became a popular slogan. Charter guarantees, the immemorial rights of Englishmen, and the compact theory of government, borrowed from John Locke's philosophical justification of the English revolution of 1688, were thrust forward as the bases of opposition. Taxation for revenue quickly came to symbolize arbitrary interference by Parliament with the internal affairs of the colonies.

But the merchants and their satellites had not intended that the colonies should strike for independence. They had too much of a stake in the established colonial order and the British commercial system. What they wished was merely a disturbance in America sufficiently jarring to cause the ministry to abandon the new policy and return to the easy-going days prior to 1763. As soon as this was done they intended

Historical Background of American Political Democracy 23

to sever their connection with the masses. But they were playing a dangerous game.

British policy, although not changing in principle, ebbed and flowed in application. When it seemed to ease, the merchants dropped their uneasy alliance with the mob, but when it bore down again, they encouraged agitation by the popular leaders. Each time the alliance was reestablished, however, they were drawn closer to the abyss of revolution. In 1774, after the Boston Tea Party and Britain's retaliatory Coercive Acts, they found themselves skidding along the brink and tried frantically to apply the brakes. But it was too late. The back-country element, recognizing in the movement against England a chance to redress the grievances they had labored under for decades, joined hands with the underprivileged of the seaboard to see to it that democracy in the form of both autonomy and the overthrow of aristocracy should prevail. When the Declaration of Independence asserted the right of revolution and the principle of the equality of man, it struck a responsive note in the hearts of both the frontiersmen and the unimportant people of the towns. Here was an opportunity to clean two Augean stables at once.

Even before independence was established in the Treaty of 1783, the initial gains for democracy had been made. They were not, however, all that Sons of Liberty might have desired. Beginning as early as January 1776 and continuing through 1780, the former colonies drafted the state constitutions which were to be the vehicles of their independence. But only Massachusetts and New Hampshire (in its second constitution) followed what has come to be regarded as the completely democratic mode of constitution-making. In these states alone, conventions, popularly elected for the specific job at hand, drafted their documents and submitted them to the people for ratification. Rhode Island and Connecticut simply modified their charters in minor details and retained them as full-fledged constitutions. In the other states, the legislatures, either with or without specific authorization, formulated the new constitutions. But only in Maryland, Pennsylvania, and Carolina were the people given an opportunity to pass judgment on the result.

In most instances, the state constituent bodies were rather completely dominated by the privileged, aristocratic classes. Consequently, the gains for democracy fell somewhat short of the promise embodied in the Declaration of Independence. While all the constitutions reflected the general influence of Jefferson's well-turned phrases, they all clung to the pre-revolutionary principle that only property-holders were qualified to participate in government. Every one restricted the franchise to property owners, renters of houses, or taxpayers. The requirements for officeholding varied from paying taxes in Pennsylvania to owning land or slaves of at least 1000 pounds' value in South Carolina. Most of the documents imposed religious tests of some kind as a condition of public preferment.

It is true that, in general, property qualifications were reduced, and that in the redistribution of land that was a part of the revolutionary movement such restrictions as were kept were not as discriminatory as previously. Yet the principle remained that government was the exclusive privilege of those who had a property stake in the community and an approved spiritual revelation. It is true that many of the pre-war aristocrats were forced to flee the country as a result of the revolution. But their places were taken by former underlings, who, after moving up a notch in the social scale, quickly adopted the identical exclusiveness they had previously condemned.

It is true that under the new constitutions the wings of the executive were clipped and the powers of the government were hedged in the interests of the people. But such limitations were more concerned with civil rights which had been threatened by England than with political rights which had been denied in colonial government. It is true that there were instances of reapportionment in the legislatures to give greater recognition to the back country. There were also instances of the disestablishment of the state church, of the abolition of primogeniture and entail, and even, by implication, of the abolition of slavery. But generally speaking, in the original thirteen states special privilege held on tenaciously in one form or another. With the possible exception of Pennsylvania, only the frontier state of Vermont, which maintained a separate existence from 1777 until its admission into the Union as the fourteenth state in 1791, boasted a constitution which paid more than elaborate lip-service to the principles of the Declaration.

Vermont, the home of the liberal, Ethan Allen, wrote into its fundamental law not only most of the best features of the other state constitutions, but some supplemental ideas of its own. It was the first state in American history to provide for universal manhood suffrage, the abolition of religious tests, and the emancipation of slaves. As a "western" state in its time, it heralded the liberal influences the West continued to contribute to American life in the future.

Taking everything into consideration, the revolutionary constitutions had made some progress toward democracy. But there was much more to be done. With all that was accomplished in even the remainder of the eighteenth century, the results of the Revolution represented a far cry from real democracy.

In spite of all the individual constitution-making the states undertook during the war-time period, none of them had ever intended to carry on in splendid isolation. Almost from the moment independence was declared, they had all looked forward to some kind of joint action to guarantee and institutionalize their collective autonomy. This determination brought them, however, face to face with the identical problem which had stumped British statesmen prior to the war. To Downing Street it had been a problem of imperial organization, the crux of which was the incorporation of political subdivisions into a general government in such a way as to maintain strong central authority without destroying local autonomy. Essentially it was the political aspect of the universal problem of the one and the many. In government, the possible extremes were overcentralization and excessive decentralization, with the ideal happy medium embodying the strength of complete union with the liberty of qualified self-expression.

Britain's mistake was that she failed to find the happy medium. With an almost perfected solution at hand in the practical relations which had developed between the colonies and the mother country, she had not recognized it. Consequently, she endeavored to meet the needs of empire by sacrificing autonomy to centralization — enhancing the one (the mother country) at the expense of the many (the colonies).

But as expressed in the Articles of Confederation, adopted in 1781, the first American attempt to solve the problem was not much more successful. If England's error was overcentralization, America's was too much decentralization. Understandably enough, the pendulum swung from one extreme to the other; whereas the British policy led to revolution, the American resulted in near anarchy. Like the British, the Americans had not seen the full implications of the embryonic federalism that was inherent in the British imperial system. They copied the rough division of power between the center and the parts, investing the Confederation Congress with authority over matters of general concern and retaining for the states authority over domestic questions. But this was only a superficial approach to the problem. In their reaction to the centralizing features in British policy after 1763, they gave the central government no power to enforce its will, and thereby created a system as weak as the British was strong. As one commentator has stated, the government of the Confederation was one of powers but no power.

The fact is that the sovereignty of the states was never surrendered under the Articles of Confederation. The relationship of the Confederation government to the states was

Historical Background of American Political Democracy 27

similar to that between the League of Nations and the national states of Europe. Based upon states rather than upon people, it could expect the measures it advocated to be carried out only if, when, and where the individual states saw fit to put them into effect. The British blunder had been to impose a unitary governmental system on the diverse parts of the empire. The American blunder was to expect the confederate, or league, principle to make unity out of avowed and acknowledged plurality.

But weak as it was, the Articles of Confederation contributed the inestimable service of holding the states together until a better plan of union could be devised. In the meantime, as the price of its adoption by all the states, it had brought about the cession to the central government of the "western lands" claimed in overlapping confusion by the individual states. The one great constructive work of the Confederation Congress was the adoption of the Ordinance of 1787 for the administration of this territory in accordance with democratic principles in so far as they had developed in practice.

Essentially, the unorganized lands in the west represented the "colonies" of the American government. In this sense, then, the Northwest Ordinance embraced the fundamentals of a distinctly American colonial policy. It is revealing in that it depicts the gains democracy had made and the limitations which still hampered it. It is important in that the liberal governmental principles of this Ordinance were extended to future continental areas as they were acquired. By such enlightened action, the government of the United States has been able to extend its authority gradually and, on the whole, peaceably over an area three million square miles in extent that embraces all kinds of differences, and yet maintain its unity. Without the common-sense provisions of the Ordinance of 1787, the territory now under a single flag almost certainly would have become completely Balkanized as the result of successive revolutions on the part of new communities against the domineering, exploitative, older ones that endeavored to hold them in leading strings.

Basic in the American policy was the principle that the colonies of the United States were not to be held in permanent subjection to the original states. As potential new states evolved out of the territories, they were to be admitted into the Union on a basis of perfect equality with the others. This merely recognized, of course, the validity of the autonomy principle for which the original states themselves had struggled against England. But its significance lies in the fact that it reveals the sincerity of the colonial case against the British empire, and the extent to which democracy in America was still identified with autonomy by those who were in the positions of power. The new "mother country" freely granted its colonies, as necessary features of a decent colonial existence, the liberty of action and the hope for the future it had fought to secure from its own "mother." But, as we shall see, it limited any further democracy to the *status quo* expressed in the revolutionary constitutions of the original states.

Even the representation, autonomy, and state equality which were granted by the Ordinance were extended only gradually. Three stages of government were provided for. The first was an arbitrary but temporary one. A governor, a secretary, and three judges, all appointed by Congress, jointly exercised the executive, legislative, and judicial powers. When the population of the territory reached five thousand free male inhabitants of full age, the first stage of government gave way to an intermediate one. In this, a limited degree of autonomy was permitted. A bicameral assembly in which the members of the lower house were elected by the qualified voters in the district took over the legislative functions. Congress still appointed the governor, but a non-voting delegate elected by the legislature in joint ballot became the territorial spokesman in Congress. When any district achieved a total population of sixty thousand free inhabitants, the third stage was reached. Under an enabling act of Congress, it was eligible to form a state constitution and be admitted into the Union on a basis of equality with the other states.

But the Northwest Ordinance contained few concessions to democracy itself. Democratic principles had to await action by the new states as they were formed. It is true that slavery was forever prohibited in the Northwest, that primogeniture was outlawed, and that a liberal bill of rights was attached to the Ordinance. But property qualifications for both voting and officeholding were also carefully written in. In fact, there was nothing to indicate that constitutions for the proposed new states would not be drafted by conventions based upon a property franchise. Similarly there was no guarantee that even if they were submitted to a referendum, more than a minority of the people would have an opportunity to express their will.

The enabling act for Ohio, however, passed by a Congress chosen at the time of the Jeffersonian "revolution" of 1800, helped somewhat. It provided that the Ohio convention should be chosen by male taxpayers of full age. Restrictive as this was, it was considerably more liberal than the custom in the states on the seaboard. The constitution adopted virtually swept away property qualifications for both voting and officeholding, but it was not submitted to the people for ratification. As subsequent western states included liberal franchise provisions in their constitutions, and as a wave of liberalism swept over the United States from the twenties on, the original thirteen states modified their constitutional requirements. Universal white manhood suffrage obtained generally by the early thirties. Decades later, the Fifteenth and Nineteenth Amendments to the federal Constitution finished the mopping-up process by at least legalizing Negro and woman suffrage in states which were adamant in their opposition.

In the meantime, the first steps had been taken to institutionalize the autonomy of the original states by forming the government of the United States. But the federal Constitution contributed little to the extension of democracy. The members of the convention which drafted it did not come fresh from the people. They were indirectly elected by state legislatures which had in turn been chosen under a restricted franchise. They represented the conservative, property-holding class. The West, the small farmers, and the mechanics in the towns were not represented at all. Both the personnel and the outlook of the Constitutional Convention differed from those of the Continental Congress which had adopted the Declaration of Independence. For the most part, the members frankly distrusted "the turbulence and follies of democracy." They were not selfishly gathered together to protect their individual interests, but they did tend to identify the interests of their class with the good of the country as a whole.

Perhaps their chief contribution was the fact that they solved the problem of imperial organization which had been so baffling to British statesmanship and to the architects of the Articles of Confederation. The key was found in a perfected federalism which recognized dual citizenship (national and state) for all persons, with some technical exceptions, who lived in the United States. The powers of government were carefully divided between the national and the state authorities, and each of these was to be supreme in its own sphere. Operating upon its own citizenry, each government was to enforce its will by means of its own law officers, its own courts, and even its own penal institutions, thereby eliminating an important source of friction.

Like those who had framed the state constitutions, the members of the federal convention intended to set up a government which was republican in form but which would not be in the control of the masses, who, as Alexander Hamilton phrased it, were turbulent and changing, rarely judging or determining anything rightly. The President of the United

Historical Background of American Political Democracy 31

States was to be chosen not by the people, but indirectly by special electors who were to be selected in any manner the state legislatures directed. The upper house of Congress was also removed from the direct control of the people by the provision that Senators should be elected by the state legislatures. Judges in the federal courts were to be nominated by the indirectly elected President and confirmed by the indirectly elected Senate. Only the House of Representatives was to be directly chosen by the people. But Representatives were to serve only two years, all leaving office at once; the indirectly elected Senators were to serve three times as long, with only one-third leaving office at a given time; the indirectly elected President was to serve four years; and the indirectly chosen judges were to serve for life. No property qualifications or religious tests were written into the Constitution. None needed to be. The franchise provision that voters for the only office that citizens were permitted to fill directly, the House, should have the same qualifications as voters for members of the most numerous branch of the state legislature automatically put into effect the franchise restrictions of the state constitutions. Probably the prohibition laid upon state action of certain kinds and the fact that there was no bill of rights in the original document have been overemphasized and misconstrued. But it is undeniable that in tone the Constitution of the United States was as inconsistent with the spirit of the Declaration of Independence as were the lip-service state constitutions of the revolutionary period.

This is not to deny that the Constitution was an inspired document for the purpose of maintaining orderly processes. Nor is there any escaping the fact that it set up a government which in comparison with that of other nations of the time was democratic beyond reproach. But the fact remains that the conservative influences in the United States had captured the revolutionary movement before it became unmanageable and had prevented its democratic implications from going to their logical conclusion in state, territory, and nation. That is why much remained to be done in the interests of democracy by way of interpretation of the Constitution and the development of democratic techniques in subsequent years.

When the Constitution was referred to the states for ratification, many of the former revolutionary leaders had serious doubts about it. Jefferson hoped that it would be adopted, but that enough states would oppose it to force the inclusion of a bill of rights. Sam Adams and John Hancock were won over to its support only with difficulty. Patrick Henry and Richard Henry Lee fought it to the bitter end. In general, the rank and file of the people were opposed to it. The back country in particular feared it. The fact is that in a straight-out referendum with universal manhood suffrage it probably would not have been adopted.

But ratification was carried out by state conventions elected, except in New York, under the usual franchise restrictions. Even so, the New Hampshire, Massachusetts, and Virginia conventions were so opposed at the time of their election that their support was very doubtful. North Carolina rejected the document outright, and Rhode Island failed even to call a convention. New York ratified only when the delegates departed from what was recognized to be the will of their constituents. Because of various reasons, probably not more than one-fourth of the adult American males voted for delegates to the ratifying conventions. A reliable estimate states that only about one-sixth of them actually favored ratification.

Perhaps the chief fear behind the opposition to the Constitution was that it created a powerful government which, falling into the hands of the vested interests, might be used to exploit the people. That this was a real danger became obvious before Washington left the Presidency. The Federalist party, representing the wealthy, conservative, aristocratic element of the country, put through a program which, with all its merits, seemed to have the interests of the few rather than of the many as its objective. With Hamilton as its high priest and an assumed superiority that was galling to the rank and file of the people, it advocated extreme centralization, "loose" construction of the Constitution, and governmental activity in behalf of business. But its actions in bond redemption, the creation of a privately controlled banking monopoly, the levying of a tariff that was protective in principle, and the imposition of an excise tax that fell heavily on the West seemed to the masses likely to deprive them of a large part of the liberty supposed to be inherent in self-government. Agriculture and labor, and the debtor group in general, clamored that they were being sacrificed to the selfish interests of commerce, industry, and finance. Because in the interests of the few it ignored the hopes and fears of the many, the Federalist party as a national political force died a sudden death.

Jefferson, taking up the cudgel for the plain people, led the fight against the Federalists in the earliest movement, under the Constitution, for greater democracy. It might almost be said that his demand was more for liberty — political, economic, religious, and intellectual — than for true democracy. Jefferson was no proponent of equality, except as equality of opportunity is implied in liberty. The essence of his particular brand of democracy was not greater participation in government, but greater personal liberty for the people through a minimum of government. The masses, after giving some evidence of responsibility, should have the ballot, not so much to control the government as to protect themselves against it. If they did not have some kind of checkrein, government would be manipulated by the shrewd and the strong, the unprincipled and the predatory. As a result, the liberties of the people would be destroyed and the wealth created by the producers of the nation misappropriated. But if the people had the power to control, they would sustain the equality of opportunity for everyone; and a great, free nation, making full use of its potentialities without let or hindrance, would forge ahead in genuine progress.

It should be noted, however, that Jefferson was not concerned with the laboring class of the towns. His was an agrarian and not an industrial democracy. A nation of free, independent, self-sufficient, landowning small farmers was the highest possible ideal. But a nation of penny-pinching mechanics and tradesmen, crowded into urban centers, squabbling and bickering among themselves, living the life of the damned, and dependent for their very living upon the uncertainties of business, was an offense to God.

Holding that government was a necessary evil, Jefferson believed that the extent of its authority should decline in proportion to its geographical removal from the people. Most governmental functions, in his opinion, were safest in the hands of local agencies. Therefore, the national government, remote as it was from the everyday life of the people, should exercise only a general police function. Rooted in this conception was not merely the state-rights principle which underlay Jeffersonian democracy, but the "strict" interpretation of the Constitution which Jefferson advocated. The powers of the federal government had been delegated and enumerated in the Constitution, and, by the Tenth Amendment, all other powers had been reserved to the states or the people of the states. Jefferson wanted no tyranny to emerge through enhancement of the central government's powers by means of Hamilton's "loose" construction theory.

Thus in the early days, when America was an essentially rural, agricultural nation, liberalism seemed best served by a minimum of government. Strict construction of the Constitution, state rights, laissez-faire, and rugged individualism were the key designs on the palladium of liberty. The undemocratic, privileged class were the friends of strong government, loose construction, the ignoring of state rights, regulatory interference, and unquestioning obedience to law. In time the Jeffersonian technique inevitably came to be identified with democracy itself, and the Hamiltonian technique with aristocracy. Fundamentally, however, it was what

Jefferson and Hamilton were seeking, and not how they sought it, that made one democratic and the other aristocratic. Ends and not means, substance and not forms, made for democracy or aristocracy. Conceivably the time might come, with a basic change in the nature of the country, when democracy could best be achieved by the use of Hamiltonian methods, and the Jeffersonian techniques would play completely into the hands of the conservatives. But that was not clear in 1800.

Jeffersonian democracy, in spite of the simplicity and informality that the President introduced into the government, did not bear much practical fruit. The so-called "Revolution of 1800" is something of an exaggeration. Jefferson himself found it necessary to renounce some of the principles he espoused, and it is difficult to find much of a break, except perhaps in emphasis, between the policies of Jefferson and of Adams. Centralization went on apace, loose construction of the Constitution was accepted by the President himself, and his political heirs placed the stamp of approval on the protective tariff, the national bank, and other hated Federalist projects. A "Virginia Dynasty" of Presidents bespoke the influence of an easy-going, landed gentry whose democracy was largely of the *noblesse oblige* variety. Their concessions to the old Federalist legislative program were the result of their belief that no great harm would be done their interests and of their disposition to be cooperative for political reasons. From their very philosophy of government, they could do little, except in a negative way, to make the government a people's government.

The great mass of the population in the settled regions of the country therefore found political democracy little advanced from what it had been immediately after the Revolution. Only in the West was democracy making much headway, and that, except for its relationship with the government's comparatively liberal land policy, had no connection with what was taking place in Washington.

As a matter of fact, the New West, together with the backcountry elements of the older states and the submerged elements in the cities, began in the 1820's to tire of the genteel democratic tradition expressed by the Virginia Dynasty. Monroe had no opponent for the Presidency in 1820, but by 1824 four candidates put in strong bids, and in 1828 Andrew Jackson was swept into the Presidency by an avalanche of votes from citizens who had only recently acquired the ballot. The common man, newly enfranchised by the rapidly increasing western states and by changes in the eastern state constitutions, had presumably come into his own. Once more conservatism had lost out through its own complacency and lack of imagination.

The election of 1828 was far more a political revolution than that of 1800. Of particular importance in this campaign was the fact that Jackson had succeeded in establishing a political combination of the West and the South against a new party which took over the old Federalist doctrines and spoke largely for the financial, commercial, and industrial interests of the Northeast. The western-southern political alliance was, generally speaking, to be the symbol of democracy and the key to political success from 1828 to 1860.

Jackson did not create Jacksonian democracy. He expressed it. His personality, his reputation, the legends which were connected with his name, rather than his dedication to a clearly thought-out political philosophy, made him the leader. The movement he eventually captured was already on the way when he galloped to the fore. It made *him*, rather than vice versa. Westward expansion, foreign immigration, a nascent labor movement in the cities, the general spirit of unrest and dissatisfaction with outworn shibboleths, the quickening of the public conscience, the seething cauldron of humanitarian reform, from all of which the movement stemmed, were the background and not the product of Jacksonian democracy.

Jackson himself was something of an opportunist. On the

Historical Background of American Political Democracy 37

major issues of the times he was likely to be all things to all men, particularly at election time. But fundamentally he hated monopoly and special privilege, as his attack on the national bank testified. Basic in his brand of democracy was the idea of more government. Unlike Jefferson, he had no fear of a strong central authority, at least so long as he exercised it. He believed in state rights, but he felt that he was the head of a nation and not a league of commonwealths. In his opinion, the President had a mandate from the people and should act vigorously in carrying it out. The Constitution should be interpreted liberally when it was to the interest of the common man, and strictly when it was not. The President's interpretation was every bit as valid as John Marshall's. The masses should have the ballot for the purpose of participating in the political process and bending the government to their will. Nor were they to be excluded from holding office. Jackson broke down the old governmental bureaucracy and for the first time admitted the rank and file to public positions on a large scale. The principle of rotation in office had his complete support, for he believed in the innate ability of the average man to handle satisfactorily any job tendered him. Under Jackson, the doctrine of equality was added to that of liberty.

But the Jacksonian democratic party, like that of Jefferson, gradually fell under conservative control. While the period of the roaring forties and the fuming fifties was one of great gains in social democracy — at least in part of the country — it was one of essential reaction in politics. The South, which earlier had half believed, or at least tolerated, the mild radicalism of Jefferson, had gone completely conservative. Under the driving influence of cotton production, it had become an aggressive, plantation-owning, staple-raising, slaveholding aristocracy, no longer apologetic for any feature in its life and no longer interested in democratic nonsense. In 1830 an attempt had been made in Virginia to stem the tide, but it had ended in failure. The new, militant South of the mid-century was a genuine vested interest of wealth, ability, and power.

Gaining complete ascendancy in the Democratic party, the South moved in to dominate the national government in a fashion that exceeded the wildest dreams of the Virginia Dynasty. Under its hard-driving leadership, the test of legislation was essentially its effect upon the South. Perhaps no one expected legislation in which the Northeast had an interest, such as the protective tariff, to be given much consideration. But a strain was put upon the allegiance of the West, which the South needed to maintain its dominance, when western interests were ignored. A homestead act, rapid organization of western territories into states, internal improvements at the expense of the national government, federal aid to agricultural and mechanical colleges, and a northern terminal for the proposed Pacific railroad, all of which represented western ambitions, were held off imperiously by the southern masters of the government. Their adamant attitude toward slavery extension likewise did them no good in a west which was willing to live and let live.

Unlike the Federalists, the new vested interest utilized the doctrine of state rights to protect its citadel. At the same time, working through the overweighted state influence in the Senate and the electoral college, it was able to maintain control in Washington long after the South had fallen behind the North in population. By 1860, the Northeast had become thoroughly industrialized and urbanized. Even the West, although predominantly rural and agricultural, had broken out into a rash of cities and industries. Taken altogether, the North far exceeded the South not only in population, but also in wealth and latent strength. But the planter minority, with its controlled Presidents, its effective check in the Senate, and its majority on the Supreme Court bench, continued to run the government in its own interests.

Like every other aristocratic, vested-interest group, however, the planter oligarchy overplayed its hand. In what

Historical Background of American Political Democracy 39

Charles A. Beard describes as the second American revolution, its minority control was smashed. Like the first American revolution, this powerful, metamorphosing movement did not consist of war alone. The second American revolution began not later than 1854, at the time of the Kansas-Nebraska Act, and continued at least until 1877, when the last of the Federal troops were withdrawn from the "reconstructed" southern states. The open break came in 1860, when the old southern-western political alliance was broken. A new northeastern-western alliance overthrew the southern domination of the government and placed Abraham Lincoln and the presumably liberal Republican party in power. As Beard points out, this was a revolution of the North against the South, and not of the South against the North. The South was in control. The North was on the outside looking in. But as a result of the election, the South was unhorsed and the North vaulted into the governmental saddle.

The Civil War, under this conception, was a sanguinary fight to see whether the revolution would stick. The South endeavored to escape the effects of the overturn by leaving the Union and setting up for itself. The North fought to realize the benefits of the new order by forcing the South to remain in the Union. Five years of destructive warfare plus the nightmare of Reconstruction completed the revolution. The power of the old, pre-war southern aristocracy was broken. The South itself went through a process of regeneration as slavery was destroyed, plantations were broken up, diversified agriculture was extended, and new industries began to appear. The old-time all-powerful Democratic party was for a time discredited and reduced to the position of a party of opposition. Apparently a new day had arrived for the common man.

It was not long, however, before it became evident that the Republican party had gone conservative. The financial and industrial interests of the Northeast slipped almost imperceptibly into control over it and made it the vehicle of their interests. Party leaders lost the common touch as they took their orders from the lords of a new economic feudal system. Mouthing democracy, they preached the doctrine of laissez-faire and hailed the virtues of rugged individualism and free competition. But the laissez-faire they wished was the absence of any control of business and of legislation favorable to any other economic group. Rugged individualism meant the right of ruthless exploitation. Free competition did not preclude the organization of huge business combines to blackjack helpless consumers through monopoly practice.

Whatever their preachments, however, the new masters actually stood for greater centralization of power and greater governmental activity where their interests were concerned. Protective tariffs, favorable banking legislation, contract immigration, subsidies to business, and crack-downs on state legislation inimical to their holdings represented their true desires. Only if strong central authority were used in the interests of the masses would they oppose it.

The average man gradually awoke to the fact that he had carried through the second American revolution only to supplant one vested interest with another. Particularly disillusioned was the West. By the end of Reconstruction, it had begun to feel that although it had won the war, it had somehow lost the peace. The breaking of the old western-southern political alliance no longer appeared to be the unmitigated good it had seemed in 1860. The farmers of the West seemed faced with peasantry unless something were done to save them. Western discontent was supplemented somewhat by unrest among the laboring men of the industrial East. Organizations of farmers on one hand and laborers on the other were undertaken to alleviate bad conditions by non-political action. But they were none too successful, for the farmers' organizations failed in their business enterprises and federal troops were called out to shoot down striking workmen. Panaceas and political nostrums of one kind or another, rang-

Historical Background of American Political Democracy 41

ing from greenbackism to the single tax, made their appearance, but got nowhere.

In the last decade of the century, the Populist or People's party, endeavoring to combine farmers and laboring men into a powerful instrument of political liberalism, forged to the front. The core of its program called for direct issuance by the government of money against crops as security, government ownership of the railroad, telegraph, and telephone systems of the country, and repossession by the government, in the interest of actual settlers, of all unused land monopolies. Subordinate demands included popular election of Senators, a graduated income tax, a postal savings system, immigration restriction, the initiative and referendum, and the Australian ballot. But the Populist party went down to defeat in 1892, as the farmers and the laborers demonstrated that they could not work together and the mass of the voters registered their distaste for third-party action. In the following election, William Jennings Bryan, running as a Democrat but bearing a modified Populist banner, was also overwhelmed. The industrial and financial leaders of the country, after the scare of their lives, succeeded in convincing the Northeast and the Middle West that his doctrines were socialistic.

Out of the welter of the late nineteenth century, however, one principle had emerged. In the new industrial day, the Jeffersonian principles of little government and state rights played directly into the hands of the vested interests. Strong central authority and increased governmental activity in the interests of the people as a whole — strict regulation of business and monopolies — collectivism rather than socialism — might bring about a degree of democracy such as the country had never known. Paradoxically, in this new day, the general Jeffersonian ends might best be achieved through the use of Hamiltonian means.

Already the doctrine of regulation had been grudgingly written into the law of the land by the Cullom Interstate

Commerce Act of 1887 and the Sherman Anti-Trust Act of 1890. The twentieth century brought the flowering of the collectivist principle. William McKinley, reelected in 1900 to carry on the nineteenth-century practices as completely as possible, gave way to Theodore Roosevelt. Roosevelt, although compromising with the "invisible government" of the nation, saw the truth that unrestrained laissez-faire and rugged individualism could result only in business overreaching itself and playing into the hands of genuine socialism, which the majority of Americans, even the underprivileged, did not want. Roosevelt felt keenly that business had to be saved from itself.

The practical achievements of the Roosevelt administrations were not great, but the President came to preach a doctrine of the New Nationalism. In essence this embraced a strong centralized government regulating business in the interests of the people and dedicated to a general program of social and economic democracy. Roosevelt's chief contribution was his agitation and education that paved the way for greater positive achievements on the part of successors who had fundamentally similar views. In 1912 he ruined the Republican party's hope that it could return to the days of McKinley. Heading the so-called Progressive party, which bolted the Republican organization when it refused to clean house and adopt liberal principles, he split the Republican vote in the election and permitted the election of Woodrow Wilson. There was no love lost between Roosevelt and Wilson at any time in their careers, but partisanship and personal animosity being discounted, their views were fundamentally similar.

Wilson's New Freedom, then, was out of the same mold as Roosevelt's New Nationalism. But Wilson was able to achieve greater results. With the Underwood Tariff, the Federal Reserve Act, the Clayton Anti-Trust Act, the Federal Trade Commission Act, the Federal Farm Loan Act, and the Adamson eight-hour-day railroad act, strong government

Historical Background of American Political Democracy 43

in the interests of the masses reached a pre-World War high. Once again the high-handed insolence of the vested interests had brought retribution.

For all practical purposes, the Wilsonian reforms came to an end in late 1916. Whether American entry into the war or the exhaustion of the Wilsonian program was the cause has not yet been determined. But the end of the war brought a period of disillusionment in which the forces of reaction were once more able to extend their influence over the people. The Harding-Coolidge-Hoover regime represented as complete a throw-back to the nineteenth century as can be conceived. It dovetailed perfectly with where McKinley had left off. For all practical purposes, there might as well have been no Roosevelt-Wilson era. Laissez-faire, except aid to business, and rugged individualism had a new heyday.

Such reaction could be supported as long as prosperity of a type continued in the country. But 1929 brought other conditions which were largely the product of a decade of shortsightedness on the part of business and the government it controlled. The Hoover administration could not bring itself to undertake strong measures of direct relief for a despairing people even in the midst of depression. It talked the language of Jefferson. Too much governmental action would destroy the liberties of the people.

In 1932, the people's penalty for disregard of all interests except those of the minority was imposed once more. In the most sweeping landslide American political history had yet witnessed, Franklin Roosevelt, with an appeal to the "Forgotten Man" and the promise of a "New Deal," overthrew the Republican regime and ushered in what has come to be known as the "Roosevelt Revolution." But the Roosevelt Revolution was revolutionary only as it is compared with what immediately preceded it. Basically, the New Deal merely carried on, although on a widely extended scale, the principles of the earlier New Nationalism and New Freedom.

Under the New Deal, the authority of the central government and the power of the Executive reached proportions never touched before. Recovery was a major objective, but reform permeated the whole program. The government engaged not merely in direct relief and the regulation of business, it went into business itself when that was deemed advisable. Acting upon the principle that prosperity could not be restored until purchasing power was rehabilitated, it undertook to "prime" the national economic pump. Money was to be forced into circulation and prices were to be forced up from depression depths. Increased incomes would presumably restore markets to something like normality. The government accordingly tinkered with the currency, embarked upon huge construction projects, loaned large sums of money, paid out virtual doles, adopted a pro-labor, pro-farm policy, and endeavored to win back the foreign markets which had been lost during the preceding decade. All along the line it sought the restoration of confidence. However, it lost the confidence of business almost entirely.

That the New Deal made mistakes was inevitable. In many phases of its activity it was frankly experimental. That it overreached itself is possible. The enormous power it exerted over business was interpreted by some as death to the ideal of reasonably free private enterprise, by others as a move toward socialism, and by still others as the preliminary to fascism. That it was dangerous to democracy is conceivable. It allied itself with some of the rottenest state and local political machines in the country. Gradually it became something of a machine itself as it welded a top-heavy bureaucracy and dependent groups throughout the country into the heavily obligated parts of a New Deal steam-roller. But that it was popular with the masses — for whatever reason — is undeniable.

The third election of Franklin Roosevelt in 1940 raised the question as to why he had run again. Was it the mere love of power? Was it that his program was not yet completed? Was it that he had failed to develop a satisfactory torch-bearer to succeed him? Was it that the new World War made it his duty to remain in harness? Or was it that he saw in the New Deal the great ideal which was needed to give point to the struggle of the "democratic" nations against totalitarianism? Was it that he saw that the war had created a situation in which the United States, under proper leadership, could secure the extension of New Deal principles to other nations in both Europe and Asia? What people, jaded with the recurrence of balance-of-power wars, could fail to fight to the last ditch for a genuinely democratic peace settlement which would promise the downtrodden of the earth a New Deal politically, economically, and socially at last?

CHAPTER 2

AMERICAN DEMOCRACY AND AMERICAN GOVERNMENT

by Albert H. Garretson

The present world crisis has made Americans aware of the fact that believers in democracy think of the United States as the place where democracy actually works. Some of them know, as many of us Americans know, that it does not work here as well as it should, that we are not entirely satisfied with the way it is applied from day to day. But they also know that we insist at all costs on not being interfered with in seeing to it that our democracy continues, and that we are resolved that it shall be steadily improved and extended. What is there about the experience of the United States with democracy that makes believers in democracy the world over watch us carefully in our experiment in self-government? Have we made any unique contributions to the practical effectiveness of the democratic ideal?

We have had great advantages. Most of our earliest citizens believed passionately in democracy; if ever the faith burned low in the hearts of some Americans, the true believers among us were always being reinforced by new disciples who had left the Old World to pledge their faith to the New World and its form of government.

Many of us match democracy in our minds with democratic public government. That is natural. We think of our constitutions, national and state, and of the structure of our public government as our democracy. And we are proud of

American Democracy and American Government 47

the great contributions that Americans have made to the art of democratic public government. But this is only part of the story. There is, after all, the whole field of private government. What have we done to make democratic government work in the church, in the family, in the business corporation, in the labor union, in the schools? These are sometimes awkward questions. But all believers in democracy know that the effort to make it work is a long, uphill struggle.

It is in the field of public constitutional government that we are most proud of our record with democracy; and we shall have to limit our discussion to this part of the problem. We have made democracy grow and we have made it work from day to day. We have discovered the necessary constitutional means, the necessary governmental organization. Now we stand ready to defend it against belittlement and against open attack, for we shall make it continue to grow and we shall make it continue to work in the changing circumstances of the present crisis.

The first chapter of this book discussed the nature of American democracy and discovered that it involved the acceptance of two principal ideas, the dignity of the individual citizen and his common participation in his government. In the present chapter we turn first to the fundamental problem of making democracy work in our public governments, federal, state, and local. It is the problem of setting up workable machinery that will enable the individual citizen to take part in deciding what the government shall do and what it shall not do. It is the problem of seeing to it that each of us shall be permitted to share in the making of governmental policies that may hurt or help us. Someone has said that most governments act on the "push the citizen and see if he hollers" system. Democratic constitutional government provides a means whereby the "holler" is heard by government officials. But the voting machinery must produce more than a record of protests and objections from the citizens. It is important that we are able to "turn the rascals out" by ballot, but we must also see to it that the officeholders who are elected in their place are instructed by the voters. It may be that, in effect, the voters simply instruct them not to do what the rascals did. This is not enough. They must be elected, not with negative instruction, but with positive instruction as well. They must be held accountable and they must know for what they are held accountable. Simple as it may seem, this is difficult to accomplish.

One of the ways that we have done it in the United States is through the two-party system, a system which produces the practical result of a rotation of politicians in office. True enough, the constitutional fathers sought, by various provisions in the Constitution, to prevent the rise of political parties. But parties arose and they have continued because they do some very important things. They provide the personnel of government, they help to formulate policies, they organize and coordinate the branches of the government, and they criticize the work of government. It is indeed difficult to imagine a successful democratic government without an effective party system. Those sections of our country, North or South, state-wide or local, where the opposition threat and criticism can come only from a minority group within the party in power—because there is virtually no chance of the other party getting into office—undoubtedly suffer from not having an effectively working two-party system. This system in the United States not only has provided a means for the individual citizen to make himself heard in determining national policy, but it has been a great stabilizing force in our national life. Each of the parties has had to prepare a program that would be more or less acceptable to all parts of the country. This has often meant "straddling" issues and avoiding problems, but the nation has not been torn apart as would be the case were there many parties, each representing a small regional, racial, religious, or economic group. This splitting up of a nation into many small parties weakens it. It happened abroad in many democracies now dead. When we

American Democracy and American Government 49

become impatient with our two-party system we must remember the difficult and complicated task a national party performs.

Each of us makes many claims on the government. We want the government to help us or we want the government to let us alone. These claims must be reconciled. The political party serves as a shock absorber between the citizen himself and his government, federal, state, or local. Any machinery that takes up shocks and adjusts differences is of great value today when the clashes among the many groups in our country are so definite and so sharp.

Not only does the political party do a rough and ready job of sifting out the claims of individuals on the party and, through it, on the government, it does the same thing among interest groups. These groups may be general, like farmers or workers or industrialists or Southerners or Northwesterners, or quite specific, like sugar growers, steel manufacturers, or druggists. More often than not, an individual citizen brings pressure on his government through some such interest group or lobby. His lobby may be able to get results where he as an individual cannot. Virtually every American is represented not by one, but probably by several, lobbies which claim to speak for him at the state capital or in Washington. To many people, lobbies are all bad. However this may be, they are powerful and not only inevitable but necessary. The day-to-day information and research which they provide have come to be significant in our government. We should realize that they are actually informal agencies in our governmental system. They do a job and we must keep an eye on how they do it and how they work within our political parties.

Political parties, of course, are held together by the common desire of the members, particularly the leaders, to get into office. A political party seeks to get its members into executive, judicial, and legislative positions so that it can carry out its program. It cannot put through its program and do what the voters want unless it produces cooperation among those three branches of our government. If the Congress or legislature is controlled by one party and the President or governor is a member of another, the rivalry may produce a stalemate. Those of us who want the government to help us will not like such a result; those who are fearful of the government and do not want the proposed action will like such a result. This brings us to the separation of powers idea, that the power of government is divided into great sections: the legislative, the executive, and the judicial. The American development of this idea in combination with the idea of democracy is a unique contribution to the art of government. Political parties, after all, were not discovered by the United States. As mentioned before, the constitutional fathers hoped to prevent their development, but they met a need in the New World democracy as they did in the Old World democracies.

In taking over the separation of powers idea, however, the framers of the Constitution believed that they were copying one of the best features of the British government of 1787. But, as we can now see so clearly, the British government in that very period was abandoning this idea in favor of making the legislative power supreme. Today the British constitution provides that the Cabinet is responsible to the Parliament, that the king is the nation's "first civil servant," and that the British constitution is what the Parliament says it is. Nevertheless, in 1787, the constitutional fathers, relying on the great French scholar Montesquieu's analysis of the British constitution and upon their own observation of the government in London, applied the separation of powers principle to our Constitution. But, being men of judgment and broad experience, they did not let a theoretical idea run away with them. They carefully paired the separation of powers idea with the check and balance idea. To the extent that we give the President the legislative power of the veto, or the Senate the power of ratifying treaties and confirming appointments, or the Congress the power to create courts and determine their procedure, we are unseparating the separation of powers. Here we see the borrowing of ideas from Europe, but the very careful adaptation of them to avoid, at all costs, a too great concentration of political power. This attitude was, of course, the result of our bitter experience before the Revolutionary War at the hands of the British imperial government in London. We have seen that one of the services of political parties is to provide a way for us to make the three branches work together and produce the results that we demand from our government.

Political parties manage to bring the three branches into harness by developing a program which they try to carry out in each one of them. They seek to elect their candidates to office in each branch and to provide a party leadership that will carry through the party program. This is possible even in a state like New York where the executive branch and the legislative branch are practically always controlled by opposite parties. In fact, it is so unusual to find the governor and both houses of the legislature belonging to the same party that it has been absolutely necessary to build up a kind of super-bipartisan government. After all, in such a case — be it almost permanent as in New York, or periodic as elsewhere — the people insist that government be carried on. And the political parties have between them developed the machinery to carry it on.

Another important development in American constitutional government has been the willingness of the people to have the courts, particularly the Supreme Court, referee the Constitution. Although nothing in the Constitution specifically gave the Court the power of judicial review, this idea was at work in our own colonial period and in the British imperial government before the revolution of 1776; and it is now thought of as peculiarly the contribution of the United States to constitutional democracy. In many democratic countries the power to interpret the Constitution is given to the legislature. This seems as unwise to Americans as our practice seems to the British. Although differences of this kind cannot be explained simply, it is at least clear that at the time our practice of giving the courts this power developed under John Marshall, the courts were thought of as the people's defenders against executive tyranny, and the legislatures were feared as being perhaps too democratic and disrespectful of property rights. This the history of the time makes clear. In Britain, on the other hand, the legislature was the people's defender against executive tyranny and the courts were not as popular as they later came to be.

If, as we stated, the fundamental problem in making democracy work in our public government is the problem of setting up workable machinery to enable the individual citizen to share in the making of national, state, or local governmental policy, what do we mean by talking about separation of powers and judicial review? This has brought us to the second large question in the relation of democracy to government. How can government be prevented from running away from the citizen who elected it? How can the servant of the people be kept from becoming the master of the people?

The powers were separated and checks were imposed from power to power in order to prevent too great a concentration of it in any one person or group. The Supreme Court successfully claimed the right to judge whether the Congress and the President were acting within its interpretation of their powers under the Constitution. These two peculiarly American practices in government — the separation of powers, and judicial review — could be said to be governors to prevent the government from gaining too much speed. Moreover, the practices fitted in with the prevailing attitude toward government at the time — that government is best which governs least.

In recent times, however, we have been asking our government to do more and more for us. Sometimes we ask for money or a loan, sometimes for protection, sometimes for regulation of our business competitors, sometimes even that the government go into business. These heavy demands have raised some perplexing problems. We still want to avoid concentrating power in a few hands, but at the same time we want quick, efficient, expert service from our government organizations. In order to secure these results we have had to rely upon the government workers in the civil service of the regular government departments. But in addition to improving the personnel of the civil service we have used the device of the independent board or commission of experts. These administrative agencies are becoming the most powerful and, in some ways, the most important arms of our government. They are made up of men who are experts in their knowledge of a particular field. As everyone knows, knowledge plus authority commands more power than authority does standing alone.

These powerful government boards and agencies that are doing more and more of the work we are heaping on our government are created by the legislatures. The state legislature or Congress usually passes a law creating the board or agency and giving it whatever power it has. It is then the duty of the courts to decide whether the legislative body had the power to pass this law and, if so, to see that the board or commission exercises its powers with "fair play" but does not exceed these granted powers.

What happens to the separation of powers theory when a modern government agency like the Interstate Commerce Commission, the Securities and Exchange Commission, or the National Labor Relations Board has executive, legislative, and judicial power all wrapped in one? What happens when one of these boards lays down the regulations or laws and then acts as policeman, prosecutor, jury, and judge? Although the setting up of those boards and agencies played havoc with some of our prized constitutional theories, the voters have indicated time and again that they want the government to do what these boards are best equipped to do; the result is that they are here to stay. The courts, of course, were highly suspicious and critical of these agencies that have power to injure as well as help private citizens. It is interesting to note, however, that the courts do not hold such a board unconstitutional because its powers are not separated. The principal test of constitutionality today is whether or not its procedure guarantees fair play to everyone who appears before it.

Here the courts are applying ideas that are fundamental to our experience with democracy. Democracy rests in the dignity of the individual, and that dignity must be honored. The citizen must be treated fairly by his government and by his fellow citizens. He has a right to know what the government intends to do to him, whether it be to tax him, draft him, take his property, deprive him of his privilege to do business, or what not. He has a right to be heard and to defend himself, to seek the counsel of his friends or, if necessary, of a lawyer. These rights run deep into the history of the common law of the United States and of England. They are not unique with us, but we honor them none the less. We are revolted when they are denied to human beings, and we understand perfectly when the courts openly use the phrase "fair play" and insist that it be observed between man and man, and between man and his government.

What other protections have we from attempted actions of the government, besides these watchdog services of the courts in holding the legislature and the Executive to the power given to them by the Constitution? The protections of our civil liberties — the rights to free speech, free press, free assembly, free choice of worship, and the other protections in the Bill of Rights. So suspicious were the early Americans when the Constitution was presented to them for ratification without the first ten amendments containing these guarantees, that before they would ratify and accept it they insisted on an agreement that these amendments be passed. Americans felt strongly about these rights then and they do today. They insist that these rights are a man's natural rights. A man is a man and he has a right to speak his mind on public questions, and to print his ideas, and to try to persuade his fellows through a free press. He has a right to assemble with his fellows, and to worship God freely and according to his choice.

Today, in addition to recognizing these rights as *natural rights* due a man as a free man, we can see very clearly the practical need for the protection of civil liberties. We said above that the fundamental problem of an effective democracy is the creation of workable machinery to translate the desires of the people into public policy. This can be done only through discussion and debate and compromise, not alone in the halls of the legislature but throughout the country. If this is true, it is necessary that every idea be presented and discussed in order that we may test its truth or falsity, its usefulness or danger to our democratic way of life. In a democracy we must trust the people to avoid error and to hold fast to the truth. Whom else can we trust? We have said that our civil liberties are ends in themselves. Men have a right to these liberties. But they are also means. That is to say, they are necessary to discovering the truth so that we can decide how to use our government to meet our demands.

We have seen the important functions that political parties perform. One of these is putting the alternatives to the voters — that is, alternatives of candidates, of policies, and of programs for carrying out the desires of the voters. This may seem elementary and obvious. It is; but it is also fundamental that the voters be confronted with alternatives. Otherwise, Hitler could claim that Germany is democratic because the German people are permitted to vote. But what is a vote if there are no genuine alternatives to vote for? Even more important is the answer to the question, who shall decide on the alternatives? The private citizen — that is, you and I — working through political parties, does this job of preparing the alternatives offered at an election. And in order to do it halfway decently, we must have free speech, a free press, free assembly, and the other protections from the government in power. We have a job to do in a democracy; we must insist that our government give us the chance to do it. Of course, most of us do a miserable job; many of us don't vote at all, and most of us who do vote are poor party members. By poor party members we don't always mean in-and-out party members. Sometimes the threat of leaving a party or even actually walking out of it is the most effective means of forcing it to put clear and desirable alternatives to the voters at an election.

Many Americans seem to think that if they are faithful voters and make an effort to vote intelligently they are doing their whole duty as democratic citizens. But voting is not enough. It is even more important that they do their part in bringing about an election situation where their vote will mean something. One way of failing to do this is to permit a political machine to take charge of a political party and rule a city, a county, a state, or a nation. We thereby make it more and more difficult to create a possible alternative to the machine. We have allowed it to get pretty close to a monopoly — it's hard to break a monopoly! Nevertheless, we know how to break political machines, although it is amazing how long we will feed such a machine before throwing it out. But we must remember that it would be almost impossible to get rid of it if we didn't have the free press, free speech, and free assembly that make it possible to get information, to criticize, and to build up the opinion that will turn the machine out of office.

We also know the value of being protected from the government's illegal searches and seizures. We rely on our courts and legislatures to see to it that these constitutional protections do not break down. We insist, in America, that our mail shall not be opened and that our telephone conversations shall not be tapped and perhaps recorded. There is nothing that brings Americans to their feet in protest more quickly than a threat to their civil liberties. There is nothing that brings the idea of democracy so closely home to us. And yet there are many who are not eternally vigilant of these liberties. Some of us seem to think, from time to time, that the civil liberties of some Americans can be permanently violated without any danger of this failure proving to be "catching." Bad examples and bad precedents may one day destroy our own liberties.

We know that the government may take our lives and our property — that we may be drafted, that our property may be taxed and even condemned. This we allow on conditions. The taking must be constitutional. It must be done, as we say, with due process of law, and in the case of condemnation of property the government must pay a fair price. Here again we rely on the courts to secure us from abuses of power by the legislature and the Executive.

We are still speaking of the ways and means that Americans have perfected to prevent their own government from injuring them. We shall return later to discuss this problem of the precarious balance between using our government and at the same time distrusting it. This question is closely connected with the problem of federalism. Many people think that our principal contribution to the development of democracy in the world has been the way in which we have combined the idea of democracy with a division of power between the national government at Washington and the governments of the forty-eight states. All Americans know that we are a federal nation — that the states have all the powers that they have not given to the government in Washington. Our neighbor to the north has done it the other way round. The national government at Ottawa has all the power that it has not given to the provinces, or states, of Canada.

What is the result of our dividing the power between the central and the local governments? It is to make each weaker than if all the power were concentrated in one government.

It is in this way that federalism is part of the solution to the problem of protecting ourselves from our government. But federalism is primarily a political device to get just the necessary amount of central government for all the parts and still permit as much local government as possible. Elsewhere in this book there is a discussion of the state-rights versus national-government argument in our history. What we are intent on pointing out here is that the division of government is, in many ways, like the separation of powers device. Instead of dividing the whole power of government according to what kind of power is to be used — that is, roughly on a separation of powers basis — federalism divides it on a regional or central-local basis. In both instances the result is an effective restraint on the power of government.

In recent years this result of federalism in our democracy has been very evident. When the voters insist that the government do something about something, the question arises: which government, the national or the state? This is a question for the courts. They will decide whether what the voters want can be done constitutionally and, if so, whether the national government or the state governments may do it. In making these decisions, there is always the possibility that the courts may decide, as they did in the first Agricultural Adjustment Administration case, that only the states may be permitted to do what only the national government actually can do — set up an adequate nation-wide farm program. Every American could see the nature of the problem when Justice Roberts, in that case, described agricultural production as "a purely local activity." If this were true, there would be created a kind of twilight zone where, practically speaking, no effective action could be taken. Difficulties like this are "got around" but they will always crop up in a federal system like ours.

One of the most common ways the national government does things that the courts have said it may not do under the Constitution is to give a subsidy to a state government for that purpose. The courts have allowed this. The social security program, for instance, is a most complicated set of arrangements, subsidies, credits, and so on, between the national government and the state governments. We should see quite clearly that indirection and "going around the mulberry bush" are the price we must sometimes pay for federalism. These rigidities in our system make expensive bookkeeping, much red tape, and delay; but they are the price we pay for splitting up the power of the people between the national government and the state governments.

Beyond the great advantage of keeping much of the government close to the people, another advantage is the fact that our federal system permits each of the states to act as a laboratory where experiments can be tried out; if found good, they can be adopted by the other states. A few examples of ideas and practices tried out by individual states and later generally accepted throughout the nation include workmen's compensation laws, the income tax, the state-financed university, and the initiative and referendum. Such experimentation is very useful when the problem does not extend outside one state. But so many of our serious problems cannot be held within a single state; they flood out into many states. And then the question must be: does the national government have the power to handle the problem? If we shifted our constitutional plan to the Canadian pattern so that the government in Washington would have all the power not given to the states, we would not improve matters much. For then we might find that a problem was truly local but that only the national government had constitutional power to handle it; under our present system the courts may find that a problem is national but that only the states have constitutional power to deal with it. No, we must realize that such difficulties are part of our decision to have a federal system and to divide power regionally in much the same way that we separate the powers into executive, legislative, and judicial in the national and state governments.

Both of these processes split up governmental power and prevent its concentration in any one place, in any one individual group.

Throughout our discussion we have noted that the citizen in our American democracy requires two things of his government: that it serve him well, but not too well, that is, to the point of controlling his every action — that it be his servant but not his master. And we have seen that the fundamental problem of a political democracy is to provide the necessary machinery so that the citizen may use the power of government. This is what we think we have done in setting up our constitutions, national and state. We know that we are remiss and careless in using the machinery, but it is here for us to use. At the same time, there is the necessity of setting up the protections and guarantees against our own government; we know that we must be eternally vigilant to preserve these liberties.

But these two demands may clash. The first one assumes that the majority of the American people can make the governmental machinery work to give them what they want, or that they can refuse to operate the machinery and continue to get what they have. Does this mean that a majority of the people should have their way if they set about getting it by operating the proper governmental machinery? Can't you hear the answers? "Why, of course," says one of us. "Well, I'm not so sure," says another. The first is thinking along these lines: "Why, democracy is the government of the people, by the people, and for the people. And if the people — and that surely means a majority of them — want something, they should have it." The second is thinking along another line: "After all, how can I be sure that the majority is always right? They might be unreasonable and take my property and my rights away from me."

These ordinary and simple reactions to the implications of democratic rule are as old as our experience with democracy. They represent a difference in attitude toward

American Democracy and American Government 61

democracy that was present in colonial times. This difference cropped up in the Constitutional Convention of 1787 and has been with us ever since.

One way of getting at the heart of this problem is to examine the sentence from the Declaration of Independence: "All governments derive their just powers from the consent of the governed." What do Americans mean by "the consent of the governed"? Obviously it must be a real consent, not consent under pressure or threats. But how does the consent take place? Does the minority consent to accept the decision of the majority, and to ordain and establish, as we did, a constitution for the United States of America when the majority ratifies it? Yes. But having consented to the Constitution, do the people bind themselves to no change in it without the consent of the government set up under it? Thomas Jefferson stated quite firmly — and how amazing it sounds today — that we ought to have a revolution, that is to say, a new constitution, every twenty years. He could not see how the consent of the people could be fairly secured in any other way. On the other side was the view that people, once having consented to the Constitution, were bound by their decision; the Constitution could thereafter be changed only by the usual complicated and difficult amendment process.

Many of our state constitutions provide that they shall automatically be brought up to date at regular intervals. That is, a new state constitutional convention shall be called every ten, fifteen, or twenty years and a new constitution drawn up or the old one amended and presented to the people of the state for their consent. But we do not think of this as a constitutional revolution in the Jeffersonian sense. We think of it as a kind of check-up or overhauling of the family car. Our federal Constitution has never had anything like an overhauling. It has been amended relatively few times since the first ten amendments were enacted. However, great historical events have, in effect, amended it — the Civil War, for instance. And, finally, the courts have changed and modified it in applying it from year to year.

This judicial review of whatever the courts consider a threat to the Constitution has frequently clashed with the idea that the people are always all-powerful and sovereign. These clashes have raised the question of whether the government is the people. If the government is legally the representative of the people and the people are all-powerful and sovereign, why can't the government do what the people ask — in spite of what the courts and the Constitution may say? Logically, this may be true enough, but Americans have shied away from the logic that a people's government should have the people's power. Our practical good sense has been unwilling to accept at face value the legal identification of government and people. Our Congressmen and legislators may be good and able men, our governors and Presidents honest and courageous leaders; but when they sit down in their offices and begin to exercise our power, we know that a certain indefinable change comes over them. Somehow an elected representative — be he a labor delegate, a corporation representative, a Congressman, or a President — changes in an office of power. We seem definitely willing that the courts may from time to time prevent him from exercising the will of the majority which elected him. Most of us continue to believe that the people — that is, of course, the majority of the people — should have the power to rule, but nevertheless we put a great many obstacles in the way. Most of us accept the full implication of majority rule, but at the same time, very practically if not logically, we protect the minority from the majority, protect all the people from what the courts hold to be unconstitutional. As a democracy we hold fast to the restraints recommended by our American experience.

Democracy has always presented this dilemma of freedom versus authority. A democratic system must permit us to keep ourselves free as individuals, but at the same time give the government enough authority to do what we want it to do. The present crisis has brought home to every one of us the problem of finding this balance between freedom and authority. For some time our government has been wielding more and more administrative power and it has inevitably clashed with individual rights of liberty and property. Today we recognize that the government will use more and more of this administrative power as it moves toward more and more of the planning required for an efficient defense. We can see clearly that there must be many changes in our democratic way of doing things. But our past record is a comfort to us. We have known how to meet great problems. Our democracy has always found the balance between freedom and authority that has met the needs of each period of crisis in our history. It has known how to defend itself from social chaos and to protect its great heritage of American freedom.

CHAPTER 3

DEMOCRACY IN THE AMERICAN ECONOMY

by Thomas H. Robinson

When it comes to satisfying our wants, we Americans are the world's most fortunate people. We have more food and clothing, more bathtubs and radios, more lipstick and permanents, more movies and swing music than any of our neighbors. Our national income in 1928 amounted to 89 billions, or to approximately $750 for every man, woman, and child in the country. Our most fortunate neighbors, the Canadians, had a per capita income of $550 in 1927. Among the least fortunate of those with whom we deal are the people of Japan, with an income of only $66 per person in 1925. Think of it. For every dollar received by the "average" Japanese, the "average" American received more than eleven. We do pretty well by ourselves.

A number of factors have contributed to our good fortune. One of these is the fact that our ancestors had the foresight to settle in such a richly endowed land. Of all the countries in the world, none can boast of such a wealth of resources as ours.

A second factor is to be found in the extraordinary scientific and technological developments in America during the past 175 years. Nature, by herself, makes very inadequate provision for our wants. A few — a very few — things exist in a condition fit to satisfy wants *and* in such quantities that all of us can take all we desire. A few more things that are in a want-satisfying condition are relatively scarce. But the great bulk of our resources must have something done to them before they can be used. We have to shape and reshape all sorts of materials to get want-satisfying goods. We have to carry these materials from where they are less needed to where they are more needed. Sometimes we have to store them for future needs. In short, we have to produce most of our goods. Needless to say, the remarkable progress of science, and its application through inventions to the task of producing goods from nature's stores, have been immeasurably important in providing us with what we want.

Still a third reason is our democratic way of life. To us, democracy means freedom — individual freedom. It means freedom for each one of us to take part in making policies that concern us. It means taking part in a way that counts. In the United States, democracy means that all 130,000,000 of us have a say, a real say, in the making of American policies. It means that American policies are *our* policies. Furthermore, democracy means that the persons we intrust with the administration of our policies are our servants, not our masters. In this respect, it means individual freedom from executive tyranny.

Of course this individual freedom is not license for each of us to do as he pleases. We have responsibilities. When *we* decide a policy, each *one* of us is honor bound to adopt it as *his* policy. The few who disagree with the many are not justified, on the pretext of their individual freedom, in thwarting the many. Those who act like the spoiled child who won't play because he can't have his way contribute to a social chaos rather than a social order, to a situation ripe for a dictator.

Needless to say, we are defining the principle of democracy, not describing how this principle actually works in practice. What democracy means and its expression in our social life may be, and sometimes are, two different things.

This democratic principle applies to all aspects of social life. Democracy can be — and in America it is — as much a part of our intellectual as of our religious life, of our art as of our education, of our economy as of our government. The principle itself was brought from Europe by the earliest colonial settlers, nourished by their descendants, and strengthened by generations of later immigrants right up to the present day. Most of the settlers who came to America were looking for greater economic, religious, and political liberty than they had at home. Most of them were refugees from an authority they disliked. And they and their descendants found in the United States a congenial environment in which their ideas of freedom and liberty took root and grew into a sturdy American democracy.

Indeed America was especially fertile soil for the growth of democracy. No long-established civilization existed to impose the "dead hand" of its past upon the lives of newcomers. And the extraordinary abundance of cheap land combined with the scarcity of labor to promote economic independence and to give individual freedom a high place in the scale of values. The frontier environment, so long a feature of this country, favored the development of a democratic, individualistic society in which a man was judged by his works and in which he was free to show what he could do.

Naturally the settlers brought much social as well as material baggage along with them. They brought much that did not stand up under the harsh abrasives of frontier life. For instance, a class system and authoritarian rule by a chosen few were tried for a time and finally given up. On the other hand, there was much that fitted in with the growing spirit of freedom. These elements lived. In the case of our American economy, with which we are especially concerned in this chapter, our inheritance from Europe in general and England in particular was very rich. Private property, reliance upon individual initiative, specialization, exchange mediated by money, and competitively determined prices as the chief guides to most of our economic activity —

these were elements brought from overseas, knit into, and made vital parts of, our American economic system.

As we have already noted, the United States is a fortunate country; but it is no Shangri-la. Despite our relative abundance, there are Americans with inadequate food, shoddy clothes, unsanitary homes, no cars, and very few tickets to the movies. Of course these people want enough food, good clothes, decent homes, cars, and a chance to sigh over Clark Gable or get in a fever about Hedy Lamarr. Yet the fact is that, fortunate as we are, we do not have the wherewithal to produce everything that everyone wants. In 1929, for instance, a year that climaxed a "golden age," one out of every five American families lived in what we define as poverty. And today, as we strain to produce the *matériel* of war, we are all too well aware of our lack of vital supplies. We know we shall have to give up plenty for the sake of our defense program. In spite of our vast resources, scarcity is still the dominant fact of our lives.

The harsh reality of scarcity, scarcity of resources and the resultant scarcity of goods, confronts us with an extremely serious problem. If we haven't enough aluminum for all the planes and all the pans we want, we have to decide how much shall be used for planes and how much for pans. If there isn't enough fat for the food and the munitions we want, we must decide what we shall do without. These "ifs" illustrate one of the most difficult problems with which Americans — and every other people, for that matter — are faced. This problem resides in the fact that our wants have no known limits, whereas our resources for satisfying these wants are definitely limited. In practice, furthermore, alternative uses exist for every resource. As a result, we are forced to distribute scarce resources among these optional uses. This predicament is what we call the *economic* problem.

To the solution of this problem, as to the solution of their other basic problems, Americans have applied the democratic principle. They have created an economic system based on individual freedom, an economic system which, they think, contributes more to the satisfaction of their wants than any other system. It is this system that we propose to consider both in principle and in practice.

At the outset, a word of warning. The first part of our discussion will be highly simplified. It will be a description of our economic organization, as stripped of non-essentials as a bathing beauty. Moreover, our description will be in terms of perfection, for we shall emphasize how a democratic economic organization is supposed to work. After all, we have some precedent for this approach. Theologians talk about the kingdom of heaven on earth, physicists have ideas about the mechanics of a frictionless machine, and football coaches dream about the play that is sure to score. Of course the theologians are aware of sin, the physicists pooh-pooh the reality of perpetual motion, and the football coaches know that the "perfect play" is only a dream. And we know, too, that our economic organization, democratic as it is, is far from perfect. But we gain considerable understanding by discussing fundamentals and by knowing how things ought to be. We gain perspective. We know where to look for shortcomings, and how to recognize them as such — the latter no mean achievement! We can tell how much the real world about us differs from the ideal. And we can get a pretty good idea as to whether a proposed reform will kill or cure.

Fundamentally, our economy is an exchange economy. We the people — to use Mr. Willkie's phrase — exchange productive resources, that is, labor and property in all their thousands of forms, for want-satisfying goods. This exchange is not direct, but is mediated by money. We the people, as the owners of productive resources, sell these resources to business enterprises for money. With this money, we the people, as consumers, buy want-satisfying goods from business enterprises. Every exchange, of course, involves an evaluation, that is, an estimate of what we are willing to give up to get what we want. In our economy, these evalua-

Democracy in the American Economy

tions are in terms of money, or prices. We have a price system.

However, a democratic economy is not the only exchange economy with business enterprises and a price system. Men sell their labor to business enterprises in Soviet Russia for rubles. Men rent their homes from real estate agencies in Fascist Italy for lira. Men receive interest in marks on investments in public utilities in Nazi Germany. Our economy is democratic not because we have business enterprises and a price system but because of our relations, as individuals, with business enterprises and because of the kind of price system we have.

Three things mark our relations with business enterprises. First, we can sell to and buy from any enterprise we please. In a dictatorship, you deal with whom you are told. Second, any of us can start an enterprise for any legal purpose we like. If we want to make electric fans for the Eskimos or ice skates for the residents of the Amazon Valley, that is our affair. But in a dictatorship, business enterprises are initiated with the permission of the dictator and produce only what the dictator says. Third, business enterprises are free to sell to and to buy from us as they see fit.

Two things about our price system distinguish it from a price system in a dictatorship. First, within very wide limits, each one of us is free to offer and to accept or reject any prices we please for goods and resources. Second, the prices that prevail are set by our freely made offers and acceptances. If you are willing to pay ten dollars for a pair of shoelaces, that is *your* business. If you turn down a hundred-dollar-a-day job, that, too, is *your* business. In any case, the prices you actually pay for shoelaces and receive for your labor must be freely acceptable to you and to the business enterprises with which you deal.

In short, in our economy the accent is on freedom. This kind of an economy is called free private enterprise.

The reasons for claiming that free private enterprise is

the economic equivalent of the millennium, or perpetual motion, or the perfect football play call for some elaboration. Let's start with the question of who gets what, and how much.

If individuals are provided with money — as they are from the sale of their resources — and if they are free to spend it — as they are — then the prices each is willing to pay indicate the relative importance of different goods to him. Moreover, it is a safe bet that each person will spend his money so that he cannot increase his satisfactions by any other combination of expenditures. None of us, for instance, will spend a dollar for tobacco if he can get more of a kick from a dollar's worth of beer. When we buy, we buy what will give us the most satisfaction. Furthermore, none of us will spend a dollar for a quart of ice cream which we can buy for fifty cents. Whatever we buy, we buy at the lowest possible price.

Of course our system does not guarantee that those who want particular goods will get them. The ability to pay is by no means evenly distributed — a point to which we shall refer later — goods are scarce, and prices will be set by the freely made, competing offers of buyers. Those able and willing to pay the highest prices get what they want; the others do without. For instance, your neighbor with ten times your income can buy lots of things you cannot afford but may want very much. Let both of you go to an auction and see who comes away with the rickety chairs and the chipped glass goblets.

However, even if incomes were equal there is no certainty that the distribution of goods would be equally want-satisfying. Individuals differ greatly in their likes and dislikes. An income that would mean ease and luxury to some would mean poverty and hardship to others. In any case, speculation of this sort is a bit futile. It just is not possible to measure one man's capacity for enjoyment, let alone compare it with that of another. You can't be sure that a string of pearls will make Mary happier than Hazel. Of course it would be very convenient to have a kind of psychic X-ray that would reveal the relative intensities of each person's wants. Maybe then Aunt Susie would be sure to give the electric train to father instead of to Johnny. And think how easy it would be to select gifts for brides! As it is, though, we have to get along with a system in which, at the prevailing prices, we spend our money on the — to us — most want-satisfying goods.

Now let's turn to the question of who produces the goods consumers want.

From our point of view, the primary job of a business enterprise is the production of goods. But from the point of view of those who run it, the primary job of a business enterprise is to make a profit — in fact, as much profit as possible. These two jobs can be done most effectively when a business enterprise produces what consumers want most. Naturally every business enterprise is on the lookout for highly profitable goods. Suppose a firm finds such an item, say plastic cars. It will pay this firm to expand its output of these cars. Other enterprises will try to produce plastic cars too; new enterprises, even, may be started for this purpose. Before long, the firm that discovered the profitability of plastic cars will have company as other firms seek a share of the profits.

Meanwhile, as more and more plastic cars are sold, consumers want them less and less, and become less willing to pay the prevailing price. Then the element of competition goes to work. The first firm to sense consumer reluctance to buy tries to make its cars more attractive by lowering the price or improving the quality or both. The other firms have to follow suit, or their showrooms will be filled with unsold cars. However, there is a limit to this competitive price-cutting and quality-improving. Business enterprises are no more equal in efficiency than football teams and bridge players are equal in skill. So, as price drops and quality improves, the profits of the less efficient firms shrink. It is but a matter of time before these firms are forced into bankruptcy or into some other line of production in which profits are greater. In any case, the net result is that the most efficient firms make plastic cars and sell them at a price too low to attract effective competition and yet high enough to provide at least as much profit as the making of any other good would yield.

Now we have to show that the incomes people get are the largest possible.

If business enterprises are to produce, they must have productive resources. But practically all resources are scarce. Moreover, practically all resources can be used for a number of different purposes. Coal can be used in a blast furnace, in a railway locomotive, or in the making of artificial rubber. Wool can be used for dresses, uniforms, or blankets. A tool maker can make tools for the airplane, shipbuilding, or automobile industries. Consequently there will be competition for scarce resources. Naturally the owners of resources will sell to those who pay the highest prices. Clearly, the highest bidders will be the most efficient firms engaged in the most profitable activities. Under these circumstances, consumers' incomes will be as high as it is possible for them to be.

To put the whole thing in a nutshell, our economy, organized on the democratic principle into a system of free private enterprise, insures that our scarce resources fall into the hands of the most efficient firms producing the most want-satisfying goods for sale at the lowest possible prices. And the owners of resources secure the highest possible prices for their resources, that is, the highest incomes to spend on the lowest-priced, most want-satisfying goods. Q.E.D.

A corollary should be added to the foregoing theorems. Our price-guided, profit-motivated, competitive, free-private-enterprise economy can function *most* effectively only if prices are free to change with every change in consumers' wants, in the willingness of the owners of resources to part with them, and in the efficiency with which business enterprises can compete. For instance, if the price of candy bars is high, consumers will curtail their purchases, but producers will take the high price as a signal to continue, if not to expand, production. Unless the price falls, there will be lots of stale, unsold candy bars. Resources will have been wasted, firms deprived of business receipts, profits reduced, and the owners of resources unpaid. If the price of a day's labor is too low, workers may refuse to accept jobs. Unless wages rise, some firms will be without the labor they want, the volume of goods produced will be smaller, prices will go up, individual incomes will be lower, and wants will be satisfied in less than the maximum possible degree. Anyway you look at it, a price that is prevented from moving up or down, when it would move up or down in the absence of interference, leads to wasted resources and to less want-satisfaction than is possible.

Such is the essence of our economic system and the way it is *supposed* to work. Such, in brief and in purely materialistic terms, are our reasons for thinking that an economic system organized on the democratic principle is the best of all possible systems, especially for consumers. After all, it is for the benefit of consumers that economic activities are carried on.

In the pattern we have sketched, some will see a resemblance to democracy in our government. Our government, we say, is a government of laws, not of men. What we mean is that we the people decide governmental policies and select the men to administer them. We vote for or against proposed policies and candidates for office; and the policies and candidates for whom the most votes are cast are selected. Our economic system, be it noted, has the equivalent of this election process. Instead of using ballots and getting election returns, we use dollars and get prices. For all practical purposes, the market is the economic equivalent of the polling booth. The analogy can be carried further. Just as political parties appeal for support on the basis of their records and promises for the future, so business enterprises campaign for the favors of consumers — the economic "voters" — on the basis of proved ability or promises to deliver the goods. Business men, it can be added, are the economic counterparts of politicians.

But with these likenesses there are important differences. A voter has only one vote on each issue and on the candidates for each office, while a consumer has as many "votes" as he has dollars. We penalize "repeating" at the polls, but we encourage it in the market place. Of course, plural voting in the market place has a very definite advantage; it enables an individual to register not only a preference for or against a particular policy but also how much he is for or against. Another unlikeness exists in the vastly more complicated task of the consumer. A voter has comparatively few issues about which he has to make up his mind, and then he has only one vote on each. A consumer, on the other hand, has hundreds and thousands of different kinds of goods among which he must discriminate; and he has hundreds, if not thousands, of dollars to spend on them. A still further unlikeness arises from the fact that governmental elections are discontinuous. They take place only on given dates, usually some time apart. By contrast, the determination of prices is a continuous process, with each price free to change at any time. In our government, policies may be insensitive to interelection changes of opinion; but in our economy, policies change as freely changing prices reflect new consumer likes and dislikes or new competitive conditions in industry.

Of course it is all very well to know how our economy is supposed to behave, but the facts of the matter are that it misbehaves. Our economic system is no more a perfect lady than the girl in the song, "There's a Little Bit of Bad in Every Good Little Girl." Indeed, there is reason to liken our system to that other young lady who "when she was good, was very, very good; but when she was bad, was horrid." On the whole, during the 1920's, our economy was very, very good; but during the 1930's, it most certainly was horrid.

Democracy in the American Economy

Much of the responsibility for the wayward behavior of our economy is ours. We the people, as consumers, must be willing to, know enough to, be able to, and actually discriminate in favor of the most want-satisfying goods. Moreover, we the people, as the owners of resources, must be equally discriminating in the sale of these resources to business enterprises. What's more, business enterprises must be fully as discriminating in their choices of goods to make, in their purchases of resources, and in their sales to consumers. To the extent that the facts fall short of these "musts," our economic system falls short of the best solution of the economic problem.

Certainly the facts do fall short of these "musts." Both as consumers and as the owners of resources, we are not willing to discriminate in favor of what is best. We are woefully lacking in the information needed to make the best choices among the many, many thousands of kinds of goods and among the numerous possible purchasers of our resources. Many of us, as individuals, are unable to discriminate even if we would. And many times we do not discriminate even if we could. Business enterprises, on the other hand, probably because they employ specialists in the art, appear to be somewhat better than people in this matter of discrimination. But even they are far from perfect. They produce goods that people do not want or are unable to buy, they pay too much for resources, they suppress competition, and so on.

Here again there is a striking parallel between the facts in our democratic economy and in our democratic government. It is a commonplace of politics that many voters do not discriminate among parties and candidates. Parties and politicians have their faithful followers just as business enterprises have their habitual customers. Moreover, not all voters are adequately informed about the issues and candidates in each election. Some voters, indeed, are prevented from voting — it may be a poll tax, or a technicality in the residence requirement, or it may be bad roads. Then, of course, some voters just don't bother to vote. And when it comes to parties and politicians, there is more than a faint suspicion that some of them sometimes do not act in the most intelligent way or from the loftiest of motives.

It is not possible, within the limits of this chapter, to give a complete discussion of our economy. But we can give brief consideration to some of its more important aspects. Accordingly, we shall devote some attention to our national income, the increase in capital goods, freedom in our economy, and the role of government in our economic life.

If we want to know how well a team plays baseball, we look at the box score. If we wish to know how well the people of a nation provide for their wants, we examine the figures on national income. As already emphasized, we Americans provide for ourselves very well in comparison with other peoples. And we have little reason to apologize for our long-time economic box score. The National Industrial Conference Board tells us that we started in 1799 with a per capita real income of goods and services worth $211 at 1926 prices, and that we ended 1938 with a per capita real income worth $533, also at 1926 prices. In 140 years we have boosted our real income some 250 per cent. That's not so bad.

However, there is another and not so favorable angle to our national income record. Whatever the mathematically computed average income per person may be, the fact remains that, in actual practice, individual and family incomes are far from equal. These incomes vary from zero and less to several millions, with very large numbers in the low-income groups. For instance, a study by the National Resources Committee revealed that in the year ending June 30, 1936, about 42 per cent of all American families received less than $1000, 79 per cent less than $2000, and 92 per cent less than $3000. The tenth of all consumer units — families and single persons living alone — with the lowest incomes received a total of a billion dollars, while the tenth with the highest incomes received nearly twenty-one and a half billions. The highest income received in the lowest tenth was $340; the lowest income in the highest tenth was $2600. More than 12,745,000 consumer units shared in the tenth of the nation's income going to those with the lowest incomes, while only 197,000 consumer units shared in the tenth going to those with the highest incomes.

But it is a comparison of these figures on the distribution of income with data on the cost of living that is really significant. We find, for instance, that in 1935–1936 it would have cost a family of four, the typical American family, about $735 to maintain only a poverty standard of living, nearly $1470 to provide a minimum standard of health and decency, and approximately $2200 for the comfort, or what we like to think of as the American, standard. Here is something to think about. In 1935–1936, even if their incomes had been spent wisely — a somewhat dubious "if" — 30 out of every 100 American families could afford no better than a poverty standard of living, only 33 out of every 100 could maintain a minimum health and decency standard, and only a bare 15 could live as we would like Americans to live. Even allowing for a wide margin of error, for the fact that 1935–1936 was still a depression period, and for the possibility — very doubtful — that our standards are too high, there is little in the foregoing figures to make us smugly complacent, however impressive our achievements since 1799.

One other point about the distribution of our national income is worth noting. It is that workers get a much greater proportion of the total income than property owners. Moreover, the workers' proportion is a growing one. Out of every $100 of income, $58 in 1899 and $68 in 1938 were paid out in salaries and wages to workers of all kinds. Meanwhile, the share going to property owners in the form of dividends, interest, rents, and royalties has remained practically constant. This share was about $12 out of every $100 in both 1899 and 1938. What is called entrepreneurial income, or the withdrawals by owners, either as individual proprietors or as partners, from all fields of business, including farming, merchandising, and professional services, declined from $30 to $20 out of every $100 of income from 1899 to 1938. This entrepreneurial income combines payments for property invested as well as for labor provided. The decline indicated is probably due largely to the increasing importance of the corporate form of business organization. There are a number of implications in these figures. For instance, contrary to a rather widely held idea, the workers cannot add greatly to their incomes at the expense of the owners of property.

Now let's take a look at capital goods, that is, goods used to make other goods. Great steel mills, vast factories, complicated assembly lines, intricate machine tools, mass-production equipment, powerful railway locomotives, tractors, trucks, ships, multi-motored transport planes, huge electric power generating plants, ingenious business machines, and the innumerable other examples of our mechanical age are to be found on all sides. We know that the accumulation of these goods has been very rapid, although figures to prove this point are rather fragmentary. We do know, however, that the value of our capital goods per gainfully employed worker was about $560 in 1880 and slightly more than $1500 in 1920. Moreover, we know that each worker engaged in manufacturing had one horsepower of mechanical energy to help him in 1869 and five in 1929.

For hundreds of years, men had used only the simplest tools and had relied primarily upon their own energy in making goods. But along about the middle of the eighteenth century, a series of revolutionary changes set in. Machinery and non-human sources of power came increasingly into use until now they dominate the industrial scene. This revolution in technology began in England and spread to other countries. And nowhere did it find a warmer, though somewhat belated, welcome than in the United States. Conditions in America favored the rapid accumulation of a vast stock of capital equipment. By all odds the most important of these conditions was the scarcity of labor in conjunction with the extraordinary abundance of natural resources in an economically undeveloped country. There was so much to do and there were so few to do it that anything promising to aid men's labors was sure of a welcome and a trial.

Yet the need for productive equipment, great as it was, was met primarily because Americans saved on a substantial scale over a long period of time. As it turned out, many of the settlers came with the idea of bettering themselves economically. They were a hard-working, thrifty lot, fully aware of the need to save. Moreover, many of them brought with them a Puritan tradition that established simple living and saving as religious acts. Another significant influence was the democratizing of education. With the spread of education came the desire for a higher standard of living for oneself and one's family. Furthermore, as people became better educated, they became better able to foresee problems that could be met more effectively by saving.

Along with these inducements to save were the buttressing facts that the protection of property and property rights was a major concern of our political and legal systems, and that the country enjoyed peace and order to a remarkable degree. Individuals could save, confident that they would be able to enjoy the fruits of their thrift. Destructive wars were few, and the savings of each generation could accumulate, to be passed on virtually intact to those that followed. Then, as savings were amassed, a series of financial agencies developed to make what was saved available for productive purposes. Savings banks, life insurance companies, mortgage houses, brokers, stock exchanges, and others provided channels for the easy flow of savings to producer.

Throughout the creation of all our capital equipment runs the spirit of democracy, like the theme of some great symphony. Sometimes it is in a minor key, and sometimes it crashes forth in all the blare of the brass and rumble of the percussion instruments. But it is always there as the central and controlling element. Thus the extraordinary development of science — itself an expression of democracy — provided ideas for industry. Saving made it possible to give concrete expression to these ideas. Emphasis upon individual freedom in an environment calling for individual initiative meant that these ideas, and others, would be tried in one way or another. The spread of education, also a product of democracy, stepped up the abilities of people to meet their problems, including the economic problem. And all these developments occurred in an economic system that was itself basically democratic. It is not at all strange that Americans acquired a world-wide reputation for resourcefulness, that "Yankee ingenuity" became a synonym for the ability to devise ways and means of solving difficult problems.

So far, we have made much of freedom in our economic democracy. Such emphasis may be misleading, for it is well to recognize that there is, in practice, considerably less freedom, considerably less democracy than we could wish. We need only to note something of the existing circumstances affecting consumers, owners of property, workers, and business enterprises to make this point clear.

There are many limits to the freedom of consumers, not the least important of which is lack of income. Certainly the bulk of the consumers are without the means of getting more than the minimum essentials, to say nothing of indulging in comforts and luxuries. But even with the incomes they have, they are restricted by meager and sometimes misleading information. Of course advertising does inform consumers about many things of which they otherwise would be unaware. But we have yet to reach that ethical plane in which misrepresentation is taboo. Moreover, advertisers have achieved such a command over their art that they can get people to like almost anything, including what has already been produced. Instead of telling business enterprises what they want, consumers sometimes find themselves in the position of being told what to like.

Property owners are individuals who have rights to the satisfactions that particular goods are capable of yielding. In general, property owners are presumed to be free to use their property as they see fit. But property rights are not, and never have been, absolute; they are relative to time, place, and circumstances. During the past century or so, and in particular during the past decade or two, there has been considerable legal modification of the rights of property owners. Zoning ordinances, relief for debtors, regulation of interest charges, and restrictions on the sale and resale of goods are but a few examples of these changes.

Other barriers to the full and free exercise of property rights, barriers that the law and our economic system do not presume, have also developed. Let us examine one instance. Under our system of free private enterprise, productive activities are carried on by business enterprises initiated by and under the control of property owners, or capitalists. This is what we mean by capitalism. As long as the individual proprietorship and partnership forms of business enterprise predominated, the system remained essentially capitalistic. Those who ventured their property in a business also controlled it. And, as a corollary of their right to control, they had the full financial responsibility for any losses incurred by their enterprises.

However, the increasing use of the corporate form of business organization has weakened this close relationship of ownership, control, and financial responsibility. The ownership of a corporation is divided into a number of shares. An individual's share in control is proportionate to his ownership of voting stock, and his financial responsibility is limited usually to his actual investment. Among the advantages of the corporation are the ease with which small savings from numerous sources can be combined to create a single, large-scale enterprise, and the possibility of specializing the functions of investment and management.

As a result of these features, conditions may develop in which persons with a relatively small share of ownership actually control an enterprise. For instance, it would be quite out of the question for all the stockholders of a large corporation to attend its meetings. In 1937, the American Telephone and Telegraph Company listed 642,000 stockholders; the General Motors Corporation, 378,000; and the United States Steel Corporation, 213,000. Furthermore, most stockholders own fewer than 100 shares, and feel helpless to exercise any influence at company meetings. But even if they wanted to have a say, most of them know too little about their company's affairs to participate in them intelligently. Then, too, many stockholders live so far from the company's head office that they find it too inconvenient and expensive to attend meetings. As a result, therefore, of the diffusion of stock ownership, most stockholders do not go to company meetings and do not vote independently. For the most part, shareholders' rights to vote either are not exercised or are assigned by a proxy to the few who are actually interested in controlling the company. These few are often management officials who have but a very small ownership interest in the company.

Some interesting developments have accompanied this separation of ownership, control, and financial responsibility. For one thing, a modification of capitalism is involved; for another, the way is open for insiders to gain at the expense of the owners. Investors have a right to expect that enterprises will be operated for their benefit. Yet the corporation permits a significant modification of this expectation. Management officials, the real controllers, with little profit to secure on an ownership basis and with relatively little financial risk, may adopt policies that benefit them, rather than the owners. It is something of a paradox that a legal device that was adopted to promote our economic system is an agency through which this system undergoes a rather fundamental change.

Freedom for individual workers in our economic system leaves much to be desired. In general, the individual worker is at a great disadvantage in the labor market. He rarely is familiar with conditions in this market; he is seldom skilled in selling his labor; and, because his income in the past has been too small to enable him to save, he is far less able to do without a job than an enterprise is able to do without his labor. Moreover, he has to deal with a specialist in the art of buying labor. And both the worker and his potential employer know, if they do not come quickly to terms, that other workers anxious for employment will be much less fussy. Furthermore, there is reason to believe that business enterprises make use of their bargaining advantages. Indeed, our system practically forces them to do so, for competition puts pressure on every firm to reduce its costs. And labor is an important cost element.

Our discussion of freedom of enterprise must be confined to a few of the high spots. In principle, anyone can undertake any business, but in practice there are legal and economic limitations to this freedom. Consider some of these legal limitations. We encourage the invention of new devices and new methods by granting a patent to the inventor. This patent gives him a seventeen-year monopoly on the sale and use of his invention. When the use of an invention is necessary for competitive success in an industry, freedom to enter that industry may be sharply restricted. Again, you and I cannot organize a bus service in our community whenever the spirit moves us. We have to prove to an agent of the government that our proposed service is both a necessity and a convenience. If a satisfactory service is already in operation, we are not likely to be allowed to compete. Similarly, we should need government permission to enter — and sometimes to leave — the railroad, telephone, telegraph, radio, power transmission, pipe line, toll bridge, and toll road fields.

Moreover, you and I cannot just offhand decide that we are going to set ourselves up as doctors, as architects, or as plumbers. We have to satisfy a representative of the public that we are qualified to engage in these callings.

On the economic side, the amount of resources needed to begin operations in certain fields is the main obstacle to freedom of enterprise. It costs money — far more than most people can raise — to enter the public utility, railroad, steel, automobile, airplane, rubber, motion picture, oil, cement, and other industries that use capital goods on an extensive scale. Even in industries such as agriculture, merchandising, and professional services, in which small-scale enterprises abound, the investment needed to undertake successful operations is a major item for most people. And in these industries too the large-scale firm is appearing and making it more and more difficult for the others.

Partly because of these limitations, some industries are dominated by a very few concerns. For instance, it was reported to the Temporary National Economic Committee that five companies controlled 40 per cent of the cement output in 1931, three companies made 80 per cent of the cigarettes in 1934, four companies produced about 80 per cent of the copper and two companies turned out 95 per cent of the plate glass in 1935, and four companies accounted for all the corn binders in 1936. It is to be noted, of course, that the amount of concentration in an industry does not measure the degree of monopoly that may exist. While there may be relatively little competition among the few firms in an industry, there may be a great deal of competition among the products of this and other industries.

However, despite concentration in a number of industries and despite various other restrictions, there is a surprising amount of freedom of enterprise. Dun and Bradstreet report that as many as 400,000 new enterprises began operations in 1937, for instance. Most of them were small, and the mortality rate was high. Few new firms lasted more than a year. Indeed, 351,000 went out of business in 1937. These figures, incidentally, provide an interesting commentary on the operation of the competitive process in our economic system, and on the way inefficient firms are purged therefrom. They also underscore the fact that, from the social point of view, it is as much the function of business men to lose money as it is to make it.

There is still another angle to freedom of enterprise that deserves attention. We have a capitalistic system of free private enterprise, that is, a system in which the owners of property undertake and control business enterprises. For a time, a single individual, or a few in partnership, could initiate and carry on a business. Then, for various reasons, some of which we have mentioned, the corporate form of business organization was widely adopted. Hundreds and even thousands can now combine freely to engage in economic activities. We take such combinations of property owners for granted.

Yet the forces that induced property owners to combine were no stronger than those that have impelled workers to unite. The individual worker is a weak bargainer in the labor market. His hold on his job is usually insecure. He became increasingly aware that his income must come entirely from the sale of his labor, for he had neither the resources necessary to go into business on a modern basis nor the likelihood of getting them. Then, with the spread of education, he and his fellows became articulate; they could voice their grievances, communicate with one another, and plan together for joint action. Moreover, the worker lived in a society in which he had a vote, was free to settle his religious questions in his own way, and could roam at will in the world of ideas; but he could say nothing significant about the conditions under which he sold his labor. And finally, with his income already too small for comfort, he was made more and more dissatisfied by alluring goods forced upon his attention by skillful sales and advertising methods. It is no wonder that the workers combined into unions to sell their labor as advantageously as possible.

From the strictly economic point of view, a union is a form of business enterprise. It is a marketing agency, just as an investment trust, a fruit growers' exchange, and a dairy farmers' cooperative are. Its policies are the policies of other enterprises, although its tactics may be somewhat different. And its officers are, in effect, business men. In the face of the fact that individuals in a system of free private enterprise are presumed to be free to dispose of their resources as they please, the bitter opposition to unions is especially noteworthy. It is only a matter of a few years since unions secured a legal right to exist and do business. And it is a fact that many business men still think of them as instruments of the devil. Many a company officer who would hand out cigars and theater tickets to the persons from whom he buys his coal would like to deal out tear gas and arrest warrants to the representatives of the union from which he buys his labor.

The reasons for this antagonism between capital and labor are many. In part, they reach back into the past when, in a class-stratified society, property owners in the upper classes had rights while the workers in the lower classes had duties. In part, they stem from the fact that our economy is capitalistic as well as democratic. Labor is not a form of property, and its sellers are not considered to have the right to dispose of it through business enterprises. Yet there would appear to be nothing in a democratically organized economy to deny to the sellers of labor what is granted freely to the sellers of property. And this even though it results in a modification of capitalism.

However, the justification of a union's right to exist is no justification of its policies. These policies, like those of any other business enterprise, have to be judged in the light of their consistency with a system of free private enterprise. While this is not the place to detail union policies, it must be observed that there is much about them that is as anti-free-private-enterprise as the best — or worst — of our industrial monopolies. Competition is anathema to unionists. No union willingly tolerates another union in the same field, and no union permits its members to compete freely for jobs. Unions insist upon the closed shop or its equivalent. Moreover, they introduce inflexible elements, such as rigid wage rates and restrictive working rules, into a system that depends upon flexibility for its most efficient operation.

There are, of course, many valuable things about unions. They do improve the bargaining power of their members. They do increase job security. They do fight for better, safer, and more healthy working conditions. They do provide assistance to members in time of need. But unions, like many other business enterprises, will have to mend many of their ways if we are to retain democracy in our economy.

The role of government in our economic system is one of rapidly growing importance. During the first century of our independence, there was comparatively little call for government to engage directly in economic activities or to regulate the way people carried on their businesses. Laissez-faire was the accepted and approved government policy. Indeed, until the latter part of the last century, there was little need for government intervention. The country was big enough for each to go his own way without getting in the other fellow's way too much. But, as the country filled up, the big fellows began to step on the little ones. And it gradually became apparent that a "hands-off" policy by government could mean the end of free private enterprise. Meanwhile, the government was urged by both the little fellows and the big ones to take a hand in what was going on. The little fellows wanted help against the big; the big ones wanted to grow bigger. Slowly, but with increasing frequency, the government began to participate in the country's economic affairs.

Most of the government's economic measures were adopted to satisfy some particularly vocal group in the community.

The result is a government economic program that is neither internally coherent nor consistent. Government takes the part of consumers by developing standards for goods; by collecting and disseminating information; by penalizing enterprises that make false or misleading claims about their products, and enterprises that sell adulterated or impure foods and drugs; by encouraging consumers' cooperatives; by regulating enterprises, such as the public utilities, that provide essential services under monopolistic conditions; by antimonopoly campaigns; and by providing a wide variety of services directly through its own agencies.

Government helps property owners in many ways. For example, companies that want to sell securities are required to furnish adequate information about themselves to prospective investors. And once an investor has put his funds in an enterprise, he finds that the government does much to make the enterprise profitable. A vast fund of information on which to base business decisions is available at the taxpayers' expense. Banks are made stronger by government inspection. Depositors are protected by government-sponsored deposit insurance. Anti-trust laws help to prevent the little fellows from being gobbled up by the big ones. Tariffs protect investors in domestic enterprises from loss due to the competition of foreign concerns. Resale price maintenance laws protect investors in some domestic firms from loss because of the competition of other domestic enterprises. Then there are bounties and subsidies which enable otherwise profitless companies to operate profitably.

Government also lends a hand to workers. Through its employment offices, it helps workers to find jobs. Through its public works program, it gives them jobs. Through its factory laws, it makes jobs safer and more comfortable. Through its workmen's compensation legislation, it provides for earnings lost as a result of a work accident. With its minimum wage and maximum hour laws, government attempts to set a floor under wages and a ceiling over hours for the benefit of workers. It guarantees workers the right to organize unions and to bargain collectively. And, through its unemployment insurance program, government provides incomes for workers during involuntary idleness.

Some of these measures, such as the development of standards, the collection and dissemination of information, the preservation of competition, and the regulation of monopolies, help our economy to operate more effectively. On the other hand, other measures are inconsistent with free private enterprise. For example, the protective tariff, resale price maintenance laws, much of our farm program, and some of our labor policies are as close to free private enterprise as Ecuador is to the north pole.

The protective tariff permits the survival of business enterprises that admittedly are too inefficient to stand the rough and tumble of competition in a free and open market. Resale price maintenance laws, called "fair trade" laws in ignorance or in a cynical disregard for the facts, likewise stifle rather than promote competition. Under these laws, a dealer who could sell a product profitably at a lower price than his competitors must nevertheless keep it up to the level agreed upon by his competitors and the manufacturer of the product.

Our farm program with its governmentally fixed prices, production quotas, export subsidies, and absorption of surpluses is alien to the spirit of our economy. Farmers used to be the backbone of our individualistic system. But there are indications now that many of them are economic hangers-on to a system of which they are important political props.

When it comes to labor policy, the government deserves a great deal of credit, especially in recent years, for the extension to workers of rights that have long been enjoyed by property owners. However, in getting rid of the inequities, it must be careful lest it throw out the baby with the bath water. It is all very well to guarantee workers the right to combine, but it is quite another thing to condone the use of monopolistic policies by these combinations. In the main, no one questions the right of workers to withhold their labor by means of a strike, any more than he would question the right of a landowner to refuse to rent his land. But it is a different matter for workers on strike to prevent others, who would like to work, from working. We certainly do not allow a landowner who won't rent to force his neighbors not to rent either.

Besides intervening in the affairs of private enterprises, government has gone into business on its own account. There are ample authority and precedent for this policy. As long ago as 1776, Adam Smith, that great propagandist for free private enterprise, declared in *The Wealth of Nations:* "The sovereign [that is, the government] has . . . the duty of erecting and maintaining certain public works and certain public institutions which it can never be for the interest of any individual or small group of individuals to erect and maintain: because the profit could never repay the expense to any individual or small number of individuals, though it may frequently do much more than repay it to a great society." As if in conformity with this injunction, government in the United States has built roads and bridges, improved harbors and dug canals, operated our postal system, coined our money and provided the basis for our monetary system, and been the mainstay of our education.

With the passing of time, government has added to its productive activities in extraordinary measure. It now builds dams, generates electricity, and distributes power. It constructs ships and operates a merchant marine. It runs a railroad. It owns the largest printing establishment in the country. It provides tourist facilities. It sells insurance, engages in banking, builds houses, markets crops, and heals the sick. In fact, there are few, if any, economic activities in which government is not now engaged. Something of the economic importance of government is indicated by the fact that, in 1937, $16 out of every $100 paid to individuals came from government. For every dollar of income received by individuals from private enterprise in 1799 there were 80 in 1937; but for every dollar that individuals received from the government in 1799, there were 1630 in 1937.

In viewing these and other evidences of government's participation in our economy, some are doubtful of our ability to maintain a democratic economic system. There are, indeed, serious threats to the continuance of free private enterprise. There is some danger, of course, in the substitution of governmental for private enterprise. But there is more real danger in the ways in which government intervenes in the affairs of privately operated enterprise. And this danger is likely to become more acute with the growing necessity for government regulation of our increasingly complex economic organization. Will government intervene to promote or to destroy free private enterprise?

The answer to this question depends upon the working of our political democracy. Past experience gives the supporters of a democratic economy plenty of reason for apprehension. Government policies are decided by those who have or control the most votes. On the other hand, economic policies are decided by consumers. Political fortunes are made by doing what voters want, whereas economic fortunes are made by providing what consumers want. In recent years, however, many of those who have been unable to make a go of it in the market place have resorted to the polling booth. And in many instances, through the power of government, they have been able to secure special privileges and favors, and to obtain income out of all proportion to their economic value. Even the Sphinx must smile at the irony of a situation in which a people willing to die for democracy willingly lose it in their economic life through its operation in their political life.

There are other dangers to our democratic system. Not the least of them is the modification or disappearance of a number of the factors that contributed so materially to the growth of democracy. While we still have an abundance of resources and are likely to do so for some time to come, our preeminence in this respect is no longer what it was. Moreover, we have no monopoly of science. And, since nothing succeeds like success, we have many imitators of our technological developments. Furthermore, the need for labor is much less imperative now than it was a hundred or two hundred years ago. In addition, now that we are an established nation, we have traditions of our own that may serve as a dead weight against which new ideas and the originality of individual initiative will have to struggle. To cap it all, we are no longer isolated from the rest of the world as we were. Whether we like it or not, we are inextricably tied up with the political, economic, and cultural fortunes of our transocean neighbors. When they get into trouble, we do too.

It is considerations such as these that lead some people to think of free private enterprise as the wave of the past. They urge that we give up the freedom of our economic system for the dictation of a planned, a centrally planned, economy. To appease us, they swear by all the gods that they will preserve democracy in government. Yet how they "plan" to live half slave and half free is something of a mystery. To political realists, the possibility that a political democracy can operate a coherently planned economic system for any length of time is remote. Reread the second paragraph above to get the idea. There is, indeed, plenty of reason to believe that the end of democracy in our economy would mean the end of democracy in our government.

For those of us who believe that democracy is the best basis on which to organize our social life, for those of us who think that free private enterprise is still the best principle on which to run an economic system, much of the foregoing will be far from pleasant. But it is of vital importance for us to know how our system actually works as well as how it is supposed to work. In fact, our awareness of the shortcomings, the mistakes, and the frustrations in its operation can be turned to good advantage. The coach who uses the Warner system doesn't give it up because his team fails to score on every play or to win every game. He studies what happened, and he uses what he learns to improve his team's play in the next game. The bridge player who uses the Culbertson system doesn't throw it over when she loses a rubber or fails to make a grand slam. She holds a postmortem on her hands, and hopes she'll remember to return her partner's lead the next time. *We* can use *our* knowledge of our democratically inspired system to make it more like the democracy we wish it to be.

CHAPTER 4

THE SPIRIT OF AMERICAN SCIENCE

by SIDNEY J. FRENCH

We have been told many times in the past that science is international in scope. So it is in its language and in the exchange of ideas in peace time. But in its applications it has become the most powerful tool of selfish nationalism known to man. It is the tool of war mongers, of those who maintain that one nation or race is destined to rule all peoples, of a dictator who seeks to sweep democracy from the face of the earth.

Science has been nourished by democracy through the ages. Now, however, it has been turned against the hand that nourished it. What, then, is democracy's duty to science? Should she seek to destroy it? Should she cultivate its application to defense and war in an effort to destroy those who seek the end of democracy? Or are there values in science which transcend war, death, and dictatorship, and must be preserved and cherished at any cost? Is there anything in America's heritage in science as well as in democracy that puts this problem squarely up to her?

There are, indeed, features in American scientific traditions and ideals that are destined to make her answer to this question of vital importance to the whole world. But only from the background of her scientific development can these features be properly appreciated.

The heritage of American science stems directly from that son of American democracy, Benjamin Franklin. He

The Spirit of American Science

was, without doubt, the most startling product of unlettered and uncultured colonial America. Bawdy pioneer or suave diplomat, crude inventor or scientist of the highest merit, idol of European ladies or of European scientists, writer of idle thoughts or author of profound treatises, man of common clay or of high degree — which was he? History has never been able to distinguish, because he was all of these — and more.

It is unfortunate that popular history has pictured Franklin as a man flying a kite in a thunderstorm to draw lightning from a cloud. His real contribution to science is far more profound; he was the pioneer in a new science, the inspirer of scientists. To him electricity was more than a mere scientific plaything, more than a philosophical concept; he made it an experimental science. He opened its door to Michael Faraday, who in turn drew back the curtains for Thomas Edison. Without Franklin there could scarcely have been a Faraday, and without Faraday there assuredly would have been no Edison.

When Franklin's new lightning rods were introduced in Europe many felt that they were a device of the devil calculated to draw down the wrath of the Almighty. To prove that he was no devil, Franklin next proceeded to calm the troubled waters. By pouring oil on rough water he noted that the surface became smooth; he explained the effect in words so modern that they might have been written yesterday.

Along with other rebellious Americans, Franklin drew down the wrath of King George III of England. To humble this American rebel, the king ordered that the sharp points on the lightning rods at Kew Palace be changed to more sightly rounded knobs. From a Franklin admirer came a clever retort indicating the king's lack of knowledge of both science and society:

> While you, great George, for safety hunt,
> And sharp conductors change for blunt,
>   the Nation's out of joint.

> Franklin a wiser course pursues,
> And all your thunder fearless views
> by keeping to the point.

The point is, indeed, paradoxical. Franklin — product of a supposedly uncouth pioneer civilization that was battling its way to freedom from Europe in government, culture, and science — was, surprisingly, teaching cultivated and scientific Europe how to apply the experimental technique in both science and social ethics. Democracy had begun to raise its voice even before it was out of the womb.

It was Franklin's stimulus that gave to England — and later to America — one of their great scientists. Joseph Priestley, the stuttering English Dissenter who had an ardent passion for democracy, decided to write a book on the history of electricity and naturally turned to Franklin for advice. Franklin advised the experimental approach and Priestley discovered therein a new passion which converted him in twenty years from a little-known Dissenter to a world-famous scientist, discoverer of the most important element known to man — oxygen. It was this same Priestley whose home and laboratory were later burned by an angry Royalist mob in England, who fled for his life from the political storm to the shores of democratic America in 1794.

America "borrowed" her first scientist from Europe. But Priestley was not the last scientist to be "borrowed," or even the greatest. Today, as in those earlier days of European autocracy and unrest, democratic America is "borrowing" heavily of Europe's scientists. From Priestley all the way to Einstein, European scientists have trickled in — some, like Steinmetz and Pupin, as lowly immigrants with fame still before them; some, like Einstein, with fame already won but with freedom ahead. Through the barren scientific years of the nineteenth century men of science came to ease America's growing pains.

The high standards set by Franklin could not persist. As a free nation, America turned from Europe to the isola-

The Spirit of American Science

tion of a rugged challenging land, full of empty space and virgin resources. It is only natural that her first task was to know her vast self, the second to feed and clothe herself, and only lastly to cultivate herself. But even in establishing herself, she was influenced by the science of Europe. The American Constitution, with its grant of freedom checked by restraint, is a graphic parallel of Newtonian mechanics. From John Locke came the introduction of Newtonian concepts into political thought. As the planets revolve about the sun, each checking and balancing the other, so, reasoned Locke, men should cooperate for balanced freedom, each dependent on the other. From Locke, Jefferson received the inspiration for his philosophy of natural rights. Adams, too, was greatly impressed by the orderliness and universality of Newton's principles. Franklin, the only scientist among the framers of the Constitution, was least impressed by the application of Newtonian principles to the affairs of men, perhaps because, as a scientist, he stood less in awe of the operations of nature than did his fellow patriots.

There was little room for pure science to flourish in young America, for pure science had been for centuries, and still was, a gentleman's pastime, not a profession. With vast stretches to be traversed, with a population living close to the earth which must be fed and clothed, with little wealth and no heritage, America must perforce turn to the practical arts. Franklin knew this; he was himself the prototype of the typical American inventor of the nineteenth century. But unlike the inventors who followed him, he was first a scientist whose inventions stemmed from pure science. He recognized the needs of a new nation when he founded the first American Philosophical Society in Philadelphia in 1743. Its purpose was to "promote *useful* knowledge," whereas that of the staid Royal Society of London, founded a century earlier, was to "promote natural knowledge."

Incidentally, it was the need for food, set against a background of revolution and Napoleonic dictatorship in France, that led to the founding of one of America's most remarkable industries. In his youth, Eleuthère Irénée du Pont had learned the art of powder-making under the greatest scientist of the eighteenth century, Antoine Laurent Lavoisier. As a side line to his great work in science, Lavoisier had taken over the decadent powder monopoly of France and had built it as a government agency into an organization that produced the finest powder in the world. It was this powder that finally won the American Revolution, that enabled the French Revolution to hold its enemies at bay, that started Napoleon on his era of conquest. It was this powder, too, that contributed in no small measure to Lavoisier's fall and eventual death on the guillotine.

In 1800, Du Pont reached America's shores, a fugitive from the shifting tides of political oppression in Europe. He had no wealth, but he had a growing family to support. His days of powder-making were long since past, but he had to earn a living, get food for his family somehow. He tried hunting but found the unscientific American powder poor. Then he realized his opportunity. As Lavoisier had made the best powder in Europe, he would make the best powder in America — by Lavoisierian methods. He built himself a "modern" powder mill on the banks of the Brandywine. It was not war but the need for food upon which America's first great munitions industry was founded. So too, it has not been war, but peace, that has built out of that munitions factory the great industry which now translates the findings of science into the language of necessity and luxury.

This was not an isolated incident; there were thousands more like it, resulting from Europe's insistence that man was not capable of governing himself. Europe's intolerance gave America her chance.

The nineteenth century is far from being a century of science in America. During those one hundred years, America produced but one scientist to rank with a Newton, a Darwin, a Lavoisier, or a Faraday. But Europe herself produced little more. Pure science as a challenging game for gentlemen was passing out with the increasing specialization of science, and science as a profession had not yet entered. It was a century of interlude.

But what America lacked in pure science she more than made up in invention, the child of science. Americans are not a race of born inventors. But in a young and growing country there was great need for invention. European methods of transportation and communication were not suited to the vast reaches of America; Europe had an abundance of labor, America a paucity. Furthermore, America set out deliberately on the democratic policy of educating the masses and thus releasing her otherwise hidden genius. Yankee ingenuity is not a myth; it is simply one expression of democracy in a new and virile nation.

Fulton adapted Watt's invention of the steam engine to navigation by water because he saw a real need for better transportation in a land whose distances were so great — and because there was money to be made in a successful steamboat. So America gave the world the steamboat.

In 1844 Samuel F. Morse put together some ideas of Franklin and Faraday and produced the telegraph. Again, communication in a far-flung, sparsely settled land provided the idea; profit, the motive. From Bell came the telephone; from Edison, the dynamo to make possible the transportation of electricity in large amounts. From Burbank, through an almost mystic sense of choice, came the application of the principles of breeding to swell the products of agriculture. From Eli Whitney came the cotton gin and the beginning of mass production. Cyrus McCormick provided the harvester as a substitute for labor on the farm. Through the century inventions poured in to substitute machines for America's lack of manpower.

Thus did America solve the problem of knowing herself and feeding and clothing herself in the nineteenth century. Inventions are as typical of our nineteenth-century democracy as the political spellbinder and the torchlight parade; they represent the growing pains of democracy.

While America invented, Europe was changing her scientific atmosphere. Science was no longer merely a part of philosophy, merely a gentleman's game. But not till 1825 could a student secure laboratory training in scientific techniques in a college or university, for no laboratories were available. Faraday obtained his training by washing bottles for Sir Humphry Davy. Carl Wilhelm Scheele, Sweden's greatest scientist, stole time and space in his employer's pharmacy. Lavoisier opened his own laboratory, endowed by his private fortune, to a few ambitious young men.

Science in Europe had sunk to a low degree shortly after the beginning of the nineteenth century. England's two great universities, Oxford and Cambridge, offered no courses in it. Only Faraday and Dalton remained to finish up the great work of Newton, Boyle, Priestley, and others. With the death of Lavoisier, France had passed her zenith in science. True, other great European scientists were on the way to break the monotony of the nineteenth century. France was still to bring forth Pasteur and Curie; England, Darwin, Clerk Maxwell, and Thomson.

But in 1825 an event of importance took place in the little town of Giessen, Germany, which gave science a new life. The first experimental laboratory in science for students was opened by the University of Giessen at the insistence of Justus Liebig. There, students could come to learn the experimental techniques of chemistry. Insignificant as this event may seem, it was to mark the beginning of a new era in science, an era of widespread experimental science with Germany in the lead.

Many circumstances combined to give Germany her dominant position in nineteenth-century science. She became united for the first time since the sixteenth century and could thus play an independent role in European culture. The lack of natural resources and a seafaring tradition led to an early attempt at self-sufficiency. The science of Newton, Boyle, Lavoisier, and Faraday had no connection with industry, whereas the science developed in Germany was closely linked with it. It was a practical working combination realized for the first time between science and industry; each stimulated and helped to finance the other. It was this combination which played an important part in wresting from England the industrial leadership of Europe as the century wore on.

So rapid was the growth of chemistry in a country which, prior to 1800, had contributed little to this science, that by the middle of the century Germany had taken a lead that was to last till the World War of 1914 finally broke her hold. So great did her prestige in science become that no American scientist, particularly a chemist, could be deemed fully educated until he had studied at the feet of German masters. Even English scientists topped off their scant training at Oxford or Cambridge with work in Germany.

As far as pure science was concerned, the nineteenth century was an era of empiricism, of fact-collecting, of tabulating, of summarizing, of testing. Few great principles were discovered, but the collection and codification of the factual material were necessary preludes to further advance. In this type of careful, accurate, painstaking work the German scientist was a master and the world owes him a great debt, for without him the progress of the twentieth century would be almost impossible. Such men as Wöhler, Liebig, Kekulé, Wurtz, Baeyer, and Ostwald reduced the chaos of organic chemistry to a beautiful sequence of logical facts. Had this happened in England, with its tradition of science for the sake of science, it would probably have remained a sequence of logical facts, quite unrelated to any practical use. But in Germany there was no such tradition. The value of science there lay not in merely seeking the truth, but in applying it to the use of men. In 1914 and again in 1939, Germany was able to prove to the world the nationalistic value of this hand-and-glove operation of science and industry.

By 1885, Germany had begun to build up her world-wide monopoly in organic chemicals and coal-tar products, a monopoly which more than any other factor opened the eyes of America to the real possibilities in chemistry in 1914–1918.

While Germany was passing into the age of chemical science, America was still inventing machines; she remained without a science which might be called her own. But industrially, she was beginning to rival Germany. Even so, the increasing specialization in science was beginning to mark America. The student laboratory was coming in rapidly under a system of democratic education for the masses. Land-grant colleges were training engineers as well as agriculturalists. As industries grew in size, the inventor was giving way to the trained technician — but not before he had established American industrialism on so firm a foundation that it could compete with that of Germany. As yet, however, there was little international competition because America was still filling her own orders; immigrants were pouring in by the hundreds of thousands.

Of inventors there were plenty; of scientists, few. America had produced no Faraday, no Newton. Or had she? It was perhaps her very nearness to the earth, to elemental things, her intentness on invention and expansion that caused her to ignore the existence of one of her greatest pure scientists of the nineteenth century. Yet the far-reaching principles enunciated by him are the very foundation stones of most of modern industry.

Crowther in his *Famous American Men of Science* tells the story which indicates all too well the greatness which America has ignored for three-quarters of a century.

After the annual dinner of a British Scientific Society held in London within the last decade, twenty or thirty of the members retired to a café in order to continue informal conversations on topics of common interest. A discussion presently arose on the relative importance of various famous scientific discoveries. Everyone became keenly interested in the many-sided question, and the arguments became more and more earnest and involved. After a time, one of the participants suggested that the results of the discussion might be clearer if they could be expressed in a mathematical form, such as a ballot. A ballot was accordingly organized, and each member was asked to write down, in order of importance, the names of twenty scientists whom he conceived to be the greatest that have appeared since the Renaissance. The orders on the separate ballot papers were combined so as to give a collective order. In this way the party's collective opinion and order of the twenty greatest scientists since the Renaissance was ascertained.

Newton was the first name on the list, Darwin was the second and Faraday and Einstein were bracketed third. The next name was Willard Gibbs. His very high place was due not to a few votes which put him first, but to uniformly high placing by nearly all the voters."[1]

Yet, in America, the name of Willard Gibbs has been presented for America's Hall of Fame twice and has failed both times to win a place.

So little are Willard Gibbs and his work known and appreciated here that the mere mention of the name draws a blank stare. "Who was Willard Gibbs, and what did he do?" Why was his name so revered in England and Germany that Clerk Maxwell preached Gibbs to all Europe, that German professors of mathematics and physics could raise no sign of recognition at the mention of any American scientist until Gibbs' name was mentioned? Why was Gibbs so little recognized in America that the students of Yale were quite ignorant of the genius in their midst? Why did industry, which now uses the principles developed by Gibbs in all their many ramifications, fail to see that money was to be made from his work?

The answers to all these questions are relatively simple. For one thing, Gibbs never became popularly known in America because he was ahead of his time. Machines were

[1] J. G. Crowther, *Famous American Men of Science*, New York: W. W. Norton and Co., Inc., p. 229.

the one phase of industry to which his principles had little application. Gibbs wrote in mathematical terms with an academic precision which few in this country were capable of understanding. Someone has said of Laplace's writings in mathematics that when the statement, "It is now easy to see," appeared, the reader could prepare himself for a tussle of several hours in attempting to understand what followed. So it was with Gibbs' work. Furthermore, Gibbs was not concerned with the possible application of his principles to industry. He was concerned with meeting the challenge of nature and interpreting her laws in a precise manner.

Finally, America was still looking to Europe for leadership in science; she was under the influence of the dominating German science and was quite modestly unaware that she might hatch a genius of her own. So firm was she in this belief that she failed to recognize the genius when he appeared.

What was Gibbs' great work? Most simply expressed it was this: He discovered the laws that control all solutions and mixtures of substances. Where do these laws fit into industry? In the making of alloys and paints, in the blending of oils, in the making of synthetic materials of many types — in fact, in almost every modern industry, except the making and utilization of machines. Gibbs in the nineteenth century laid the foundations for our industry of the twentieth century. Not industry alone has now discovered his importance; his principles apply equally well in biology, in medicine; the human body with its many complex mixtures and solutions is, perhaps, the greatest exemplification of them.

The sorry story of Willard Gibbs is all too enlightening as to the state of pure science in America in the latter part of the nineteenth century. America was still grubbing out the forests, building railroads and telegraph lines, flinging her wealth of natural resources around like a child turned loose in a library of rare volumes. She had as little time for the cultivation of pure science as she had for the cultivation of fine music, art, or literature. She was still an adolescent.

But in the invention of machines she led the world. The sewing machine, the typewriter, the harvester, and a thousand other products of Yankee ingenuity were balancing the labor shortage and furnishing food, clothing, and work for the flood of immigrants. Large industries were rapidly replacing handworking shops as rapid transportation systems paved the way for the concentration of production. We were reaching the age of Trusts and Combines; great wealth was flowing into the hands of a few men.

It seems paradoxical that great wealth should often prompt its possessor to endow institutions not designed to produce wealth. But such is often the case. By the beginning of the twentieth century, accumulated wealth had begun to flow back into normal channels through the hitherto dry arroyos of pure science and art. Thus began America's development of pure science.

Astronomy, one of the first of the sciences to profit through this system, can scarcely be called a practical science. It is, indeed, an expensive science calling for elaborate equipment; only with the most powerful telescopes can the limits of space be pushed back to discover what lies beyond. The machine age in democracy has truly given America her leadership in astronomy. The endowing of institutes of medical research has given her the leadership in this field. Great foundations like the Carnegie, Rockefeller, and Guggenheim have all had incalculable influence in building up American science as well as American culture.

We may not all agree that the donor should have the right to dispose of his wealth as he sees fit, but we can agree that, in the main, democracy has functioned unusually well in such instances. The wealth has gone into building up the future, not into dissipating the present.

Near the end of the nineteenth century, the sciences of physics and chemistry had apparently reached dead ends.

Everything that could be weighed or measured had been weighed, measured, and recorded. Conclusions had been drawn; Newton's hypotheses had all been checked, verified, and vindicated. "Finis" could be written to the science of physics.

The facts of chemistry were carefully catalogued in Germany. The periodic table predicted that there should be only ninety-two chemical elements. All but a few of these had been discovered and studied exhaustively. What was there left to do? Germany was handling the discovery of new organic compounds well and might be trusted to continue that fine work. The possibility of synthesizing new organic compounds was about exhausted — so thought the empiricists. F. P. Venable, American historian of chemistry, wrote in 1893, "It can scarcely be expected that the chemistry of the future will progress with the rapid leaps which the passing century has witnessed. . . . The chemistry of today is no longer synthetical; the third quarter saw this rise to its highest point." [2]

How wrong a historian can be when he attempts to look into the future is fully evidenced by the chemistry of the twentieth century. Its progress is to that of the nineteenth century as the progress of a pursuit plane to an ox-cart. The synthetic chemistry of the last century was nothing but a preface to a mighty book, the chapters of which appear in ever-increasing length and without apparent end.

Physics, too, has opened a new book, the preface of which was written in the immortal discoveries of Becquerel, Curie, Thomson, Ramsay, Soddy, and a host of others. No longer is physics primarily concerned with weighing and measuring matter, with the aspects of its gross structure. It is probing into the very heart of the atom to discover of what stuff it is made; to discover the mechanism which holds it together; to discover the trigger which may release its bound-up

[2] F. P. Venable, *A Short History of Chemistry*, Boston: D. C. Heath and Co., p. 144.

energy. As organic chemicals were synthesized in the nineteenth century, so physics now synthesizes atoms, but on a smaller scale. Gone is the lethargy of the physicist, for the thresholds of new discoveries lie all around him.

In these great shifting movements of science that started as the present century swung into place, America played no part. Radium had no significance in machines or in any other industry. It would not pull trains or make shoes for immigrants. The interiors of atoms, like the interiors of stars, were of no immediate concern to democracy or the problem of food and clothes. Germany was making synthetic organic chemicals and sending them to America for consumption. Why, then, should we bother to make them? They were of minor importance — so we argued.

But beneath this apparent indifference to science was a dawning consciousness of its importance. Markets in the machine age were finally reaching an apparent saturation point. The centralization of industry had increased the importance of the technical man. The lessons of science and industry taught by Germany were making some impression. At first, only those technical men who could turn ideas into dollars were wanted; then gradually the thought sifted through, that before ideas could be turned into dollars there must be fundamental concepts, and these stemmed from pure science.

One of the greatest factors in making American industry research-conscious was Thomas Alva Edison. But not until 1917 was this lesson finally learned. Edison was the last great product of a century of invention. First and foremost he was an inventor, not a scientist. Unschooled in the fundamental principles of pure science, he was a striking example of the usual trend reversed. Invention led him ultimately to some important scientific truths and made a scientist of him. Mr. Ford's statement, "Edison was a scientist, but also he was a man of extraordinary common sense," carried its own implication of American industry's opinion of the scientist in an era of mass industrialism. Because industry had grown up without invoking the aid of science, it is often assumed that science is still a plaything far removed from industry. But that statement applied to eighteenth- and nineteenth-century science, not to the science of the twentieth century. Mr. Ford is himself a scientist of the Edisonian type and it is quite natural that he should take the point of view he does. Yet, without the discovery of the *principle* of the internal combustion engine, there would be no Ford automobile today. It is of course equally true that without the Yankee ingenuity of a Henry Ford, the *principle* of internal combustion could still be nothing but an abstract concept.

The point which Mr. Ford does not emphasize is that the applications made by the Edisons are based upon the discoveries of the Faradays, the Lavoisiers, and the Newtons. If all scientists were "practical" men, great segments of science — those which show no immediate prospects of being turned into dollars or into benefits for mankind — would remain forever unexplored. Yet some of these supposedly useless segments, these scientific toys, have eventually found the most surprising applications to the needs and uses of man. The world is suddenly becoming conscious of the fact that physicists in their target-shooting at atoms, in their "playing around" with cyclotrons, may soon discover processes that will render our present means of producing energy as obsolete as the windmill.

The polarizing crystal has long been an interesting curiosity to the scientist; now it shows promise of revolutionizing our lighting methods. For years scientists played with electrical discharges in Geissler tubes. Now these tubes cast their pink neon glow along the store fronts of every main street in America. Soon they will light our homes.

Yes, Edison was a great factor in shifting the American outlook in science. But let us fervently hope that this shift will not do us more harm than good. Let us hope that the Newtons, the Faradays, the Lavoisiers, the Darwins, the

Gibbs, the Einsteins will not disappear forever from the earth.

In fact, therein lies America's great future in science — to see to it that such men have a haven in a world of strife to work as they please and on what they please; to see to it that they do *not* fall under the dollar pressure of industry; to see to it that they do not starve because their products are ideas that lack a potential dollar sign. We have made a fine start in this direction through such organizations as the Institute of Higher Learning and our numerous scientific foundations, but we must do more — much more. It is not, as Mr. Ford's statement implies, that pure science refuses to soil its hands with grimy industry. It is that we must keep open those avenues which apparently lead nowhere but which through a sudden turn may reveal a new panoramic segment of science never before known to exist, a segment in whose soil may grow many useful ideas for the betterment of man.

We cannot expect industry to bear the load of this type of research, nor should we expect to rely on benevolence in a democracy. Yet modern industry is shouldering a surprising amount of the burden today in a somewhat incidental manner. Research toward a certain end often opens up new avenues which may have little connection with the objective of the industry. Often these avenues are passed by, sealed up, and we must wait many years for results that might have had great value in some other field.

For the sake of the future, we cannot afford to turn all our scientists into "practical" men. We must have some — as many as possible — who will stop to explore the supposedly blind alleys. Our great universities fostered by democracy must see to it that there is room in their laboratories for these men. They must not be alarmed by the cry that university scientists are far too theoretical and lack practical common sense. If this cry of "wolf" is heeded, we shall find our science, which is still in its infancy in point of time, going the way of German science today. True, the universities must train technical scientists for the needs of modern industry, but they must do more: they must train scientists who can resist the lucrative lure of industry and shut themselves up in ivory towers. We cannot forever continue to burn the fuel of present accumulated science; someone must gather new fuel.

The first World War was the final blow that drove home the wedge of industrial research started by Edison. It showed America her great weakness in certain segments of applied science. It revealed our total dependence on Germany for organic chemicals of all kinds, for laboratory equipment, for optical instruments, and for many other products of science. Germany had successfully and quietly tied the whole world to her scientific apron-strings. Few who lived through the early days of that war will forget how hard it was to get even an aspirin tablet, how the crude American-made dyes ran with the water and faded with the sun. Few military men can forget the apparent magic with which Germany could convert her drug and dye industry into a munitions industry overnight. Here was careful planning. Even more startling is the revelation of the close coupling of German science and industry in the present war.

Not only did World War I finally open America's eyes to the importance of science in industry, but it also gave her the opportunity to try out her science in industry, particularly in the field of organic chemistry. With an energy that is little short of astounding, she went to work in this field. The great quickening of the pulse of applied chemistry in America dates from the shock of the first World War.

There was no assurance, however, that America would be able to maintain this new advance once the war was over, for Germany would seek to regain her lost market. It took another important factor to put this new type of industrial adventure on its feet and well out in the lead. This factor was the end of the period of physical expansion. Industry could no longer depend on a rapidly increasing population, on the extension of railroad and telegraph lines, on the cutting of forests or the mining of ore. The age of the automobile was well started; the radio and the electrical refrigerator were coming in. Even these could not offset a major depression. Only the new chemical industries were equipped to face this change. They were not depending on the principle of mass production; they were *substituting* new products for old, synthetic for natural. Moreover, these products were better adapted to man's use than the natural products. Therein lay the great strength of this new synthetics industry. With it comes a new type of industrialism, one which places the technical scientist in the key position. As an indication of the significance of this new industry for both the present and the future, we need only think in terms of nylon, vinyon, synthetic rubbers, plastics, light alloys, glass fabrics, sulfanilamide, and a host of other new synthetics developed largely in this country.

The true significance of the technical change taking place around us has hardly dawned as yet. We are in the midst of an industrial revolution which promises to be far more significant in its reaction on industry and on social relations than that which came with the early machine.

This is a revolution in which the sciences of physics and chemistry are playing major roles. It is bound to leave its deep marks on democracy. It may even destroy her by its production of great new scientific forces, or it may preserve and promote her as the only possible type of civilization capable of controlling these forces for the use of all men. Whatever it does, it will not leave democracy as it found her. Democracy herself will have to change profoundly.

That America has finally come of age in science is evidenced on every hand. That she leads the world today in science, both applied and pure, is no idle boast. We are too close to the present to judge whether we have produced in the current generation or two a Newton, a Faraday, or an Einstein. But the names of Millikan, Michelson, Lewis,

Langmuir, Lawrence, Urey, along with several dozen more, are significant in pure science. Chamberlain and Moulton have given the world the planitesimal hypothesis to replace Laplace's unworkable nebular hypothesis as an explanation for the origin of the solar system.

In biochemistry and medicine, America has forged well into the lead. With true democratic principles, she has first provided the world's highest proportion of medical practitioners to care for the health of her people. Through the influence of her medical foundations she has focused sharp attention on the long-neglected field of medical research. One of the most unique organizations for the fostering of research in biochemical fields is the Wisconsin Alumni Research Foundation. The Foundation was started by Steenbock's discovery that the vitamin D content of certain foods could be greatly increased by subjecting them to ultraviolet light. The discovery was patented, and the major income from the use of the patent is placed in the Research Foundation to be used for fostering further research.

This is an example of practical working democracy, an example of what can be done on a larger scale to foster the pure research of the future.

This great progress in science has taken place so suddenly that we are still wondering how we got there. We are still looking back toward Europe and wondering just what has happened to turn America from a humble follower to a vigorous leader. The French phrase for almost anything that happens is *C'est la guerre!* It was the war that threw the leadership in science, as in many other fields, on America's doorstep. Leadership in science she accepted; leadership in other important fields she has rejected. But the leadership in science would not have remained in America had she not been prepared, through many unconscious years of building toward it, to assume it.

Our educational system has trained technical workers to bring power not to the state but to themselves; it has pro-

The Spirit of American Science

vided the emolument, the stimulus, the time, and the freedom for scientific training and research. Independence in thought and action accounted for a century of invention to meet our specific and peculiar needs; invention gave rise to a consciousness of the need for science and its value in human affairs. Wealth acquired through invention flowed back through the channels of pure science to build up the power-head of energy needed to vitalize science.

As the child suddenly reaches manhood without being conscious of having acquired the necessary attributes of manhood, so America finds herself of age in science without having been conscious of filling in the necessary background.

However, this sudden increase in the tempo of science in America is not without its dangers to American democracy. Our Constitution was written for a pioneer country, sparsely populated and widely scattered. Like a gas, the molecules of American life were far apart, each moving in its own sphere, an independent unit. Collisions were relatively few. Every scientist knows that the laws applicable to a gas cease to operate when the gas is condensed to a liquid. The individual particles are no longer independent, no longer free to follow separate paths. They become merged into a common pattern, and even their fundamental properties are changed to suit the needs of the aggregate. The more individualistic the molecules, the greater becomes the necessary modification of their character.

Civilization has been condensed by science during the past half century till it is no longer a far-flung gas. We are no longer human molecules operating in our little independent spheres; we are parts of a pattern and our conduct must be modified accordingly. It is this that democracy must ultimately recognize and for which it must make due allowance if it is to survive in this crowded world.

True, we are committed to democracy, but not to static democracy. No static form of government can hope to endure for long — history is full of records of the fall of static states. In place of the individual freedom of older democracy must come correlated freedom; in place of independent effort, coordinated effort. Politically we are conscious of the need for such changes, but individually we resist the compressing force of science. Our scientific achievements have outstripped our social abilities to adjust.

The compression of civilization by science has brought men into more frequent conflict with one another. Eventually this should breed greater tolerance, but in the interval it breeds more wars. It is an unfortunate consequence of science that it places immense physical power in the hands of unscrupulous men. A simple adaptation of the scientific products developed for peaceful use suffices to convert them into terrifying weapons of war.

When the Wright brothers first flew in their "box kite with an engine in it" at Kitty Hawk, they had nothing but peace in their hearts and minds. Yet the airplane has become war's most destructive weapon. The tractor tread was invented in America to plow the sodden ground better. A simple adaptation made it the basis of the modern war tank. The radio, developed commercially in the United States for reaching across great stretches of country, has become war's most powerful propaganda agent. The telephone and the telegraph have both played important roles in war. Peace-loving America has contributed more than her share of war's deadly weapons.

Shall we, then, stop discovering and building these new scientific instruments of peace to prevent their adaptation to war? The answer is, of course, no! Modern scientific warfare is no more barbarous than war fought with bayonets, spears, or poisoned arrows to those engaged in it. The principal difference is that the war front has been extended to include all civilians of the warring nations. This extension may even have beneficial results. Nations will become less eager to fight, knowing that their entire population must be on the receiving end of the war. Alfred Nobel, donor of the famous prizes in peace and the sciences, made his fortune through the invention of dynamite. He believed — and sincerely — that the most successful way to end all war was to make war so horrible that men would refuse to fight. Thus far his theory has not been proved true, but nevertheless considerable evidence supports the idea as war continues to take heavier and heavier tolls of civilian life, as civilians as well as soldiers of the line become dead heroes.

Nowhere has the close connection between science and war been more clearly recognized or more aptly applied than in Germany. The close relation between science, industry, and government has been largely responsible for her mighty war machine. Under the Nazi regime, however, science has given way to technical adaptation. Hitler is burning the accumulated fuel of German science in one great conflagration.

Scientists have always claimed immunity from political strife, and in the main they have been granted it. Even the bloody French Revolution spared the lives of its scientists regardless of their views, except for Lavoisier. But in Germany today, no immunity exists for scientists. It is assumed, *a priori*, that no one but a Nazi can be a good scientist. In the Nazi version, Einstein is just a dogmatist. Born, Schrödinger, Jordan, Heisenberg, and Sommerfeld — Jews who have given the world the magnificent modern theory of the atom — are all merely physico-mathematical acrobats.

Hitler himself regards science as of little consequence; this is evident when he writes concerning education in *Mein Kampf,* "Our first aim must be the development of character, especially of will power, and a readiness to take responsibility; scientific training follows far behind." Hitler's attitude toward science is incomprehensible. Why has he deliberately sold Germany's great heritage of science for a sorry mess of technical immediacy? Was it because he regarded it as part and parcel of international Jewry? Or did he hope to adorn Nazism with its robes? The ill winds upon which he has cast

German science are blowing it straight into the arms of the democracies. If the process continues for long, Germany, like Japan, will become a nation of imitators, a nation of adapters. Whatever Hitler's reasons, the world stands to lose by this ruthless destruction of cherished treasures. Unless the United States or some other democracy is prepared and ready to take over the functions of tabulating, coordinating, and classifying scientific data that Germany has done so well for a century, the world will suffer a setback comparable to the fall of Roman civilization.

Hitler's attitude is at variance with that of all the other dictators of modern history. Napoleon subsidized science heavily. Mussolini, until he came under the domination of his stronger partner, encouraged science in the vain hope that Italy, barren of natural resources, might achieve synthetic self-sufficiency. The attitude toward science in Soviet Russia is in sharp contrast to that of Hitler. As in Germany, science works for the state but in a different manner. Russia takes the long view; she encourages pure scientific research. She has taken her pattern from pre-Nazi Germany and from America. Bernal in *The Social Function of Science* estimates the following total percentages of the national income spent for scientific research of all kinds:

Soviet Union	0.8%
United States	0.5%
Germany (1930)	0.13–0.17%
England	0.1%

Russia has been quick to recognize the value of scientific research. This recognition has grown out of practical scientific needs. All the funds for research come directly from the government. In the United States, on the other hand, the national government provides but a small proportion. In Russia, even more than in the United States, science is taught in the schools from the lowest grade up to the highest. Popular information on it is widely disseminated. There is, of course, a high degree of coordination in her science because of dictation from the top. This coordination is lacking in a democracy.

The contrast in the attitude toward science in Russia and Germany today is both marked and somewhat paradoxical. Germany, who spent a century building her magnificent edifice, is doing her best to destroy it in a generation. Russia, with no traditional roots in science, is cultivating the soil carefully and assiduously. She still has far to go; but with a continuance of her present policy, she may well become America's greatest rival in science in the future.

We return to our original question. What is democracy's duty toward science? Must she destroy it? Must she use it as the dictators use it? Or must she preserve it at all costs?

Destroy it she could not. Even were she to control the world by force, which of itself would destroy democracy, she could never put an end to the advance of science. It is inherent in the nature of man to discover new facts, learn new ways, and build new things. Legislative prohibition of science would be not farcical but extremely dangerous; bootleg science would become the tool of power wherever science was outlawed.

Democracy must use science as the dictators use it — for the present at least. If not, there will be no democracy — and no science as we understand it. Fortunately, America's heritage and tradition in science make this possible. Invention and mass-production methods can meet the threat of mechanized warfare. This threat must be met with all our Yankee ingenuity and the fullest application of technical science possible. That is the immediate necessity for democracy, but it is not the ultimate necessity.

The importance of science to man must transcend war, death, and dictatorship. Through the science of the future lies a highway to peace. The shadows of war point up the destructive factors of science, but these same factors, remember, were born of peace and will return to peace. Drug factories may be converted into explosives plants overnight, but this must not blind us to the fact that drugs have saved far more lives than explosives have destroyed. Chlorine as a poison gas has taken lives in war, but it has saved countless thousands because it kills bacteria as well as men. Arsenic compounds have been used as poison gases in war, but arsenic in the form of salvarsan has brought hope to hundreds of thousands afflicted with syphilis. Sulfanilamide and its newer allies are closely related to explosives; but at present they represent man's greatest hope for life. Shall we abandon research on them because they might conceivably be used in war?

The airplane rains death and destruction over Europe at the moment, but it has also made possible the discovery of new lands; carried vaccines and drugs to inaccessible, stricken areas; brought help to those laid low by storm, pestilence, and earthquake; carried children to the deathbeds of parents; carried good will across oceans; welded together peoples of different cultures; and saved men from icy deaths in oceans and lakes. The radio may be the greatest agent of propaganda known to man, but it is also the greatest agent of education. As it unifies nations, so it may be used to unify continents and the world. In time of flood, fire, and famine it directs help to stricken areas. It can become the greatest agent of peace and good will known to man.

Tractor treads rumble across Europe on tanks, but far more of them rumble across brown fields on agricultural machines. Nitrates form the basis of modern war explosives, but far more of them are used to fertilize these same brown fields that the world may have food to eat. Let us never overlook these facts and many similar ones when we condemn science for the role it plays in war.

We can never reach world self-sufficiency through the brutality of war; we merely shift the areas of self-sufficiency. We may never be able to reach it through science either, but this avenue offers more hope than war. The ultimate goal of science must be that man shall know himself and his environment and, through knowing, be able to control himself and his environment to the ends of living more fully and more richly with his fellow men. To such a goal democracy can subscribe without equivocation; dictatorship cannot. Is there any hope of reaching this goal through science? There is; but it is a hope that can be fulfilled only through cooperation, only through the continued careful cultivation of science for the benefit of man, not for his destruction.

Germany, once the world's benefactor in science, has become the world's destroyer through science. To her former role the democracies must fall heir. There is no other way. There is no question as to what democracy's role in science must be during the immediate crucial future. She must be the protector and guardian of pure science. She must provide the ivory towers where "impractical" scientists may sit and dream their dreams. She must offer a haven for all scientists driven forth from other lands by oppression.

If we make vitamins by the ton today, tomorrow we may be able to guarantee a balanced diet to every man, woman, and child on earth. As we tap the atom today, we may be able tomorrow to provide energy to operate the world's machines at a fraction of the present cost and thus supply shelter and clothing for the whole world. These are the goals for which democracy must work in science. They are the only goals worth while because they are the only ones that can ever insure permanent peace on the earth.

CHAPTER 5

THE SPIRIT OF AMERICAN ART

by ALFRED KRAKUSIN

When the average person is asked to describe what first comes into his mind at the mention of the word "art," he usually describes a picture that has nothing to do with the American scene. His ideas of art are usually based on some knowledge of a few European paintings which he remembers rather vaguely. Most of us have been exposed to European paintings which may have been more skillfully painted than our native products. The artists who created these well-known works may perhaps have been more intuitive, more inspired, more romantic.

But let us take a look at the American art scene. Here are works by such men as Thomas Eakins, Winslow Homer, Caleb Bingham, to mention a few of the early great ones. These men have established what we are proud to recognize as the backbone of the American tradition in painting. They may not have been as subtle as their European contemporaries, perhaps not as imaginative; yet they have offered us, in place of intricate delicacies and dubious sophistication, robust values that we are happy to recognize as healthy and purposeful. These are values that belong to a nation reared in the Calvinistic spirit. This matter-of-fact thinking is a solid tradition. It has an inner core of stern Puritanical morality that is not easily snapped. In the hands of these straightforward men, painting in America has always been a legitimate enterprise, not merely an artistic exercise. It is a

The Spirit of American Art

form of work that these men have gone into for practical reasons. Their attitudes and motives are observable; the result is not superficial.

That there is an essential American character to American painting is because it was our good fortune to have had men like Homer, Bingham, Eakins, and others during the middle and latter part of the past century who did not have delicate temperaments. Their make-up did not go to pieces after the first shock. Fortunately they were not of such intricate and delicate construction mentally that they were easily disturbed by the crudities of their time. They took these realities in their stride. These men were not clever painters nor were they artistic fellows; whenever they lean that way they step out of character.

When American painters begin to subdue their real personalities and substitute for them something that is unnatural, we find a sharp cleavage between what is truly our own and what is borrowed. Benjamin West, Gilbert Stuart, and other nineteenth-century artists who painted battle scenes are in this category.

The strong, moral, and strangely masculine attitude observable in American realistic painting that appeared less than a hundred years ago proves that there is an intrinsic value in this authentic American stream. When this attitude crosses the streams from Old World sources this value is disturbed. This masculine quality has a special meaning to us in America. It is as American as baseball, Ring Lardner, barber shops, horseshoe pitching, and the like. It is the quality that suggests directness and simplicity, and holds out for truthfulness above all things. It is often as provincial and domestic as an old shoe.

As this country felt its early growing strength and the promise in its potential boundaries in the "roaring forties," there appeared on the scene more citizens with independent points of view who pushed westward and settled there because they were adventuresome and highly individualistic.

Evidence of this individualistic temperament showed itself whenever some group or groups felt that the part of the country in which they were living was not democratic enough for them — they packed up their children and their tools and went westward. The Civil War played no small part in releasing restless groups from the East for these adventuresome extensions of our borders.

This attitude and this direct courageous effort of the more adventurously-minded are reflected in the paintings of some of their contemporaries who were also rugged individualists owing no debt to any established school of painting. The experiences of these first seekers of pure democracy and the spirit with which they met their trials are depicted simply and without embellishments by our first realistic painters. At no time in these early accounts, in paint, of those settlers before and after the Civil War is there any attempt to suggest the heroic. The simple matter-of-course recording of the outpost experiences indicates a natural desire for restraint, a natural denial of dramatics. All the homely experiences that would naturally follow from these new and often bare beginnings are seen in such paintings as Caleb Bingham's shallow boat calmly drifting down the river with the typical settler, his wife, cat, and a few belongings taking the new world as they found it. Homer's painting of country children in their schoolhouse and at play in Mark Twain's childhood days is another frank, non-dramatic, or non-sentimental document of these new and vigorous days.

These experiences that we label as fundamental American experiences go back a great deal further than the middle of the nineteenth century. But unfortunately the painters who left us records in paint of our seventeenth and eighteenth centuries were either job-lot itinerant portrait painters, or derivative English academy painters who satisfied the leisure class of our few large cities and towns with portraits that were diluted versions of the English academic paintings of the time. These same derivative painters also went in for the so-called battle-piece picture; this is really a watery English version of an American battle and, as such, need not interest us except as to who won or lost. Our architecture of these early periods records the sturdy, singularly nationalistic values of the time far better than do the affected historical paintings.

Too much cannot be said of these beginnings of the great tradition in American painting. Winslow Homer and Caleb Bingham are but two of our pioneer spirits whose works express this business of seeing the American scene through realistic, unaffected eyes. In their work we recognize, now more than ever, reflections of the truly authentic beginnings of our national character.

Homer and Bingham were not men who retired to a Bohemian garret to paint romantic, genteel pictures. They were both robust, outdoor types. Homer lived and worked not only as a good newspaper correspondent for *Harper's Weekly* during the Civil War, but as a lonely, enthusiastic painter of the rocky, wave-battered Maine coast. The sea and the tough Maine fishermen who went to sea and battled the elements for their daily livelihood are shown with restrained drama. We see, almost for the first time in Homer's work, an essential rough and ready quality that is a distinctive native product. These bearded American fishermen are hardy, rocklike men. Homer makes no attempt to romanticize them; rather, he tries to record dispassionately their staunch character. It is important to realize that there is a sturdy bond between this hard-working outdoor painter and these gnarled sea-bitten fishermen.

In Homer and Bingham we have good, honest-to-god journalism. There is an authentic ring to this journalism which we could recapture today and not be the losers. Academic painters contemporary with these two had other fish to fry — oily portraits and those wispy romantic treatises in paint that our grandmothers recognized as genteel painting. A few men avoided these dangerous European habits; they found no pleasure in slithering wet paint about in a romantic frenzy. It is as though they said, "Here is a job to be done; here are the tools to do it with," as a frontiersman would when he saw a lot to be cleared. They would not tolerate any false, tricky effects as a result of a self-conscious service to art.

Bingham's pencil sketches for a painting of a small country town on election day (*A Verdict of the People*) are the most amazingly honest pieces of observation of our Josiahs, and Lemuels and Elmers, typical Americans in action back in 1840, that this country will ever see. There are no excessive imaginative values in these sketches, no dramatic exaggeration; they have a factual quality that is so genuine that one can almost smell it; it is as American as corn-on-the-cob.

There were others who went farther west than Bingham and left us more of this heritage. Samuel Colman painted with more than ordinary skill the typical emigrant train fording a shallow stream out in the far mountainous west; the spirit of these early pioneers is brought to life again. Frederic Remington captured in an authentic spirit the Wild West with its lean leathery cowboys and their ponies. Though he is at times a self-conscious illustrator, he nevertheless is thoroughly American in the integrity of his observation. His cowboys are as hardy as the terrain that they must guard. Remington places the first emphasis on the picturesque quality that these high-spirited early cowboys unconsciously attain. This emphasis is of a high caliber and permits no affectations. The bucking bronco, the tautly roped steer are pictured with a dash that could not be anything but picturesque in spite of the painter. The toughness and necessary bravado that accompanied these incidents again reveal the hardiness of temperament that had to more than hold its own out in this wild, savage country. Here we find emphasis on the fact, on the deed done, rather than any clever manipulation of words. The scenes are as direct and as meaningful as an old-time six-shooter. Remington's friendship with

Teddy Roosevelt, the Rough Rider, ex-cowboy, and wildly enthusiastic horseman, is a clue to his temperament.

The painters of this period who self-consciously threw in their lot with European ideals sacrificed unnecessarily this robust, realistic, and masculine integrity for some shoddy romantic concepts that, in the last analysis, were foreign to them. These derivative painters became involved with *nuances* and subtleties of thinking that revealed their innocence in adopting Old World ideas. They established salons where so-called artistic people gathered and traded shop talk in a diluted European sense. These genteel groups, found mostly in the East, held their noses gingerly at the very mention of realism. Realism implied crudity and directness which these cultured groups thought ungentlemanly and therefore offensive.

These strong values and this attitude perhaps recur nowhere as strongly as in the paintings of Thomas Eakins, a contemporary of Remington. Though an eastern painter trained in the academic tradition, Eakins nevertheless followed closely in the footsteps of Homer, Bingham, and others by refusing to adopt mannerisms of presentation. He, like the others, instinctively shied away from tricky thinking. His intelligence recognized the artificialities that were then prevalent in the American painting scene as fostered by academic groups. He realized that these weakening factors were foreign to him and he felt it beneath his masculine dignity — this was no small thing in the seventies and eighties — to indulge in these unnatural mannerisms. Eakins conscientiously brought into his work an uncompromising attitude toward all affectations; combined with this is a stern Puritanical element that belongs historically to the American scene.

Though Eakins lived and worked during the greatest part of his life in Philadelphia, a city of polish and refinement, he gives us a realistic picture of an age which, in his hands, is not clouded in mists of sentimentality. He offers us, in the sum total of his work, a record of the transition between the provincial occupations of the early settlers and the more sophisticated pursuits of people in established towns. His work spans the development of the earlier healthy outdoor habits into an enthusiasm for those sports that would naturally interest the matter-of-fact man of leisure, the man who, though city-bred, took to rowing, hunting, sailing, etc., as a natural diversion. The world that Eakins paints is an essentially masculine world. He sees his contemporaries, men and women in various stations of life, as a sometimes stodgy but nevertheless real and conscientious observer. His concept of man is the practical concept that concerns itself with man and all he does that can be measured in a concrete fashion. Therefore when he paints men hunting, rowing, fishing, or playing chess, he reveals that he is in deadly earnest about these activities. Because he knows the men and their habits from the inside, he is able to impart a native and distinctive ring to the activities which he portrays. Singlehandedly he sums up in paint the point of view of most Americans who felt that they had a distinct stake in their own backyards. Unencumbered by any sense of obligation to the past or to foreign sources, Eakins, like Whitman and Emerson, was able to formulate a highly individualistic philosophy. His practical approach to the world he knew indicated an underlying evaluation that we recognize as extremely significant today. It was a lonely road for Eakins as it was for Whitman, but Eakins possessed the fortitude to travel it. This is especially noticeable when we compare his work with that of his contemporaries. His completely frank evaluation of the people of his times is refreshing when considered against the background of genteel affectations fostered in the sentimental eighties and nineties. It boils down to an incorruptible point of view, a singular value that belongs to the American scene of yesterday in a very special way.

The American tradition is that much more solid because of Eakins. It might comfort some Americans who are on speaking terms with the great in European art and are a little loath to accept this plodder after truth, to know that he is permanently lodged with the immortals of art in the Louvre. "A prophet is not without honor save in his own country." Eakins was one of those rare spirits who believed that life had meaning in his time. We can sense this conviction and the fundamental principles behind it that bind him to us and to the truly authentic American tradition. This is not a stale, dispirited, limited point of view.

Eakins' painting, *The Swimming Hole,* shows his characteristic approach to a typical American scene. This picture need not be described in any detail, for it is much as the average American who has swum in an old swimming hole would imagine it to be. But it is necessary to point out that this was painted by a man who, though trained academically in the best tradition, gives no academic performance. There is no attempt to idealize the figures. These are not nude figures posed in the classic manner; on the contrary, the very ease of the positions assumed by them shows that Eakins could not help showing a zest for this lazy, summer diversion. There is no effusive observation, no attempt at romancing. There is instead a solid, substantial pleasure in recording a traditional American pastime when men and boys swam in the creeks and rivers without benefit of a well-cut swimming suit or the comradeship of smartly costumed girls. The landscape in this picture does not contribute any romantic values; it is there simply as a background for this prosaic activity. There is no feathery touch to the trees or the water. The landscape is almost boring at first glance, in its seemingly dull and heavy-handed observation. Nevertheless, one is aware, after a short time, that here is an unrelenting, uncompromising attitude toward a simple scene that shows us the very nature of the man.

Eakins' restrained attitude reveals the innate dignity of the American point of view. Modern American painting can be evaluated and measured by the yardstick unconsciously set up him. His point of view, in the light of present-day happenings, may seem too moral or perhaps a little Puritanical. Those of us who have gone too far afield from this seemingly all too simple morality, who suspect this disciplined restraint as old-fashioned, might do well to investigate the irrational and hopelessly confusing points of view that are being entertained today, points of view which in the last analysis must be labeled as foreign to the national character. Eakins' brand of Puritanism is not narrow and bigoted. It is a form that sternly avoids animalism and excess sensualism. Eakins was a rebel in his time. He objected violently to the bigoted groups who thought that using nude models in teaching drawing and painting was inexcusable sinfulness. This broadening of the old Puritanical point of view, while retaining the sane moral core, indicates the healthy morality that Eakins stood for. Through his work we can again recognize certain fundamental values in our national beginnings. These are important stones in our foundations.

The most famous of the painters of Eakins' day was James McNeil Whistler. Of all Whistler's paintings, the most popular one is, of course, that of his mother. Immediately we are aware of an unbridgeable gulf between Eakins and Whistler. Whistler is claimed as an American painter by those who feel that our culture needs his romantic, impressionistic touch. One cannot dismiss him with a word. He was a skillful painter who, after studying and living in France, rocketed to success in London by combating a deadly academic school with a freshness of wit and a paint brush, both of which were highly impressionistic in a derivative sense.

John Singer Sargent, born in Europe of American parents and also wholly trained by European artists, successfully interpreted European ideas in matters of procedure. The most brilliant exponent of the *premier coup* style of painting, he was trapped by his own virtuosity; his uncanny photographic eye became the despair of his host of imitators.

Sargent and Whistler have left their marks on the academies of today, but their influence is waning and is being replaced by influences that are, unfortunately, just as foreign. The academies seem to want no part of Americanism as such. They are ready to take over a diluted form of foreign styles and mannerisms provided they are not too extreme. Above all, "Be skillful" is their motto. Virtuosity still holds the spotlight and the market place.

Portrait painting need not concern us too much. There have been too few first-rate contributions to the character that we are trying to identify as the typical American, and of these Eakins provides us with the most intensely honest characterizations. Portrait painting has always permitted too much virtuosity; this business of being adroit is alien to the national character. When we speak of successful portrait painters we have a tendency to stress the success rather than the painting aspect. Much could be said about one man's skill in painting magnificent details that may add up eventually to an apparently successful whole, as opposed to the skill of another portraitist who does the same thing in a different way. It is too easy to criticize the portrait-painting profession. There is a place for it, to be sure. Portrait painters fulfill certain demands placed upon them by success; and since they are well paid and salons continue to hang their works and give them prizes, they can take care of themselves. It is a problem not of challenging the profession but of inquiring into this corrupt use of paint. Sargent called it a panderer's profession. Most portait painters could purchase their souls back again by painting one portrait that pleased them unreservedly, not the sitter or the sitter's family.

The line of American realists did not die out with Eakins. Twenty-four years after he painted *The Swimming Hole,* another American painter tackled the same type of scene with perhaps more obvious gusto. Overlapping Eakins at the turn of the century was George Bellows, an enthusiast, like Eakins, for all healthy outdoor activities as well as sporting events. When Bellows painted a picture of forty-two scrawny city boys diving and swimming in the river, with a large water-soaked crumbling raft as their diving board, he exhibited the same zest for this unadulterated, freshly human experience as Eakins did in a more restrained fashion. This most marvelously spontaneous painting by Bellows makes us share again a common point of view that should warm the heart of every American who remembers his childhood. The Bellows painting at first seems to be more buoyantly alive in its free impressionistic vitality than the Eakins, yet when one comes back to the Eakins version there is something that is basically more substantial. Like most of Eakins' paintings, it is better than it first appears.

Like Bingham, Homer, and Eakins before him, Bellows set out to do an honest workmanlike job. All these men had a common will to do a job with all the integrity at their command. They all had something to say that they considered vital, and they had so much character and conviction that they refused to say it cleverly or irrationally. They are in the American tradition because they thought it unreasonable and undignified to be obscure and evasive in their presentations.

Bellows, like Remington, was at times a self-conscious illustrator and therefore could not deny himself a swirl of the brush. This tendency toward the dramatic in some cases indicates the explosive drive that characterized so many of Bellows' paintings of sporting events. It is as if he said, "I am enthusiastic about all this that is happening about me; I must show my enthusiasm," while Eakins might have said, "I am enthusiastic but that is my business. This is my way of saying it; take it or leave it." This attitude that avoids exhibitionism and callow imitation at all costs is an ideal that we should continue to foster.

At the turn of the present century the "ash can" school of painting was born. George Bellows was a direct offshoot of this group of common-sense illustrators and painters who were derisively called "ash can" painters by critics because they rebelled at affectations in painting and painted more realistically and with greater integrity than their more artistic contemporaries. Calling themselves the "rebels of 1908," John Sloan, George Luks, and six others made up a small but vital band of dissenters to the slavish French Beaux Art imitators. Some of this group unfortunately succumbed to the call of romanticism, even though it was their own brand. The realists of this school claim our attention because their high-spirited interest in the American scene does not flag for a moment. Sloan, Luks, and Bellows added rich chapters to the Homer and Eakins tradition. Their all-out enthusiasm for the American way of life is heartening because it is a natural zest for life as they found it. Their practical turn contributes to an honest, healthy, tough, and unaffected journalism. These journalistic efforts are part and parcel of the big-city scene as described in some of the short stories by O'Henry, a contemporary of this group.

This top-flight journalism is best shown in Bellows' fight pictures. Like Eakins before him, Bellows took the fight game seriously, reporting it excitedly in paint. His now famous *A Stag at Sharkey's* is a picture of two third-rate heavyweights slugging it out at a third-rate fight club. The drive and fight depicted in this typical American sport scene has all the drama that has ever been packed into a blow-by-blow account heard over the radio today. One of his last paintings vividly pictures the famous fight between Jack Dempsey, then champion heavyweight, and Luis Firpo, the Argentine challenger. The incident that Bellows chose to record is now pugilistic history — when Firpo, after taking a tremendous pounding, suddenly unleashed a terrific right that knocked Dempsey out of the ring. This extraordinary incident naturally appealed to Bellows' sense of the dramatic and he made the most of it. In *Taking the Count,* Eakins in the preceding generation had recorded a knockdown more objectively, with no inner excitement; his *Between Rounds* shows, with the utmost conventionality, a corner of the fight ring with a fighter being given advice and fanned with a towel waved by a second. Both Eakins and Bellows were unrelentingly factual. Eakins' reserve seems cold in contrast with Bellows' dramatic flights, but they both liked the game; though Bellows enjoyed letting himself go in paint as he did in his *Forty-Two Kids,* he measures up well with the more restrained Eakins.

These new observers of the American scene seem to enjoy themselves as men rather than as self-conscious painters who must squeeze pleasure out of their trade. Bellows, Luks, and Sloan seem happy in the world that they know and live in. Theirs is a new optimism which we can recognize as another direct contribution to the national characteristic desire to enjoy life as a day-to-day experience. They show the type of courage necessary to oppose intrenched groups whose philosophies they consider alien to American life as they knew it intimately. The healthy outbursts of energy that one senses in these realists prove their unshakable belief in the vitality of the American scene as they saw it.

John Sloan painted city people, not the fashionable, well-dressed, genteel groups, but the masses who do the work. He shows his happy state of mind in his painting of three unimportant working-class wives drying their hair and gossiping on the roof of one of the red brick tenements that have always been part of a big city. Sloan was skillful enough to paint these three women more temptingly, but like his matter-of-fact predecessors he refrains from tricky brush work and gives us an intimately vital account of a brief moment in the lives of these typical women. The informality of the composition and the painting would lead the less discerning observer to the conclusion that this is only a small, unimportant, sketchy bit of *genre* painting. But viewed in the light of his affected contemporaries, this work reveals the painter's unconscious good humor, his happiness as he records this commonplace scene with the utmost disregard of conventional artistic method and procedure. This is a large attitude, this business of being in sympathy with one's fellow men without censorship or any indication of class consciousness. Is it any wonder that the salon groups could not take to this essentially democratic point of view? Sloan went on to paint the back alleys in Greenwich Village, the clotheslines, the crowded windows, the scrawny alley cats, and the street children making a snow man in a cramped space. All are done with obvious pleasure; though these paintings are more than twenty-five years old, there is an unchanging quality in them, as there should be in these honestly evaluated typical street scenes.

This is the American idiom. There is in all this work a freshness of spirit that indicates the sheer pleasure of being alive. This may not be art in any "aesthetic" sense, it may not be what the average person expects of salon pictures; but it is within our field of familiar experience, it is alive, vital, healthy, and good for the soul.

Sloan commented on many of the various types that intermingle in the great swirl he knew as New York. His painting of the crowds visiting their favorite saloons, men and women on a Saturday night in search of fun, is full of good-humored, shrewd comment. His famous painting, *McSorley's Bar*, is a simple, unpretentious record of an old-fashioned saloon in all its dull masculine glory. Sloan does not choose the pretentious red-plushed barroom of his day; he depicts a simple, straightforward saloon interior that tells us all we need to know about all the saloons of that period. The interior is musty, drab, and casual — the type of place that did not go in for fancy drinks or fancy fronts. Like most of his work, this picture has such an authentic ring that we are reminded again of his conscientious desire to be truthful above all else.

George Luks, another of this group, paralleled Sloan's enthusiasm for the local gentry. By giving more attention to individual figures than to groups, Luks suggests a greater interest in the subsurface inner character without being too self-conscious about it. His paintings of middle-aged women and men slightly in their cups are good-naturedly alive. Luks, like Sloan, was completely uninhibited in his friendly presentation of people who find pleasure in an occasional nip. The genuine sympathy and deep understanding of human nature that Luks exhibits in his work indicate the type of American who is generous in his appraisal of human frailties. He shows so much pleasure in painting a slightly tipsy old woman that one realizes at once that only a person who has been very close to this sort of experience could so thoroughly understand it.

This large, gusty good humor is a sign of our painters' coming of age. This important note struck by Luks and Sloan indicates a characteristic tolerance that more than offsets the bigotry of the age on the one hand and the effete idealism on the other. Such largeness of spirit is found in men who have lived and evaluated their life and the lives of others in a spirit of fair play, no censorship, no moralizing. There is strength in their observations; the proof of Luks' capacity for observing and recording inner character with intensity is shown in his portraits of outstanding men of his day. This genial "Hail fellow well met" took life in his stride and painted street children with the same intensity of feeling. There is a tenderness in this broad-shouldered painter's *The Spielers,* a picture of two grinning little girls dancing on the sidewalks of New York. Here he gives us an opportunity to realize the depth and weight of his special brand of humanity. No one who was not truly a great liberal in practice could have conceived this fresh, spirited, and superbly happy picture. It indicates the quality of our own kind of healthy, good-humored optimism as a national characteristic. This is one of our most important native products. It is a rare talent, this ability to record without the slightest affectation the living grin that stems from the large-souled happy personality that Luks had. Here again we find genuine love of life and deep understanding of the forces that make it worth while. Luks' broad morality gives us another peak from which we can watch the American scene and find it inspiring. For these reasons this painting alone will stand with the classics of all time.

If painting in the first quarter of this century has any meaning for us it can be traced almost wholly to the activities of these realists. Their logical successors, their students, and imitators did not have the strength of character or the principled convictions that these rebels had. Their passing from the American scene seemed like the last of the old guard dying off.

For twenty years after the first great efforts of these giants, the American art scene was one of great confusion because of an influx of European ideas based on the modern schools of painting. In themselves these ideas were a revolt against the French academic procedures, one that made the revolt by Sloan, Luks, and others in this country seem mild by comparison. This complex rebellion against the slick, affected schools of painting appealed so much to the young men who were looking for a cause and a chance to voice their radicalism that they took it as their own, although it was alien to them. The result was unbelievable confusion for some two decades, coupled with the distress brought about by the first World War and its disastrous aftermath. The calm, reflective, direct spirit of the average American was jostled out of existence by the tremendous forces alive at that time. This fact, in itself, is proof of how much the American is a realist at heart; he could not escape to an ivory tower during those violent days. He reacted to the insanities at large and was unable to get his breath back until the world as a whole quieted down.

There were a few men who, because of their largeness of outlook, were not too violently disturbed by the hysteria of the cities. These men went their way, finding comfort in the American scene, recording their pleasures simply and directly as the realists before them had felt that they must do. For these men the world was not at an end. They saw the world of inner America with clean, unjaundiced eyes. And they were deeply moved by what they saw, for they realized that, in spite of the turmoil that the country was going through, there was a constant change from the awkward rural stage to the fast-moving industrial stage. There were still signs of the old intermingling with the new — mid-Victorian houses elbowed by garages. The incongruities that arose out of this confusion provided some of these men with food for thought. Their dispassionate point of view and healthy inventory-taking give us an amazing record of our lives in the early twenties. They saw with sympathy and deep understanding the curious dignity that existed in the architectural monstrosities of the Victorian Gothic age. They were the first to recognize the ghosts that inhabited these absurdly elaborate residences and to evaluate correctly their connection with the American scene. Again and again their work shows a native tolerance and enthusiasm for the everyday experience regardless of where they found it; these men were instinctively aware of the drama that existed in all of it. They provide evidence of renewed faith in the American way of life that is part of the tradition started by Homer and Bingham.

Charles Burchfield and Edward Hopper are two men of this caliber who quietly and without much fanfare went about their business, not knowing each other, yet telling the story of America as they saw it with directness, simplicity, and insight. To them it was not a process of self-conscious nationalism as much as concern about the world that they knew so well and liked in all its phases. They did not choose their material fastidiously but found all phases of life grist for their mills. Their contributions to our understanding of our way of life is marked by a high form of discriminating observation; they have eyes for the strange but typical moments in our civilization that we are inclined to rush past without seeing.

The Spirit of American Art

Burchfield possesses a marvelous sense of realism that can penetrate the shoddiest, most down-at-the-heels suburban back street. He is able to inject rich imaginative values into these bleak uninspiring scenes. The deserted farm houses that are the tragedy of so many American valleys are seen with complete sympathy by this man who realizes down to his core what they once meant as landmarks of life. The consummate technique that he brings to painting these scenes shows the painstaking care that is needed to tell poignantly the story of these deserted homesteads. Since he possesses instinctive imaginative powers, he accentuates the rawness of this tragedy by painting the full-blown, wild, luxurious vegetation in contrast with the weather-beaten, sagging house in all its desolation. Burchfield has an eye for the seasons as we know them in the northeastern part of the country, and for the strange moods of the day, but not the slightest bit of sentimentalism. He is able to record with great sympathy the dramatic loneliness of old Victorian Gothic houses on the gloomy, gray days that we know so well as part of our familiar scene; one can almost hear them creak and moan in Edgar Allan Poe fashion.

With quiet dignity and sympathetic insight, Burchfield paints a middle-class family at their evening meal as seen through the windows of a tacked-on kitchen in a suburban industrial row in mid-winter. The warmth and meaning that he conveys in this homely scene are a reaffirmation of the substantial values that give any work of art a universal appeal. One need not go much further than this backyard scene to sense that, like the good company that preceded him, Burchfield is content with his subject matter. Give him the neglected phases of American life and he will show you drama that is heart-warming. He does not have to look beyond his own valley for inspiration; it is around him in great abundance, and he has an eye for every detail.

Edward Hopper, also of our day, is a direct offshoot of the "rebels of 1908." With unbelievable thoroughness he reduces his observations to their barest elements. He is so persevering in this attitude that once again we see the shades of Eakins' relentless dignity. Again we see an American painter who feels that it would be beneath his dignity to subscribe to any procedure that was clever or facile. Hopper maintains a painstaking moral point of view whose strength offsets all the virtuosity that he has exhibited without restraint for many years. He approaches his work with a conscientious, clear-headed energy that is again a reminder of our national character. With all this discipline he manages to capture facets of American life that escape his skillful, ambitious contemporaries. A single light in a darkened building on a summer night, with a lone figure half in the shadows, gives him an opportunity to record this small island of humanity in the large mysterious dark that envelops it — another clear indication of superb insight into the small incident whereby the seemingly undramatic becomes highly dramatic in the hands of Hopper. He has also observed and managed to capture with curious affection the strange, lonely, dispirited character of an uninhabited street, as seen in thousands of small towns on a Sunday morning when even the air seems dead. The apparent ugliness of the pressed-tin store façades of small-town buildings waiting for the first signs of life did not cause either Hopper or Burchfield to shudder. Both men were aware of a legitimate awkwardness in these small things; it was this awareness that contributed to their understanding of the American scene.

Thomas Wolfe wrote of these small clumps of mean little houses scattered over the country at crossroads and along unimportant highways. He too saw them, not as dirty, inconvenient, haphazard hovels, but as a man starved for human society might see them — a sign of humanity, of potential companionship. One feels a strange beauty here; and if Santayana's definition of beauty holds — "pleasure regarded as the quality of a thing" — we should be grateful for these pungent observations.

The Spirit of American Art

These observations are not casual comments. They are sharpened on the painters' bitter resentment at superficial and trivial expressions. These men searched and finally found the basis for their understanding through their own insistent effort, not by any slick short-cuts. There is a deep-seated toughness to their observations that is in the American tradition.

Out of the great Midwest in the late twenties came a group of men who were interested in the study of painting. They went to Europe to further their studies, as was the custom at that time. Some of them stayed in Europe literally and figuratively, and were lost as far as American painting was concerned. A few others returned to their homeland and their native Midwest and not only found themselves but rediscovered their real enthusiasms for their valleys, plains, and countrymen. These men were aware of the need for the life they really knew as youngsters, and they set out to record it with renewed enthusiasm. They sensed the naturalness of their native background more intensely because they had time and opportunity to compare it with alien experiences. Coming home like the proverbial prodigal, they threw themselves whole-heartedly into the business of painting without affectation their midwestern skies, arid lands, and the strong Puritanical people that made this tough part of the country theirs. Their work shows this fresh evaluation of the rugged stock that held on to these vast expanses of soil. And today we realize pointedly their ability to understand the hidden drama in this relationship of man — American man — to the land, the soil. It was not so much that these men took on a self-consciously rural point of view as that they knew instinctively that the story of this large expanse of the American scene was just as vibrant, just as dynamic as the intellectual gymnastics practiced in the painting world on the eastern seaboard and in Europe.

Of this small group that returned to their own, three are outstanding in a special way: Grant Wood, John Stuart

Curry, and Thomas Benton. All had ample opportunity to decide for themselves where their true selves lay, and to a man they relinquished the hold that the modern painting movement, as fostered in France, had upon them. With typical American integrity they shook off these alien influences and settled down to being themselves — genuine native products with a deep and renewed affection for the American scene.

Grant Wood takes his Midwest as he finds it, for better or worse. In his now famous *American Gothic*, he paints, without the slightest affectation or desire to be picturesque, a farmer and his wife as native types. It is a stern, extremely serious document, direct, sincere, straightforward. These are the people who not only make up our Midwest but have the character to hold it together. In one sense, this painting is the summation of the intrinsic values in Eakins' work. These people are gaunt; they are as lean in their appearance as the pitchfork held by the farmer. They are sturdy and practical in character. The picture is as direct and homely as the store-bought overall and apron that the man and woman are wearing. This homeliness is not self-conscious. There is no evidence of a corrupt use of paint or a desire to paint brilliantly. It is again a denial of slick subtleties. Wood is like Homer and Eakins in feeling that slickness and subtlety are undignified and alien to the national character. *American Gothic* is not so much a glorification of the homeliness of these two unnamed individuals as it is a new attempt further to evaluate the virtues that exist in the native temperament. Here again is the tough, direct point of view, the practical morality based on our fundamental understanding of utilitarianism.

Wood did not come by this point of view easily. Like Burchfield and Hopper, he not only resented superficial habits and customs as they were presented by unthinking painters, but he was also disturbed and irritated by the artificial mannerisms that are prevalent in small towns with their slavish imitation of big-city doings. Wood expresses this impatience in his now equally famous *Daughters of the Revolution*, a painting of three small-town clubwomen having tea (with the little finger well out) in honor of the Revolution — and of George Washington crossing the Delaware. Though it is an ironical comment, he saves it from being vicious by a sane touch of humor. A healthy criticism is intended here and it is brought off most successfully.

When painting landscapes, Wood turns his valleys and open ranges of prairie over in his mind and then patiently makes a record of them on canvas as if he were taking inventory. The woods, trees, and vegetation are no longer affected by the accidents of rain and transient light and shade, but are collected and placed with great care on the canvas so as to indicate the special meaning that all these parts have to Wood. No small detail is ignored; he cherishes the fence and the telegraph pole as well as the budding stalks. It becomes *his* valley through a deep-seated concern that is based on strong-principled convictions.

John Stuart Curry, like Wood, traveled to Paris and after absorbing foreign points of view rediscovered himself in his native Midwest. He too does not adopt this new point of view without some criticism of certain provincial habits and customs. Like Sinclair Lewis, he pokes more than a little fun at the stern old-fashioned hysterical habits found in small western towns. In his satirical painting of an outdoor baptism in Kansas he manages to recapture the intensity of the old-time revivals that were so much a part of these rural scenes twenty years ago.

But Curry is not always satirical; sometimes he is in dead earnest. His *Tornado over Kansas*, for instance, describes a typical midwestern farmer's family running for their lives to an underground shelter, with the twisting, swiftly moving tornado in the background. Yet this is not just a factual document, nor did he paint it merely because it had dramatic value. Curry records, in this powerful scene, an element of living dangerously which the farmer in a tornado belt must take as a matter of course. The meagerness of this existence is shown in the just sufficient clothes, the typical ramshackle backyard. The story is told in a hard-boiled fashion; there is no outcry for sympathy. The strong, lean farmer and his sturdy wife, though frightened, will come out after the blow and, with their children, begin where they left off, if there is anything left to begin with. This has large implications. There is something in this incident that parallels the pioneer spirit of the first settlers in this tough, unyielding country. Here again we find conviction and the strength of a rediscovered point of view.

Thomas Benton, another Midwesterner, extends this reliable record both in his murals and in his easel paintings. He is at times indirect in his telling because of his interests as a superlative craftsman in the mechanics of painting, but he is an American with a conscience when he paints the Midwest.

Benton also survived his academic training both here and abroad. His recent self-imposed pilgrimage across the length and breadth of the states gave him an opportunity to depict many of the tragic inequalities in the midwestern panorama. Curry comments realistically in the *Tornado over Kansas* on the hardness of the midwestern farmer's life, but Benton sees not merely the farmer, but the sharecropper, the mountain folk, the disinherited of the land. Last but not least he sees the Negro with his bare past and bleak future, with his unpainted shack and unbelievably meager possessions. These comments show no irrational resentment. Benton's desire is rather to evaluate correctly the American scene which he understands so sympathetically. He consciously uses many devices to get his message across. This interest in the social status of the lowest wage group lends extra force to his statements. The fact that he can also romanticize these experiences takes the curse off their sometimes unhappy sociological implications. Benton is always uncompromisingly tough in his observations of American types and this places him firmly in the solid American tradition.

While all this enthusiasm and factual recording is taking place out west, a new native realistic evaluation of our eastern big-city life is occurring in the east. In the late twenties and early thirties, Reginal Marsh, Paul Cadmus, and Ben Shahn, among others of the first rank, commented in traditional fashion on that violent, highly accelerated scene presented by the city of New York. We said above that John Sloan recorded this scene faithfully and realistically at the turn of the century. These contemporary painters know and understand the city from the inside in its present-day extravagance. The strange paradoxical life that makes New York City a throbbing, vital, civilized American metropolis on the one hand and an unresolved mixture of alien forces and ideas on the other, offers dramatic possibilities that are probably not equaled anywhere else in the world today. In Sloan's day, the city had these forces to contend with and these ideals to absorb, but at a much slower pace. The life of this city now moves at such an accelerated tempo that only the metropolitan newspapers can keep up with its multiple changes and violent momentum. The groups who in their own weird way contribute to the strange vitality that one senses in New York are part and parcel of this remarkable fusion that theoretically should be explosive but actually constitutes the most exciting democratic panorama the world has ever seen. The unconscious democratic ideal is observed by our realistic city painters and they do their job in a typical American fashion, with energy, integrity, and relentless realism.

Marsh, like Benton, often comments on the sociological aspect of the scene, which is more desperate in a large city like New York than it can be in the rural areas. He paints the down-and-outers lining up for soup in front of a waterfront mission. The empty-faced hordes who make up the seamy side of a city's population are recorded with Rembrandtian fidelity. He relishes the city's millions at play at Coney Island, swimming in the Hudson, and taking their fun where they find it. He does not feel superior to the tastes of the no-class millions. He enjoys the burlesque shows with the lonely sex-starved men, commenting wryly on the shoddiness of the performance, performers, and costumes. He takes us to Harlem and points out one tall, lithe High Yellow girl swinging down the street in her sleasy but proudly worn Sunday dress. There is fight in his observations. The integrity observable in his work points again and again to a high order of morality that has not been relinquished since Bingham and Homer.

Paul Cadmus, one of the younger American painters, turns his eye on the vicious picture that makes up the brazen, unprincipled habits of unabsorbed and unabsorbable thousands. He is one of the really hard-boiled younger generation that sees the animalism present in so many phases of unprincipled city activity. He can indicate with savage precision the relationships that exist between morally deteriorating individuals in a big city. He suggests savage overtones in his cold observations of such a seemingly unimportant subject as men and women milling about in a cheap cafeteria. He observes with a tough masculine eye, though he has grouped the figures dramatically. His truck drivers, mechanics, and the other American types found in industrial sections are so intensely realistic at times that they are capable of making one feel uncomfortable by the strength of their presentation. They don't come any tougher than Cadmus. One of his latest paintings of a strike scene is such an intense American labor document that one feels forced to take sides. Cadmus, like Marsh, is impatient with halfway observations. He is irritated by the observable frustrations in city life and he violently yet honestly shows his resentment at unnecessary artificiality.

Cadmus in his viciously contemporary point of view can be compared with the typical American reporter who wants

The Spirit of American Art 145

no part of what he suspects is phony. Few city reporters have the acid in their make-up that he has. Cadmus can be accused of not being sufficiently detached and objective. He has been exposed to our contemporary forms of radicalism which, brooking no halfway measures, are found in their most violent aspects in large cities.

This concept of violence which is more of a city manifestation than a rural one, brings Ben Shahn's work to our attention. His crisp, incisive observations of criminals held by the police in the way characteristic of big-city police permits us to see one side of our world that is usually ignored by painters. Shahn possesses great detachment even though he is capable of painting controversial subjects. His observations of first-generation types at play in crowded city streets in surroundings that do not suggest play startle one with the unbelievable keenness of his observation. He is as tough as the others, but his point of view has extra force because of his singular capacity for understatement. His criminals lined up for the day's going-over on the powerfully lighted police platform, with their twisted caps and their heavy, coarse faces, remind us of an accumulation of candid photographs of city criminals printed from day to day in the metropolitan newspapers.

Many native-born American painters have succumbed intellectually to the brilliant theories advanced by the advance guard of modern painters stemming from France. Some have survived as Americans without owing too great a debt. Others who are Americans though of foreign stock are devoting themselves to the American scene with such intense enthusiasm and such penetrating power that they more than offset the native Americans who have gone astray. A self-conscious effort is sometimes discernible in their works, but this is only natural since they cannot eliminate the Old World stream of thought with one gesture. Their observations are always legitimate, though sophisticated in a strange way attributable to the unconscious hold the other world still has on them. In their enthusiasm for the land of their adoption they have rediscovered phases of American life that have escaped the attention of our native citizens and painters alike. They have always included a feeling of responsibility in their observations. Luigi Lucioni, Raphael Soyer, and others have bent their energies to sensing the inner meanings of the scenes about them.

Lucioni, a meticulous painter, has adopted the State of Vermont as his special province. This typical New England state with its rugged beauty and green valleys is seen again in all its special rural glory through the eyes of this first-generation American painter. With the most patient enthusiasm and detailed interest he has recorded its hills and valleys. His inner romantic temperament has stamped itself on his many canvases of the rich landscape that is Vermont. The graceful elms are featured in so many paintings in their special glory. Although the unbelievably detailed realism that Lucioni can get into a canvas is poetic and slightly Italianate in character, it is nevertheless Vermont rediscovered by a fresh, unjaded eye. His enthusiasm over an unpainted barn, typical throughout the state, with its unpainted sagging silo, makes us aware of the intrinsic relationship between these barns, the people, also slightly weathered, and the soft deep valleys. He paints the faraway blue hills exactly but not sentimentally. Emerson's statement, "I like a man who can admire a fine barn as well as a fine tragedy," takes on added meaning in Lucioni's detailed, warm description of these New England barns that Emerson knew so well. Lucioni has managed to recapture the freshness that will always exist in these valleys when seen through the eyes of men at ease in these simple relationships. There is a tightness to his observations that makes one realize the permanence that these buildings represent. This is not a fly-by-night impression but a deep-seated awareness of the stability that is present in this part of the country. It recalls the feeling the first settlers must have had after they decided to erect their homes and barns and live here permanently.

Raphael Soyer, another first-generation American painter, depicts with great tenderness and sympathy the homeless, the jobless, and the hopeless of New York City. He cannot be as direct and objective as Marsh. His realism as opposed to Marsh's occasional toughness is always tinged with an acute sense of responsibility for these floating wrecks of humanity. He has no desire, as Cadmus has, to picture the nastiness that is often seen in this beaten and frustrated group. He approaches his subjects with the most abject humility without losing the strength and inner power of his presentation. The Old World stream that runs through Soyer imparts an air of slight melancholy to his countless metropolitan figures. He has an eye for the subtle relationship between the hard, unpredictable world and man's feeble adjustment to it.

We owe a great deal to this self-conscious effort of these first-generation Americans to show us their enthusiasm for our way of life. They have a legitimate right to their form of presentation, for they cannot help including some of the Old World thinking that is part of their make-up whether they want it or not. Alexander Brook and Ahron Bohrod are other first-rate examples of this group. They paint the American scene with a sympathy and sophistication that can be traced at times to another world. Like Lucioni, they have rediscovered phases of Americana that have escaped the attention of our native citizens, and we should be grateful to them for broadening our view of those large scenes we know as America. They replace other dyed-in-the-wool Americans who have sacrificed their native points of view for a self-conscious form of presentation based on slavish imitations of European painting.

Little has been said about the imaginative powers of American painters. Realism has been stressed because it shows, through the rugged temperaments of our truly American painters, how much of our strong national character can be depicted by this direct and straightforward technique. The traditional desire to avoid sentimentalism and affectation is so much a native product that we must start with that as our first landmark. This matter-of-fact, moral pursuit of truth above all else was coupled at times with a strong imaginative sense that was never awkward but gave inner meaning to some of the most realistic painting.

A giant among these imaginative painters was Albert Pinkham Ryder, a contemporary of Eakins. Ryder was not an impressionist, but he inhabited a world that can be described only as a dream world. Though he lived among the so-called Bohemians of his day in the unswept studio that was typical of that period, he did not ape them in painting in an inspired frenzy. He took his work as seriously as the ancient monks took their vows of chastity, poverty, and obedience. With continual industry he developed an individual manner of painting which, like Eakins' style, denies affectations in procedure. In the most painstaking way he slowly developed his ideas on small canvases, ideas that are impressive today because of his capacity for sustained thinking. His unique ability to work at one canvas as long as eighteen years indicates the incredible patience of the man and his faith in his ideas. The ideas he presented are not many or too complex. They reveal that he had an intuitive feeling for the mysterious relationship between man and nature that indicates a firm belief in the inner world as he knew it introspectively. When he paints a small canvas showing a single sailboat manned by a solitary figure on a moonlit sea, he is able to suggest almost miraculously a cosmic importance to an unimportant incident that reveals monumental power. His strange interpretations of scenes in Shakespeare's plays show a talent for a slightly macabre imagery that is not too distant from Edgar Allan Poe's weird tales. It indicates his interest in associated ideas borrowed from literature and music. His importance as a painter lies in his deep insight into the mysteries that surround him.

This sounds un-American in contrast with the realists, but it stems from the man himself and not from any borrowed source. Ryder single-handedly gives solid and sustained meaning to the idealism characteristic of his day. We need to know this strange but not incongruous painter because, like the realists, he saw his problems honestly and with the greatest patience tried to solve them. This resulted in the formulation of a philosophy which, though not entirely clear and extremely personal, nevertheless can give us an approach to the imaginative world that we know is just as important as the realistic world. His was not an escapist philosophy, but one that yielded deep satisfaction to one interested in discovering his true relationship with nature, a field that admits no national boundaries.

American painting has been called provincial and primitive by some who have in mind the complexities of European thinking as indicated in the large body of European painting. It is true that our country's early painters could record nothing but what they knew and saw about them — the domestic, provincial habits and experiences that would be natural in sprawling, brawling villages and awkward towns. That they observed all this with honesty and good humor is characteristic of the realistic, unaffected American tradition. We still feel close to these attitudes; those who are honest with themselves will continue to feel close to them for some time to come. The paintings of those early days were not intended to be artistic triumphs any more than Mark Twain's *Tom Sawyer* was intended as a self-conscious literary triumph. They were meant to record, as Mark Twain does, the essence of life as it was lived then, with no window-dressing. This American brand of good humor is a national asset of no mean proportion; it indicates the native tolerance that is so much a part of our democratic point of view. This ability to grin and chuckle should be kept before us at all times, especially when the grin is directed at ourselves. In the light of present-day uncertainties those painters who are capable of sensing the need for this light-hearted though not necessarily light-headed point of view should be cherished, for they offer us stability through their friendly observations.

Sloan, Luks, Wood, and Burchfield, among others, have at times felt the necessity of commenting, wryly perhaps but nevertheless in good fun, on the activities in our daily lives that make us chuckle with them. This distinctly American trait of poking fun at one's countrymen is another indication of our democratic equilibrium. We do not have to look far afield to see that those countries that have decided that democracy is outmoded and must be replaced by some other form of government have forced this good-natured criticism out of the public eye. The people in those countries still make jokes and sly comments, but they do so with the greatest secrecy and always at the possible expense of their personal safety.

In our democracy, the talent for free and uninhibited expression is not confined to men painters. Peggy Bacon and Doris Lee, to mention only two of our first-rank women painters, also work in this humorous vein. Peggy Bacon, often satirical in both her writings and her paintings, has nevertheless a deep sympathy for the underprivileged groups. While she shrewdly exhibits the acid in her disposition when she relentlessly exposes the conceits and the deceits of the salon groups and their heavy-set mink-coated patronesses, she has that rare gift of seeing the humor in a small burly Italian junk man putting a discarded garland of wilted flowers on his horse's head on the first spring day. Like her magnificently drawn, scrawny alley cats, the sad and resigned horse is depicted with such sympathetic candor that the incident has universal appeal.

Though only a few of our many paintings have been mentioned, the average American need go no further to satisfy any curiosity he may have about his world as seen through the eyes of native painters. Painters today are no longer provincial and primitive, nor do they exhibit any false idealism. They are ever ready to criticize and to reject the shoddy thinking and false fronts of our time. They offer, though, a deep abiding affection for all phases of the American scene as they know it intimately. Their comments are honest, courageous, tolerant, and energetic. They are imaginative enough but at the same time do not lose themselves in a dream world. They have the good habit of keeping their feet solidly planted on the ground they know so well. They are tough, practical commentators whose humanitarian instincts set them apart from the overly sophisticated and brilliantly scintillating figures of the contemporary European scene. We can count on them to register impatience with any deviation from the moral integrity that made such shining examples of Homer, Bingham, and Eakins. Grant Wood, Hopper, and Burchfield, to name but a few, offer us — as they will for some time, even beyond our own generation — conclusive evidence of the essential rightness of the American scene as viewed by individualists who are not self-conscious nationalists.

It should be unnecessary to add that no other country would tolerate the expressions of these men, their humor, candor, and general "take it or leave it" kind of observation. The countries that have felt this freedom of expression inimical to their policy have by various devices forced this buoyant liveliness out of existence. A program concocted by party officials has been subtly introduced to direct the painter. He is encouraged, of course, in the type of painting that reflects the political or military glories of his state. What a sad task it must be, even for the believers, to paint countless adulatory portraits of leaders whose facial features are pulled this way and that, so that they will look honorable, just, triumphant, heroic, inspired, and invincible, all at the same time! The fair-haired portrait painters in these countries have to combine the task of neat but not gaudy plastic surgery with a flair for writing obituaries in paint. The stuffy academician is likewise encouraged, for his amiable nonprovocative pictures are used by the state to prove that a culture still exists. The truly representative dynamic voices are quickly and ruthlessly suppressed.

This state of affairs has existed for so long in some of these countries that not a single reputable expression in paint has appeared. The authentic, spirited painter, realizing that he could not serve two masters — the state and what he knew to be right and worth recording — simply closed shop and called it a day. The result is a long barren era that reflects perfectly the general condition and temperament of the members of those nations. The painters, like all the other men in the arts, are sensitive barometers that clearly indicate the strength of the storm of "state above all." When they first begin to creep out from under cover again, we can rest assured that the state has become reconciled to the need for liberal expression.

CHAPTER 6

THE SPIRIT OF MODERN AMERICAN LITERATURE

by JOHN B. HOBEN

"I say we had best look our times and lands searchingly in the face, like a physician diagnosing some deep disease." Theodore Dreiser? Dos Passos? Perhaps the words of John Steinbeck? No, it's Walt Whitman — that raw-boned, raucous old liberal, chief guide for American authors these past seventy years!

In poetry Whitman's energetic credo and practice help to make articulate such divergent poets as Robinson, Frost, Amy Lowell, and Sandburg, who do not imitate their master's rhapsodic style but who have more freely chosen their subjects and manners of treatment because of Whitman's revolt. American novelists and dramatists, while not oblivious to foreign influences, have increasingly followed the critical realism of *Democratic Vistas* in their reporting and evaluating of American life.

Like all revolutionists, the Long Island prophet had his blind spots. Writhing against the complacency and smugness of the genteel gods he shouts: "America has yet morally and artistically originated nothing!" More true perhaps than most of us care to admit, but certainly an overstatement which neglects in the field of literature itself the creative and indigenous contributions of Ben Franklin, Thoreau, and Melville. Despite his limitations, Whitman provides a pattern and point of view for this critical discussion. He projected his vision of democracy into the future and challenged his successors to make of it an American way of life which eventually would reconstruct and democratize all society. To what extent have modern American poets, novelists, and dramatists realized Whitman's cosmic dream? That is our basic problem.

No son of a privileged class was Walt Whitman. Born in 1819, a date coincident with the birth of Lowell, Whitman had no generations of eminent men attached to his family tree. His father was a Long Island farmer-carpenter, his mother a modest Quaker. He was but one among nine children. With little more than a snatch of public schooling he started out as office boy and printer's devil. At thirteen, like Franklin, Howells, and Twain, he found his Yale College in a print shop. Three years as a country school teacher, then back to journalism. By 1846 he was editing the Brooklyn *Daily Eagle*.

When the Democratic party swung over to the support of slavery, Whitman bolted and joined the radical Republicans and in so doing lost his editorship. A journey down the Ohio and Mississippi to New Orleans, a brief job, and a love affair (mythical or factual), and he was back in Brooklyn by 1850 with a seething host of American impressions and a chief ambition to express "my own physical, emotional, moral, intellectual, and aesthetic Personality, in the midst of, and tallying, the momentous spirit and facts of its immediate days, and of current America — and to exploit that Personality, identified with place and date, in a far more candid and comprehensive sense than any hitherto poem or book."

First and foremost Walt Whitman aspired to be the poet of American democracy. How well he fulfills his primary purpose can be determined by examining *Leaves of Grass* — our literary Declaration of Independence — first published in 1855 and revised and republished frequently.

Democracy was no meaningless word to Walt Whitman. He was essentially a Jeffersonian. He had an abiding faith in the masses and like a good equalitarian accepted all men as brothers. Boss and bootblack, Baptist and atheist, professor and freshman — all must have an equal opportunity for self-realization. Only when men are free will the gifted and the deserving rise to the top.

Produce great Persons, the rest follows . . .
Piety and conformity to them that like,
Peace, obesity, allegiance to them that like, . . .

Individualism is the primary theme. Time and again it surges to the foreground. It may be in the key of Emerson, as in "Song of Myself":

I know I am solid and sound,
To me the converging objects of the universe perpetually flow,
All are written to me, and I must get what the writing means.

Frequently, in the earlier poems, it beats Tom Paine's "gong of revolt" or Thoreau's anarchy.

Whitman was also a good Jeffersonian in his fear of the federalistic consolidation that devours local and state rights.

To the States or any one of them, or any city of the States,
  Resist much, obey little,
Once unquestioning obedience, once fully enslaved,
Once fully enslaved, no nation, state, city of this earth, ever afterward resumes its liberty.

There was no gap between his political thinking and his literary theory. The latter is as democratic as the former. All men are potential poets. No poem is an end in itself, it is a beginning in self-discovery; and thus both the true state and the poet function for the fullest development of the individual. Form is derived from within the nature of the material and the spirit of the poet, and the best style is the most simple, the most natural, without rhyme, meter, or superficial ornament.

His conception of the purpose and function of the poet was not always successfully practiced. Discount the stretches of mawkish sentiment, undigested impressions, and exhibitionism, and he still stands as the first great American poet to celebrate the stature of common man and to extol "the glory of the commonplace."

I believe a leaf of grass is no less than the journey-work of the stars . . .
And a mouse is miracle enough to stagger sextillions of infidels!

This expansive affection for the familiar and uncelebrated aspects of American life is the chief source of Whitman's genius. It rides the Brooklyn ferry, embraces the resistless pioneer, honors the athletic body, and whispers with rare tenderness when the lilacs bloom in April recalling the death of Lincoln.

Walt Whitman's faith in democracy was no eighteenth-century fragment sewed to his breeches. In the radical forties he was as rebellious as a left-wing Abolitionist, as blatantly optimistic about primitive virtues as a Rousseau; but the awful tragedy of civil war and the sordid aftermath with its maladministration, deceit, and corruption transfigured a left-wing journalist and a passionate poet into a mature prophet. In *Democratic Vistas* (1871) he criticizes realistically, struggles with doubt, and emerges triumphantly.

Sloughing off his exuberance, he sees much work to be done before the perfect state will arise. Government must do more than merely preserve the rights of each citizen. To produce a cohesion between state and person a broader, more practical, and ethical program of culture is demanded. Then man, "properly trained in sanest, highest freedom," will grow in his constructive use of liberty. Toward the realization of this ideal, art and literature of the future must be directed.

Poets to come! orators, singers, musicians to come!
Not today is to justify me and answer what I am for,
But you, a new brood, native, athletic, continental, greater than before known,
Arouse! for you must justify me.

The Spirit of Modern American Literature 157

Can you find another such poet and prophet of democracy in the brood to follow?

Leaves of Grass produced no immediate revolution. Emerson approved. Thoreau and Alcott were enthusiastic. Lowell smirked and declared that this sort of thing wouldn't do. Whittier gingerly dropped his copy in the fire, confident that the American public would not be hoodwinked by such rubbish. So the old gods of Beacon Street had their tea at the Saturday Club and turned out an occasional translation or metrical romance *à la* Walter Scott. When they began to drop off in the eighties and nineties, they were followed by a group of disciples who fled from Walt Whitman and all that was sensuous and real.

There was actual romance in the West. While the nation was trying to bind up its wounds, native American ballads about hoss-thieves, famous engineers, and ladies of pleasure were spreading like plantain weed. Andy Jackson's West awoke. John Hay's "Jim Bludso of the Prairie Belle" did not have Longfellow's polish, but the "infernal roar" of the old side-wheeler and Jim's heroics caught the public fancy. Even Bret Harte turned aside from his memorable short stories long enough to slide one boot on the rail.

> Say there! P'raps
> Some on you chaps
>   Might know Jim Wild?

The truest poet of the 1870's came out of the deep South. Sidney Lanier, Georgia-born, knew what it was like to fight against terrific odds. A natural musician, he bore arms for his South, was confined in a federal prison, and emerged from the war with his health ruined and his fortune wiped out. He died from tuberculosis at thirty-nine, but not before he had established himself as the most articulate voice of the South. Technique as intricate as Swinburne's fuses with a passion for Spanish oaks and luxuriant mosses to make "The Marshes of Glynn" one of the best nature poems in

American literature. Lanier's heart ached for the poverty of the southern farmer and laborer in poems of social protest like "Corn." Musician, novelist, hack-writer, teacher, and representative poet — old Walt would be proud to claim him among his brood.

The poetry of social protest broke out in the West about the time Walt Whitman died. The "Go West, young man" boom was in full swing by 1890. Millions lured on by the boom dream settled on semi-arid lands and struggled to raise crops confronted by droughts and plagues of grasshoppers. Eggs were selling for four cents a dozen. No wonder that a little verse in the San Francisco *Examiner* (January 15, 1899) was copied the world over:

> Bowed by the weight of centuries he leans
> Upon his hoe and gazes on the ground,
> The emptiness of ages in his face,
> And on his back the burden of the world.

Markham's "The Man with the Hoe" with its simple starkness is a far more eloquent denunciation than the bombast that gushed from the lips of William Jennings Bryan.

Once more the drums had sounded and the people in the street were raising questions about our big-stick attitude toward the Philippines. At the turn of the twentieth century a young professor at the University of Chicago, William Vaughn Moody, lashed out against imperialism in "An Ode in Time of Hesitation" and "On a Soldier Fallen in the Philippines."

Yet, all in all, these pickings from 1855 to 1900 represent a pretty sterile crop when one recalls Whitman's dream of a vigorous poetic range and an abundance of fresh themes. Not until 1912 was there anything like a spectacular outburst.

In this year there appeared in Chicago an unpretentious monthly, *Poetry: A Magazine of Verse,* edited by Harriet Monroe. Its purpose was to introduce the work of unknown poets and to provide an outlet for experimentation. By 1917 sales had jumped enormously and America suddenly became poetry-conscious.

It was fashionable in the twenties to discuss Amy Lowell and Imagism. Miss Lowell walked her "garden paths" in her "stiff, brocaded gown," enjoyed a brief fad, and faded. One cannot substitute a creed or novelty of expression for genuine emotion. There were, however, some first-rate poets whose early work appeared in *Poetry*.

E. A. Robinson identified himself with no particular school or movement. This quiet New Englander tramped the New Hampshire hills and the crowded streets of New York speaking sparsely, thinking deeply, and observing people with a sympathetic insight that penetrated surfaces to reach the soul.

Flammonde, the castaway, can save others but not himself. Miniver Cheevy "wept that he was ever born":

> Scratched his head and kept on thinking;
> Miniver coughed, and called it fate,
> And kept on drinking.

Fatalist or idealist, realist or romanticist, when E. A. Robinson died in 1935 America lost her outstanding poet of the twentieth century.

In the age of gin, jazz, and Theodore Dreiser a Middle Westerner by the name of Edgar Lee Masters resurrected the corpses from a small-town cemetery to castigate the pettiness, hypocrisies, and maladjustments of life. His fight was not so much against the individual Elmers, Berts, and Toms as against the morbid mass pressures that warp the growth of the individual. Critical realism has gone no further in poetry than it did in the *Spoon River* anthologies. Breaking away from traditional subjects and forms, Masters had novelty galore but lacked creative depth.

Vachel Lindsay in many ways was Walt Whitman's disciple. Trudging along the highways of the West, trading a verse for a loaf of bread, he was *of* and *for* the people; his abiding purpose was to evangelize America in the name of art and beauty. He chose his themes from folk heroes like Andy Jackson, Abe Lincoln, and John L. Sullivan, from Salvation Army reunions, from the irrepressible Negro, and he set them dancing to a ragtime rhythm. A democratic poet and one of our best loved.

Although both Robinson and Frost were New Englanders, Robert Frost's roots go down deeper in New England soil. As Louis Untermeyer so aptly put it, "Where Robinson, in his reticent disclosures and reminiscent moods, often reflects New England, Frost *is* New England." The Vermont farmhouse, the apple orchard, and the birch are not excuses to spin morals in the fashion of nineteenth-century nature poets; they are merely simple, homely facts which Robert Frost transmutes into art. Whether telling a tale about a rural character like the hired man or writing about a New England custom as in "Mending Wall," his style is conventional and colloquial, but always simple and genuine.

The story of Carl Sandburg is a tribute to Walt Whitman's dream. His father was a Swedish immigrant who worked in the Galesburg railway shop in Illinois. The son rose to eminence as a great American poet and biographer. He knew the hardships of life. Milk peddler, porter, laborer, dishwasher, harvest hand — such experience qualified him to speak for industrial America. It is next to impossible to drive northward through Gary, Indiana, without thinking of "Chicago":

> Hog Butcher for the World,
> Tool Maker, Stacker of Wheat,
> Player with Railroads and the Nation's Freight Handler;
> Stormy, husky, brawling,
> City of the Big Shoulders . . .

But Sandburg is not always hard as nails. Listen to him strum his guitar and chant the ballads of the West, or turn to "Fog" and find his tenderness.

> The fog comes
> on little cat feet.
>
> It sits looking
> over harbor and city
> on silent haunches
> and then moves on.

Sandburg's poetry does not have Robinson's degree of consistent performance but it does have a deeper, more humane sympathy. The downtrodden are not analyzed, they are championed.

There have been many omissions, some important; but here is a brood of poets that represent main currents in American poetry from 1855 to the present. Are they continental? Have they justified the democratic spirit of Walt Whitman?

Longfellow's *Hiawatha* was published in the same year as *Leaves of Grass*. To those familiar with the New Poetry, Longfellow is apt to appear prosaic and bookish. He could not write about his contemporary land because he was out of joint with it — "This is a dreadful country for a poet to live in," he wrote in his *Journal*.

Thanks, however, to bold pioneering and cultural changes within the United States, the modern poet's vision has been sharpened and expanded. Sandburg finds beauty in the din of a steel mill, Frost in a rusty strand of wire on a Vermont fence post, Lanier in a web of Spanish moss. No longer is a poet confined to geographic section, to a few well-established forms, or to the perfumed diction of the genteel school.

No, America, 1941, is still far from measuring up to Whitman's projected dream; but collectively her poets have liberated their medium and come to grips with facts. In so doing they have been fulfilling a social function. A fine poetic tradition, with a unity and diversity truly democratic, but to date Walt Whitman remains America's Continental Poet!

On December 17, 1877, the *Atlantic Monthly* gave a memorable banquet in honor of Whittier's seventieth birthday. The scene takes place in the Hotel Brunswick of Boston. The dais is covered with celebrities — Toastmaster Howells, Longfellow, Emerson, Whittier, Dr. Holmes. Just below the salt sits one of the speakers for the occasion — a young eccentric with prairie-fire hair and a nose like a spinnaker — who had just published *Tom Sawyer,* and was winning a reputation as the Wild Humorist of the Pacific Slope. After several speeches Howells introduces the Westerner as "a humorist who never left you hanging your head for having enjoyed a joke."

The speaker, instead of presenting bouquets of roses to the venerable men of letters, spins a tall tale from the point of view of a hard-boiled old miner of the Sierras whose peaceful cabin had been turned into bedlam by three uninvited "littery" men. "Mr. Emerson . . . a seedy little chap, redheaded," Mr. Holmes weighing three hundred with "double chins all the way down to his stomach," and Mr. Longfellow "built like a prize-fighter" had just raised hell in general, according to the old prospector.

They were pretty how-come-you-so by now, and they begun to blow. Emerson says, "The noblest thing I ever wrote was 'Barbara Frietchie.' Says Longfellow, "It don't begin with my 'Biglow Papers.'" Says Holmes, "My 'Thanatopsis' lays over 'em both." They mighty near ended in a fight. Then they wished they had some more company, and Mr. Emerson pointed to me and says:

> "Is yonder squalid peasant all
> That this proud nursery could breed?"

He was a-whetting his bowie on his boot — so I let it pass. Well, sir, next they took it into their heads that they would like some music; so they made me stand up and sing, "When Johnny Comes Marching Home" till I dropped — at thirteen minutes past four this morning. That's what I've been through, my friend. When I woke at seven they were leaving, thank goodness, and Mr. Longfellow had my only boots on and his'n under his arm. Says I,

"Hold on there, Evangeline, what are you going to do with *them?*" He says, "Going to make tracks with 'em, because —

> "Lives of great men all remind us
> We can make our lives sublime;
> And, departing, leave behind us
> Footprints on the sands of time."

But there was silence — a stony silence — a silence "weighing many tons to the square inch," says Howells. Longfellow listened with a "pensive puzzle," Holmes scribbled on his menu, and Emerson, "holding his elbows," listened "with a sort of Jovian oblivion of this nether world in that lapse of memory which saved him in those days from so much bother." Laboring under such terrific handicaps, the speaker finished. Suddenly the frosty atmosphere was broken by the hysterical, blood-curdling shriek of a single guest who fled the room.

What was the trouble? Mark Twain pondered the question the rest of his life. Viewed today, the speech stands as one of the greatest after-dinner speeches of all time. But the humor went flat on this particular occasion because two divergent types of the American mind had clashed. To the Brahmins Twain appeared rude, vulgar, and coarse. To the Westerner the Brahmins seemed old, provincial, and hopelessly out of touch with these United States of the Gilded Age.

The Pacific Slope humorist dropped some of the biggest incendiaries on Boston, which had been the hub of literary America for a generation, and played a strange role in the search for a new center and a new emphasis.

From the end of the Civil War until his death in 1910, Twain, first native author of importance born west of the Mississippi, recorded faithfully and tragically a fundamental contradiction in the American mind. On the one hand he clung to Cornelius Vanderbilt's "rugged" interpretation of individualism: "Damn the law! I got the power, ain't I?" In his zeal to multiply a comfortable income he speculated in wild adventures with the same audacity and ruthlessness shown by Jay Gould and John D. Rockefeller whom he worshiped. On the other hand he detested these "Robber Barons" because of his equalitarian idealism. Twain's potential flashed between the poles of Commodore Vanderbilt and Henry George and finally was short-circuited.

Some day a book will be written entitled *Mark Twain, Journalist*. As a printer's apprentice on his brother's paper, the Hannibal *Journal*, as a newspaper man who worked for papers from San Francisco to New York, he gathered up continental impressions like a gigantic vacuum sweeper and stored them away in a memory that was phenomenal. His best style was always that of an ace reporter with a feeling for the colloquial, the pungent word.

"The Jumping Frog of Calaveras" (1865) — that tall tale which first gave him a taste of fame — was a human-interest story derived from an actual yarn he heard from a backwoods miner. *The Innocents Abroad* (1869) grew out of hundreds of letters which the correspondent for the *Alta California* sent back while touring Europe and Palestine. It proved a "natural" because of the novel sagebrush slant on European culture. Europe is the foil for the naïve Westerner who finds the Parisian billiard cue "so crooked that in making a shot you had to allow for the curve or you would infallibly put the 'English' on the wrong side of the ball." His first stage in literary development was as a reporter of the American scene.

Then, thanks to the capable guidance of Howells and others, the reporter turned his attention to recording, a bit wistfully and with his characteristic exaggeration, that wealth of earlier personal experience. The nineteen-day trip over level continent, deserts, and mountains behind six plunging mustangs, "jackass" rabbits, and the Nevada prospector are all recaptured in that saga of the frontier — *Roughing It* (1871).

Two years later with the aid of Charles Dudley Warner he blossomed out with his first novel, *The Gilded Age* (1873) —

a terrible bit of fiction with a superb title and one great character in Colonel Sellers, the financial wizard with his stovepipe hat and a "tongue like a magician's wand," a favorite Yankee type right down to W. C. Fields.

Returning to the mood of personal narrative, he tapped his richest vein in *Old Times on the Mississippi* (1875), *Tom Sawyer* (1875), and *Huckleberry Finn* (1884). The last took him ten years to write, and in spirit belongs with this group that reveals the joys and tribulations of boyhood and youth in Hannibal, Missouri, and subsequent pilot days.

Huck Finn is a much better novel than *Tom Sawyer* in its wider canvas, its tighter suspense, but it falls apart after the advent of the "stumblebums" — the King and Duke. *Huck* is a grand boy's book. What a relief after so many years of domination by Louisa Alcott and Horatio Alger to hear a kid say, "Ah, nuts!" instead of "Merciful Heavens!"

Throughout this first period of Twain as reporter and recorder, a mood of wistfulness has been deepening into melancholy. The superstitions that plague Nigger Jim and the strait-laced conventions that hamstring Tom are sometimes written in bitterness. Consequently Twain's second phase of romanticism and growing despair cannot be completely explained in terms of the personal tragedies which befell him, although they quickened and intensified it.

Huck is genuinely a boy's book. *The Prince and the Pauper* (1880) is excellent reading for both old and young. The author has the detachment and the control of his theme as in no other of his stories. Curious that the equalitarian message of his best satire has been so frequently missed! Put rags on the prince and robes on the pauper and their own kin cannot tell them apart. *A Connecticut Yankee* (1889) is also written with a passion for justice but Twain's hope for the human race is definitely waning. The Middle Ages provide no haven for a fugitive from the era of Yankee ingenuity outside of the exemplary life of the peasant's champion, Joan of Arc.

The last dark sketches of "the damned human race" — *The Man That Corrupted Hadleyburg* (1899), *What Is Man?* (1906), and *The Mysterious Stranger* (1916) — have value for the psychoanalyst who wishes to explain the short-circuit in full, but are of little literary value because Sam Clemens had lost control.

Mark Twain will always hold a high place in American literature because one can make of him what one wishes. Humorist, cynic, materialist, realist, romantic, equalitarian, "rugged" individualist, he failed to diagnose the diseases of his time because he was too badly infected by them, but in his life and work he left us a true portrait of a bewildered age!

The toastmaster who introduced Mark Twain at Whittier's seventieth birthday banquet has suffered undeservedly at the hands of some twentieth-century realists whose popularity today is due in large measure to his groundwork in the nineteenth. By leading the revolt against the popular F. Marion Crawford heroic tale and by encouraging American novelists to get their roots started in their own contemporary soil, Howells still deserves his well-earned title: "Dean of American Letters."

Because he said that he preferred to call a spade "an agricultural instrument" and believed that our native authors would find "the smiling aspects" of American life more profitable as themes than the sordid, he has frequently been damned as a Pollyanna. His advice to young authors was, in effect: Write about the commonplace and the usual for only "fools wonder at the unusual." Don't ape Flaubert or Dostoevski! You're not a French or Russian novelist living in a crowded and downcast country; you're in the United States where the average citizen is law-abiding and reasonably well off and wishes to feel somewhat the better for having read your books.

This is the kind of common sense which every modern pornographer should read in *Criticism and Fiction* (1891).

This is the sort of counsel which the editor-in-chief of the *Atlantic Monthly* from 1871 to 1891 gave to Mark Twain, Henry James, Hamlin Garland, Stephen Crane, Henry George, Frank Norris, Booth Tarkington, and others.

Howells realized that different authors were equipped to observe and portray different phases of life and it is a tribute to his tolerance that he could extend a helping hand to a young western farmer who knew the drab, squalid existence of the agrarian class and longed with all his soul to protest against it.

So Hamlin Garland, moved by the same impulses that produced Markham's "The Man with the Hoe," pushes his realism a step beyond Howells':

> I grew up on a farm and I am determined once for all to put the essential ugliness of its life into print. I will not lie, even to be a patriot. A proper proportion of the sweat, flies, heat, dirt and drudgery of it all shall go in. I am a competent witness and I intend to tell the whole truth.

And he did! The young radical of the 1890's wrote some short stories in *Main-Travelled Roads* (1891) and *Prairie Folks* (1893) that for acrid realism are unsurpassed. How completely Garland broke the popular hold of the genteel realists can be demonstrated by comparing his portrait of Lucretia Burns in "Sim Burns' Wife" (1893) with Henry James' description of Mrs. Monarch in "The Real Thing" (1893).

> She rose from the cow's side at last, and taking her pails of foaming milk, staggered toward the gate. The two pails hung from her lean arms, her bare feet slipped on the filthy ground, her greasy and faded calico dress showed her tired and swollen ankles, and the mosquitoes swarmed mercilessly on her neck and bedded themselves in her colorless hair.

James, on the other hand, had fled to England to study his themes because he could discover no cultivated civilization, no aristocracy in the United States.

She looked as if she had ten thousand a year. Her husband had used the word that described her: she was, in the same order of ideas, conspicuously and irreproachably "good." For a woman of her age her waist was surprisingly small; her elbow moreover had the orthodox crook.

Hamlin Garland, whose death in 1940 caused scarcely a ripple, believed in portraying the flaws, the drabness in our social order because he was at heart a reformer who believed in a better future. He has had numerous kin, critical realists whose problem novels have attacked almost every conceivable social evil, but Upton Sinclair, Sinclair Lewis, and John Steinbeck are sufficient to demonstrate what has been done by this school.

Upton Sinclair is the most vigorous propagandist and the feeblest novelist. If you want a brilliant socialistic treatise on the smell of the meat-packing industry, read *The Jungle* (1906); an attack on yellow journalism, read *The Brass Check* (1919); and so on for thirty volumes. The difference between propaganda and art can be sensed by anyone who contrasts Sinclair's two-volume documentation of the Sacco-Vanzetti case, *Boston* (1928), with Maxwell Anderson's tragedy, *Winterset* (1935).

In 1930 the Nobel Prize in Literature was awarded to Sinclair Lewis, a far more talented novelist and an author whose popularity has been such that "Main Street" and "Babbitt" are indispensable words in our common speech. After flaying Gopher Prairie and the fly-brained booster, he strips the religious hypocrite, the Reverend Elmer Gantry, and lets him dangle in the spotlight of what he really is. In these early novels Lewis seems to take a sadistic pleasure in victimizing his characters, and the critics had just made up their minds that he was a cynic when he brought out his greatest novels, *Arrowsmith* (1925) and *Dodsworth* (1929).

The message of Dr. Arrowsmith is not that of a cynic. In his heroic pursuit of scientific truth, he symbolizes a faith. If America is loyal to the clean, uncompromising spirit of research, she may yet erect a culture rather than a clogging civilization based on the shifting sands of material success. There is hope even for the old Zenith plutocrat, Sam Dodsworth, who, after losing his fickle wife, Fran, starts to rebuild his life on firmer foundations.

When Lewis forgets his principles to the extent of identifying himself with real Americans — not caricatures — he is at his best and he is one of our best; but he has written no significant fiction since *Dodsworth*.

John Steinbeck's *Grapes of Wrath* (1939) dissolves the hardships of the migratory Garlands in the 1870's into mere trivialities. According to the revolutionary script of this young Californian, impoverished herds of dustbowl farmers driven from Oklahoma and Kansas wander like famine-driven cattle in quest of a promised land. When Pa Joad first sees California, he exclaims: "God Almighty! . . . I never knowed they was anything like her." But the grapes that dangle so promisingly before the Joads' eyes prove "Grapes of Wrath."

One may question the accuracy and justice of Steinbeck's observation, the strained finale, the lack of characterization; but the novel of social protest reaches its bitterest culmination in the hellish persecution of the Joads. Not a happy ending for Walt Whitman's saga of the "resistless restless" pioneer.

Another school of realistic novelists a bit different in hue from the Garland tradition prides itself on its uncompromising scientific attitude — usually mechanistic determinism — its immunity to social conscience, and its fidelity to individual, personal observation. This group, of which Stephen Crane was the American founder, has been called naturalistic because of similarities to the French novelists of the nineteenth century, Zola and Flaubert; but one is on safer ground to label the authors "hard-boiled realists" and let it go at that.

When there are fourteen children in a family, even in a

Methodist parsonage, it is inevitable that one of them will kick up his heels. Few Bohemians, however, have made as interesting dents on literary conventions as Stephen Crane — a famous author at twenty-four and a dissipated corpse at twenty-eight.

Maggie is a fearless yarn about an Irish girl who is trapped by a brutal environment. Fleeing the slavery of the sweatshop, she becomes a bartender's mistress, a prostitute, and finally commits suicide. The book is the first American novel about the big city slum. Crane's revelations were too potent for the publishers of the nineties and had to be privately printed.

Today the debunking of war is an old story reminiscent of John Dos Passos, Ernest Hemingway, and a host of others, but when *The Red Badge of Courage* appeared in 1895 is was a novelty. Appomattox was the subject for screeching declamations; the real filth and terror must not be allowed in print — it wouldn't be patriotic! But young Stephen Crane dared to write the truth. The amazing thing is that this novelette succeeds where so many of his followers have failed, and this in spite of the fact that the author knew nothing about the Civil War except what he heard from veterans and read in historical accounts.

Like Jules Romains in *Verdun,* Crane confines himself to one battle, but unlike the French author he assumes the rigid point of view of a sensitive farmer-boy recruit. The reader never discovers who wins the fight, for that dwindles into insignificance beside the effects of the terrifying incidents on the mind of Henry Fleming. Crane achieves the results of honest reporting combined with a highly unified point of view. Henry is the victim of forces over which he has no control. This device, so frequently questionable in the art of Sherwood Anderson, is completely convincing in *The Red Badge of Courage.*

Theodore Dreiser as the twelfth son of German immigrant parents contended with poverty and unremitting toil during his boyhood, was persecuted for his ancestry during the first World War, and hounded for his frank portrayal of sex in *Sister Carrie* (1900). No wonder that he finds life a grim matter of tooth and claw!

An American Tragedy (1925) in the strict sense of the word is the best naturalistic novel to come off a press in the United States. Dreiser pitifully and sincerely records the crime and punishment of Clyde Griffiths. The impact of the story does not rest upon style nearly so much as on the careful selection of factual material building up to the pathos of the trial scene. The true indictment is not against Clyde, the weakling, but against an American society which tolerates the cheap evangelism and ballyhoo that breed the superficial standards of our Clyde Griffiths. When Dreiser sticks to reporting and forgets his sophomoric editorializing, he is in the front rank of critical realists.

Out of the shattered illusions of the World War epoch emerged a third group of novelists who have gone berserk. In Caldwell's preoccupation with incest and murder, Faulkner's mania for sex perversion, and Hemingway's glorification of a moment of sexual pleasure snatched in the midst of violent action, the world becomes a madhouse where the maladjusted rave with fearful consternation. In his latest novel, *For Whom the Bell Tolls,* Hemingway shows signs of sanity. Roberto and dependable old Anselmo have the dignity and stature of men — not animated biological urges.

Among these spokesmen for our "Lost Generation," one and only one comes to grips with the temper of his times — Thomas Wolfe. This six-foot-six-inch North Carolinian literally and figuratively towers above his contemporaries. Some day he may be considered on a par with Herman Melville.

While walking in the gutter he never loses sight of the stars. He has indelible impressions of the morgue-like tenements with their green painted halls and dim gas jets, but he also attends "the voice of forest water in the night, a woman's laughter in the dark, the clean, hard rattle of raked gravel, the cricketing stitch of midday in hot meadows, the delicate web of children's voices in bright air."

After grappling with problems such as the meaning of life and the "spiritual disease poisoning unto death a noble and a mighty people," his thoughts and feelings began to tumble out a bit chaotically at first in *Look Homeward Angel* (1929) and *Of Time and the River* (1935). By 1938, the year of his death, he was beginning to integrate his experience and his style assumed the flexibility and magnificence of Whitman's finer poetry.

You Can't Go Home Again (1940) is one of the great American novels. It is Wolfe's autobiography told in the words of Monk Webber, but it is more than that; for every conceivable type of individual, from the forgotten harlot to life's favorite son, becomes articulate. And Wolfe has a message in this posthumous book:

> I think the true discovery of America is before us. I think the true fulfillment of our spirit, of our people, of our mighty and immortal land, is yet to come. I think the true discovery of our own democracy is still before us. And I think that all these things are certain as the morning, as inevitable as noon. I think I speak for most men living when I say that our America is Here, is Now, and beckons on before us, and that this glorious assurance is not only our living hope, but our dream to be accomplished.

A pessimist who had feared that hatred, slavery, and poverty would destroy our American culture, after thirty-seven years of questioning arrives at the same conclusion that Walt Whitman expressed seventy years before!

Most of the realists in fiction from Mark Twain to Thomas Wolfe failed to see life consistently and as a whole, but they did make an honest effort to render truthfully what they believed to be the actualities of life. Thus they achieved a tremendous expansion in subject materials and an almost limitless freedom in expression. Even though they could not agree on remedial treatment, they have made America conscious of her diseases. Like good sportsmen, the novelists have pursued the hare of truth over the hill and through the bog. What if the quarry does escape? The chase has been more invigorating than sitting at home and dreaming of the days of yore.

By 1900 the nation had conquered its inferiority complex in poetry and fiction, but not in drama. The enthusiastic revolt in the American theater did not really burst until 1915. Of the many possible explanations for the long delay, several deserve comment.

A flourishing theater has always been one of the last arts to emerge in a culture. The production of plays is a relatively complex and expensive business dependent upon a theatergoing public and a concentration of population and wealth. The pietistic objection to the theater as the devil's vestibule was a Calvinistic attitude that kept thousands of New Englanders from ticket windows up to the twentieth century; it is only within the last year that Broadway producers have started to experiment on a large scale with Sunday performances. In the good old cavalier South, where a playhouse was established as early as 1716, the moral objection was less prevalent but so was the necessary concentration of population and wealth.

The United States has turned more frequently to England and France than to other countries for fresh impulses, critical sanctions, and models; but the English and French drama of the nineteenth century was, for the most part, a sterile source. Hence when new voices did arise across the Atlantic, they spoke in the Scandinavian tongues of Ibsen and Strindberg, in the German accent of Hauptmann, Schnitzler, and Sudermann, in the Irish lilt of Synge or the blarney of Shaw, or in the Russian cadence of Chekhov. It took time for the American ear to attune itself.

About four months before the *Lusitania* went down in

1915, a handful of drama enthusiasts founded the Washington Square Players which developed into the now famous Theatre Guild of New York City. A year and a half later, while the Battle of the Somme raged, a group of playwrights and artists established the Provincetown Theater. Of the few organizations which sprang up earlier and the flock which appeared after 1915, the Theatre Guild group and the Provincetown Players are most representative because they illustrate functions, complementary at first but later fused into one.

The Provincetown clan on its first bill produced O'Neill's *Bound East for Cardiff* and was primarily concerned with cultivating native dramatic talent. On the other hand the pre-Guild organization was more internationally minded; it included Maeterlinck's *Interior* among its first offerings.

Although these random observations pursue the native tradition, it must be emphasized that the modern American theater, born when the lights were going out all over Europe, has been cosmopolitan in spirit and function. Today in another era of black-outs, the Broadway theatergoer finds an English play, *The Corn Is Green,* competing for popularity with the 100 per cent New Yorkerish *Pal Joey.*

Legends stick to the name of the foremost figure in our new theater like burrs to the coat of a sheep dog. Is O'Neill a twentieth-century Villon never quite happy unless he's tossing beer bottles through windows? Is he a man-hater who skulks in his island retreat generating Swiftian bolts against his fellow man? These questions along with the herculean task of tackling a comprehensive evaluation must be put aside in preference for a view of Eugene O'Neill's relationship to the realistic attitude which we have traced through poetry and fiction from the days of Walt Whitman.

According to George Jean Nathan, O'Neill detests playgoing and averages about one attendance every seven years. But this does not mean that America's foremost playwright, who has contributed more by way of technical experimentation in the art of play production than any predecessor, is ignorant of the institution that feeds him.

O'Neill was born in 1888 in a hotel on Broadway and Forty-third Street; one could have tied one end of his clothes line to the fire-escape of several famous theaters. His father was a popular romantic actor who toured widely in *Monte Cristo,* and the boy's first seven years were spent in an atmosphere of grease paint and dingy small-town hotels. Add to this the fact that he served as assistant manager of a road company and in 1914–1915 studied play production under the excellent guidance of George Pierce Baker, and it is evident that Eugene O'Neill was well acquainted with the ways of the theater before he threw in his lot with the newly organized Provincetown Players.

Another aspect of his life should be stressed. In those years of vagabonding after his dismissal from Princeton in 1907 and before his enforced rest in a tuberculosis sanitarium in 1912–1913, he had no serious thought of taking up writing as a career although he was a newspaper reporter for a brief spell. He did not clerk in a mail-order house, clean out stanchions on a cattle boat, prospect for gold in Honduras, or while away time in waterfront dives with any thought of converting the lusty stream of life into literary channels.

While learning his craft O'Neill experimented with one-acts, drawing heavily upon weather-beaten sailors for subjects and developing the violent aspects of sea life with a realism which approaches that of Conrad. In his initial stage Eugene O'Neill is closely identified in spirit with the Crane-Dreiser school of novelists and his favorite pattern is to dramatize the struggle of underdogs who are doomed from start to finish.

In *Beyond the Horizon* (1920), his first full-length play to reach a commercial theater and the first of three to win the Pulitzer Prize, the two brothers Robert and Andrew are trapped as inevitably as Clyde Griffiths in *An American Tragedy.* The brother with the voyaging spirit is compelled to stay on the New England farm and the naturally endowed farmer goes to sea.

Of all O'Neill's dour studies in frustration, *The Emperor Jones* (1920) is tops for sheer dramatic suspense. Brutus Jones, sophisticated and arrogant dictator of a hive of ignorant West Indians, has one weakness — superstition. Through eight episodes, to the gradual acceleration of the tom-tom, Jones' superstition swells into fear and finally into a mad terror from which there is no escape even in the depths of the jungle.

> What — what is I doin'? What is — dis place? Seems like I know dat tree — an' dem stones — an' de river. I remember — seems like I been heah befo'. (*Trembling*) Oh, Gorry, I'se skeered in dis place! I'se skeered. Oh, Lawd, perfect dis sinner!

There is but one solution — a silver bullet in a demented brain!

Along with Brutus Jones, O'Neill has created a thoroughly convincing character in Anna Christie, the waterfront prostitute. To call the play "the truest, the most searching and the most dramatically consistent study in realism that our playwrights have produced" is ridiculous; but of all his twenty-odd full-length plays, *Anna Christie* (1921) is the only one in which a character instead of an idea regulates the growth of plot. Anna seems to win a moment's happiness in her honest love for a sailor, but her creator hastens to add that it will prove only a snare and an illusion for the Old Devil Sea will triumph in the end. Brutus Jones is a coward; Anna is an Anglo-Saxon heroine who will keep her chin up in the teeth of any gale.

> Don't bawl about it. There ain't nothing to forgive anyway. It ain't your fault and it ain't mine. . . . We're all poor nuts. And things happen. And we just get mixed in wrong, that's all.

From *Desire Under the Elms* (1924) to *Mourning Becomes Electra* (1931) O'Neill has been subordinating such materials as the decadence of New England and the pathological character as objects for literary treatment. Although present in almost every play, they tend to become a plausible background across which the cyclone of human emotions rages. Maxwell Anderson, America's second most famous playwright, has also moved away from the literal and grim realism of *What Price Glory* (1924) to the lyrical but none the less dramatic affirmation of the futility of revenge in *Winterset* (1935). Significant as this revolt of O'Neill and Anderson is, it cannot be called representative of the main current in our modern theater.

In the rebellious twenties when H. L. Mencken was shouting to the boys to cudgel all the boobs in America's "boobocracy," the stage had its share of social cudgellers. Elmer Rice protests against Mr. Zero's bondage to his adding machine. Paul Green chafes at the white man's laws, prejudices, and cruelties that enslave the Carolinian Negro. Sidney Howard's *They Knew What They Wanted* presents a common-sense solution to a lonely Italian's desire for an heir and the public reception of the play proves that Victorian squeamishness is well-nigh dead.

1930 began with 86 per cent of the opening shows failures. Not until the New Deal created the Federal Theatre Project in 1935 did the American drama push ahead to new frontiers. Although we are still too close to evaluate the interesting experiment which Congress terminated in July, 1939, the relief measure kept thousands of actors and artists busy and brought the legitimate drama to the people for the first time. By 1930 a fresh crop of experimenters — Orson Welles, Clare Boothe, Thornton Wilder, John Steinbeck, Clifford Odets, and William Saroyan — brought vitality to Broadway. Let's look at a few of the playwrights of the hour.

Clare Boothe's satire of the Park Avenue female with her catty gossip over the teacup and under the drier is no Schopenhauerian indictment of the sex, but it is a most subtle achievement in maintaining a neat balance between ridicule on the one hand and honest reporting on the other. *The Women* (1936) ran for 657 performances — respectable enough when compared with any play save *Tobacco Road* — and as a sophisticated bagatelle about the women with "jungle-red" claws demonstrates that not all the beasts dwell on Jeeter Lester's Georgia farm.

Neither is Thornton Wilder's *Our Town* (Pulitzer Prize, 1938) a great play, but it does broaden the horizon and destroy the illusion that all villages are Main Streets. The simple poetic realism of the first two acts degenerates into sentimental metaphysics in the third, but not before Wilder has indelibly projected the picturesque New Hampshire town.

There's an early afternoon calm in our town: a buzzin' and a hummin' from the school buildings; only a few buggies on Main Street — the horses dozing at the hitching-posts; you all remember what it's like. Doc Gibbs is in his office, tapping people and making them say "ah." Mr. Webb's cuttin' his lawn over there; one man in ten thinks it's a privilege to push his own lawn mower.

In 1938 the New York Drama Critics' Circle selected Steinbeck's *Of Mice and Men* as the season's best play by an American author. Although George S. Kaufman adapted the book to the stage, it was written as a novel intended for dramatic production and needed only the ingenious settings of Oenslager and the supreme acting of Broderick Crawford as Lennie to make it a hit.

Of Mice and Men as a stark bit of social protest is to the stage what *Grapes of Wrath* is to the novel. Between Lennie, the demented migratory harvester with the strength of a giant, and George there exists a friendship, the product of months of working together on California ranches. Lennie is harmless enough, or would be, if only he and George could buy up ten acres with a shack, a chicken run, and a rabbit hutch. But every time they sight their Promised Land, Lennie's fondness for soft and helpless things gets them in trouble and they move on in search of another job. When the wife of the boss's son makes advances to Lennie, the play plunges to its terrible conclusion — George has to shoot his only friend to save him from the lynching party. And Steinbeck would have us believe it's all because "guys like us got no families. They get a little stake and then they blow it in. They ain't got nobody in the world that gives a hoot in hell about 'em."

In 1939–1940 London's Old Vic closed with Shakespeare's *Tempest* to the accompaniment of bombs, and the American theater was once more confronted with the task of keeping the light burning. Robert Sherwood identified himself with the gallant stand of the Finns to demonstrate the totalitarian threat to the democratic ideal. *There Shall Be No Night* is a flaming propaganda play, but it could have been much richer. It is a tragedy that Dr. Valkonen is composed of so much sound and so little flesh and blood. The outstanding playwright of the two past seasons was not Sherwood, but the rambunctious Saroyan, who won both the Critics' and the Pulitzer awards in 1940.

This young Californian, the son of Armenian immigrants, has a zest for life that holds a bewildered audience spellbound. *The Time of Your Life* when lifted from the stage wilts like an Oriental poppy. Nick's Frisco dive with its fantastic medley of hoofers, cops, Bret Harte-ish prostitutes, disillusioned drunks gives birth to no convincing character, to no significant idea, but it seethes with vitality. Where there's life, there's drama!

In the past twenty-five years the American theater has risen from a relative nonentity to a position in the front rank of the theaters of the world. The work of one of its adolescents, Eugene O'Neill, may yet become a milestone in the development of the drama comparable to Ibsen's work.

From the Civil War to the present America has had her prophets of hope and her prophets of gloom, her dreamers and her doers. Ebbing and flowing like the recurrent theme of a great symphony, a spirit persists, best defined and epitomized in literary expression by Walt Whitman.

He did not look upon his day as the fruition of his all-embracing democratic faith — far from it! Instead he exposed the hatred, greed, and vanity of the Gilded Age just as his followers have attacked the malignant growths ever ready to destroy the spiritual roots of this nation.

Consciously or unconsciously this faith in democracy has been the dominant concern of our modern poets, novelists, and dramatists. Earnestly they have striven to reveal life as it is, for in awareness of facts abides the beginning of self-discovery. Bitterly they have flayed the arrogant and ignoble, because of their conviction that every common man should be free to grow in the constructive use of liberty and that in human value no one man should be superior to any other.

CHAPTER 7

EDUCATION IN AMERICAN DEMOCRACY

by George E. Schlesser

Someone has said: "He who monopolizes the knowledge of a country will be its governor in fact, whatever may be the constitutions and laws." If this is true — and who can doubt it — it follows that a successful democracy presupposes a successful educational system. That some sort of education is necessary to democracy is acknowledged by our political requirement that all voters must be able to read. But this is a minimum requirement and, in itself, not enough to guarantee anything like a successful practice of political democracy. Those who vote should be able not only to read but to understand the many issues for and against which they are called upon to vote.

Equal educational opportunity for all citizens is still an unrealized goal, but America has done more than any other nation toward making her educational system universal in scope and democratic in practice. In the course of providing schools which would give equal opportunity to all, we have made many unique contributions to the theory of education. It is the purpose of the present chapter to discuss some of these contributions, and to indicate how the educational policies and practices of the present were brought about.

As we look around us today we see many different kinds of schools. Some are controlled by the state, some by the church, and some by private individuals or boards of trustees. Public schools are supported by the state and are free; private schools are supported by endowment and tuition; and parochial schools are supported by the church and tuition. But schools vary not only in the way in which they are supported; they vary also in purpose, program, and procedure. Some schools teach a classical curriculum, some a wholly vocational one. Some teach mainly arts and sciences, with social problems relegated to extra-curricular activity; some concern themselves almost exclusively with social problems, touching only incidentally on the arts and sciences. In some schools the method is one of the rote memorizing of facts, in others it is essentially one of reflective analysis. Does all this diversity represent strength or weakness?

Henry Suzzalo, former president of the Carnegie Foundation for the Advancement of Teaching, wrote that this wide range in performance was to be taken not as confusion in the professional mind, but as a clear indication that free experimentation in America is a complicated but indispensable substitute for the simplified orders of a political and educational bureaucracy. "And who that is American would have it otherwise, complicated and confused though the situation may seem?"

Some well-intentioned people, in looking for a way out of this apparent confusion, have sought prohibitive legislation. This non-experimental type of solution is hardly one that fits the democratic scheme of things. The best way out would seem to be through the comparison of the consequences of the different practices, and the continuous selection and combination of those that seem best. This is the way that America has handled the problem historically and her choice seems amply justified in terms of all the consequences. Many types of schools, curricula, methods, and policies did not meet the needs of the people and so died out. With variation and selection came evolution and progress.

The first schools in this country were far from democratic institutions. The early settlers brought their own customs with them. Hence it was only natural that these early schools should be patterned after those in Europe. Since people in the various sections of America came from different European countries and from different social strata, there were wide differences in educational policies and practices in New England, the Middle Colonies, and the South. The schools of New England, at first parochial, were soon to start the democratic tradition in education. The schools of the Middle Colonies were to remain parochial for some time, and the schools of the South were to remain largely aristocratic and private until after the Civil War.

Benjamin Franklin's schooling illustrates well the system of education which prevailed in New England in colonial times. Like the majority of young boys, Franklin served an apprenticeship at a trade — in his case the printer's trade — because he could not afford to attend the private schools for the training that would lead to one of the professions. In his time the "free" Latin Grammar Schools were far from free, and were available to relatively few people. Those young men who were destined for a profession usually learned to read in a private Dame school run by some woman in her kitchen for a few pennies per day per head. Later they attended a Latin Grammar School if they could afford it.

By Franklin's day some progress toward free, tax-supported schools had been made, but it was slow. Massachusetts had set the foundation for this type of school in 1647 by passing the "Old Deluder" Law, a law designed to thwart "one chief project of that old deluder Satan to keep men from the knowledge of the scriptures." It provided that every township, "after the Lord hath increased them to the number of fifty householders," should appoint one of their number to instruct the young in reading and writing. The teacher was to be paid either by the parents of the children or by a general tax. It was ordained further that "where any town shall increase up to one hundred families or householders they set up a grammar [i.e., Latin] school."

In the two schools thus provided for, support was permitted by either tuition or taxation, but no school was supported to the extent of being free. They were open to all who could pay for them. Compared to the present-day public schools that provide free education for all, these early schools were not democratic, but they were moving in the right direction. Needless to say, the quality of instruction was usually not very high, the schoolmaster generally being preoccupied with other pursuits to augment his meager salary.

Such were the schools of early colonial times, even in the more democratic New England. Most of them were under the control of the church through the Ecclesiastical Society, which was usually synonymous with the town government. Control was local. While there were a few private schools in addition to those partially tax-supported, education was available to most young people only through the system of apprenticeship which was part of the colonists' European heritage.

Three general trends are observable in our educational history since earliest colonial days. First of these is the secularization of education, removing control of the public schools from the church. The second is centralization, reducing local control and providing higher standardization. The third is the creation of a completely free system of elementary and secondary education. Let us consider each of these tendencies more fully.

Secularization of the schools became increasingly urgent as the number of religious sects in this country grew more numerous. In communities where there was but one religious sect, church control of schools might have worked out satisfactorily. But more and more persecuted religious groups were coming to America and the number of different denominations increased rapidly. To have each church establish its own school was sheer economic waste. Imagine a town of three thousand inhabitants supporting perhaps twenty different schools! This many different churches still thrive in some small communities.

The change from religious control of the schools to state control was gradual. For a time it was accelerated by an apparent decline of interest in religion. The Age of Reason provided a philosophical mood that aided and abetted the trend toward secularization. The doctrine that "all men are created equal," which had become a part of Jefferson's political outlook, provided a new axiom for education that tended to democratize the schools. Not long after the Declaration of Independence had stressed the equality idea, the Constitution, in providing freedom of religious expression to all, distinctly forbade Congress to establish any state religion. This automatically precluded the practice of public taxation for religious purposes and led to the separation of church and state. Denying the right of the church to tax and giving local government this right, together with a law like the Massachusetts law of 1647 permitting tax support of schools, led inevitably to the secularization of education.

However, the battle was not easily won. The early 1800's were to see many religious revivals and many new immigrants coming to America, bringing new religious faiths with them. This renewed interest in religion soon led the church to challenge the idea of state-controlled schools. Massachusetts opened the attack with lusty salvos from the pulpit and press. Horace Mann came to the defense of state-controlled schools and did much to save the day for secularized education. Many states denied aid to sectarian schools in their constitutions; sectarianism could not long withstand such economic pressure. State boards of education were established as early as 1837 and no amount of clerical objection was able to overthrow them. Originally they had little real authority except to make investigations into school conditions, but they gradually gained the type of authority they have today.

Illustrative of the economic pressure which hastened the process of educational secularization was the fight that occurred in New York City in 1840. The Catholics, Jews, and other sects applied to Governor Seward for a division of state funds so that schools could be established to provide teachers who spoke the same language and practiced the same religion as their newly-immigrated patrons. The legislature deferred action on the question until 1842, when, quite unexpectedly but in harmony with the precedent set by certain other localities, it established a city board of education and passed a law providing that no portion of the school funds should be given to church schools. Although this did not prevent the growth of parochial schools supported entirely by the Catholic Church, it did assure a non-sectarian control of the public school system.

The problem of the relation of religious instruction to general education still bothers educators. Separation of church and state did not satisfy everyone. The Catholics, influenced by Thomistic philosophy which taught that the supernatural was superior to the natural (secular), felt strongly enough about the matter to continue church (parochial) schools at their own expense. Protestant and Jewish groups reconciled themselves to teaching religious and moral theory outside the public schools. Recently, however, there has been a movement to put religion back into the schools. This takes the form of what are called "mixed schools." Pupils are grouped by faiths for their religious instruction during part of the regular day by the minister, priest, or rabbi, then brought together again for secular instruction. As recently as 1940 a provision permitting these mixed schools was passed in an omnibus amendment to the New York State constitution. There is a danger that the movement may result in the religious cleavages and disputes that secularization sought to overcome — certainly something to be guarded against.

The disadvantages of church control of the schools are many; hence we cannot help but be grateful for the course of events which brought secularized education into general practice. Under church control educational expense would be exorbitant because of the variety of institutions that

Education in American Democracy

would have to be supported. This would mean a definite lowering of teaching standards. Even greater difficulties could arise from encouraging each church to run its own school. Instead of sharing differences of opinion with regard to religious ideas, children would tend to become less and less tolerant. It is doubtful if any church wants consciously to encourage such intolerant religious attitudes as prevailed in the countries from which our ancestors sought refuge.

We have said that secularization of the public school system was one advance which our forefathers made in educational procedures. Another was the centralization of control. This is really a corollary of the first, for church control originally meant local control. Other factors which tended to decentralize the schools had also been at work. When our ancestors first settled in a town, they established schools and apprenticeship systems. But people did not always stay settled in the town; groups moved out to established separate parishes of their own. The difficulty of traveling from one place to another prevented children from being sent to the town school. Hence it was expedience that led to the idea of a "moving school." The traveling schoolmaster, as immortalized by Ichabod Crane, taught a few months in each parish. As parishes grew in size and economic strength, district schools were established.

By 1766 Connecticut permitted the towns to divide into smaller, semi-autonomous districts. The town school societies thus lost their power of centralized control. The result was a rapid multiplication of school districts, with a one-room school in each. In the 73 towns in Connecticut in 1775 there were only 190 School Societies, while in 1838 there were 1706 districts and one-room schools in these towns. Similar decentralization was taking place in many other states that used New England schools as a pattern. Naturally the education furnished by these many diverse school centers went from bad to worse. As one commentator on the situation has expressed it: "Only bare rudiments were taught by teachers often ignorant and sometimes brutal, by methods mechanical and dreary."

A good description of the typical district school is given in the autobiography of Samuel G. Goodrich.

> We were all seated on benches made of slabs. . . . As they were useless for other purposes, they were converted into benches, the rounded part down.
> The children were called up, one by one to Aunt Delight who . . . required each . . . to make his manners, which consisted of a small, sudden nod. She then placed the spelling book before the pupil and with a pen-knife pointed one by one to the letters of the alphabet, saying "What's that?" I believe I achieved the alphabet that summer. Two years later I went to winter school at the same place kept by Lewis Olmstead — a man who made a business of ploughing, mowing, carting manure, etc., in the summer and of teaching school in the winter. Reading, writing and arithmetic were the only things taught, and these indifferently — not *wholly* from the stupidity of the teacher, but because he had forty scholars. . . .

The poorer the instruction became, the less interest did the people of the district take in the schools. School authorities hired the teacher who would teach for the longest time for the least pay. The teachers were usually men who either had been unsuccessful in some other line of work or else were using teaching as a stepping-stone to one of the other professions. Interest in school affairs finally reached so low an ebb that the first officer of the Connecticut State Board of Education was able to say in his report of 1838: "In six of the largest societies in the State, the annual meeting of 1837, duly warned, was attended by 3 persons." The average attendance in ten districts with a total of 18,000 voters was eight people.

As usually happens when things grow bad enough, some people become interested in reform procedures. Far-sighted leaders let it be known that some towns kept no schools for several years at a time, that educational inspectors were shirking their jobs, and that the only remedy lay in providing good state boards with increased authority to standardize educational techniques. Like secularization, this was not an easy achievement; but with the general establishment of state boards of education the problem was well on its way toward solution.

We have mentioned the fact that besides secularizing and centralizing the schools our forefathers did much to democratize them by developing really free schools that provided equal opportunity for all. We all know that until relatively recently people of great ability were often deprived of even good elementary training because they could not afford it. Benjamin Franklin could not afford schooling for more than two years even in Boston, where educational opportunity was more available than elsewhere. Even later than this, Abraham Lincoln was denied schooling beyond one year for financial reasons. The schools needed improving and secularizing, as we have seen; but these could not have been brought about apart from state support through taxation, which was motivated largely by an interest in democratizing educational opportunity.

Shortly after the Revolutionary War our national Congress gave a great impetus to free schools by establishing national land grants, proceeds from which were to be used as a permanent educational endowment. The idea that the income from these funds would be large enough to support schools entirely was abandoned in 1825. Leaders soon saw that the only solution to the problem of equalizing educational opportunity was direct taxation.

Those battling for free schools had to overcome two practices that had been borrowed from Europe. One was the system of "pauper schools"; the other was the "rate-bill" idea. Pennsylvania's experience with pauper schools is illustrative of the problems which such a system presented.

The constitution of Pennsylvania, adopted in 1790, provided for a state system of pauper schools. If parents would declare themselves paupers they could send their children to a private or church school specified by the state, the expenses being paid out of a poor fund raised by taxation. Most poor people were too proud to declare themselves paupers and, since no public school existed, they found themselves unable to provide any education for their children. In 1829 a report to the legislature indicated that of 400,000 eligible children in the state, only 150,000 attended any kind of school. To improve conditions a permissible free school law was passed which permitted a child to attend school not longer than three years at public expense; however, the law was repealed within two years.

Only after a great struggle between the state senate and the house of representatives was a Free School Act finally passed in 1834. Every ward, borough, and township in the state was made into a school district. Each district was given the right to accept or reject the provisions of the Free School Act. State financial aid was given those districts which were willing to accept the amount of state control demanded by the act. Fifty-two per cent of the districts accepted at once, and by 1873 the last remaining district fell into line. Elementary schools were required to be in session for four months during the year. Pauper schools were thus rendered as unnecessary as they were unsatisfactory.

In other states the question was one not of destroying the pauper school system but of abolishing rate bills. Under the rate-bill system parents of children who attended school paid all the costs of instruction not covered by the school fund. Since these expenses were almost as great as those charged by the larger endowed private schools, the system worked against providing any educational advantages for the poor. The rate-bill system had to be abolished before real free schools could be achieved. One by one the various states did drop the system, but not until after the Civil War did the South finally abandon it.

During this time high schools had developed, the first one

being established in Boston in 1821. Although many taxpayers protested loudly against paying for such advanced education, the famous Kalamazoo decision of 1872, handed down by the Supreme Court in favor of the State of Michigan, removed any doubt that taxes could be levied by communities for the support of high schools. This decision completed the struggle for a system of free, tax-supported, nonsectarian public schools, both elementary and secondary. Out of a basic belief in the worth of the individual and the equality of men had come an equalitarian educational system.

State control of the school system has so standardized our educational requirements that today every child must attend some school until he is at least sixteen years of age. In some states, textbooks, supplies, health inspection, and transportation, as well as instruction and buildings, are furnished without charge to student or parents. In many states it is possible for a student of average ability to go from the elementary grades through college without paying a cent for tuition. Behind this fact lies a story of genuine progress, as a glance at our educational history has indicated.

There have been criticisms of the expansion of the state government's role in education. Such criticisms usually point out the advantages of decentralization. It is said that less central control would provide for more experimentation and greater initiative on the part of those who run the local schools. Moreover, it is pointed out that decentralization is a practical way of preventing any single state or national propaganda from becoming effective. In view of the distinct advantages which central control has brought about, however, such criticisms seem relatively unimportant.

How far should centralization and support of our school systems go? The movement from church to state control was one step. Will the federal government eventually assume the control now held by the several states? It is unlikely that this can happen in the near future, although vague, tentative steps in that direction are being taken. Federal aid for educational projects has been provided by the N.Y.A.; the C.C.C. and W.P.A. have also been interested in educational training. Still further aid by the federal government is conceivable — always, of course, at the risk of bureaucratic ends, as happened in Germany. This would undoubtedly be a major calamity which those who favor decentralization of school authority would view with alarm; but the dangers of becoming too nationalistic in our educational aims can surely be overcome by other methods than resorting to decentralization again. The disadvantages of local support and control are too numerous to tempt anyone in that direction.

Provided that the matter of school policy is not entirely removed from local boards, the increased standardization which federal support and control could bring about might be distinctly advantageous. Poor states would profit by sharing the educational advantages now confined to states with higher incomes.

For those who like to speculate about long-term possibilities, there is of course the remote chance that education will some day be supported and controlled on an international scale. A world league may well find international education a primary requirement for mutual understanding between nations. An international league with power to tax nations for funds to support an international education society is not inconceivable.

The Functions of Education

We have seen how the American people, because of their desire to equalize educational opportunity, have created a free, public-supported, non-sectarian system of education extending from elementary school through college. Nothing, however, has been said about the kinds of knowledge they wanted. The changing functions of the schools as they adapted themselves to changing conditions is as important a story as the struggle for free education itself.

The early colonists seemed to think that about their most important task in this world was to prepare for a future existence somewhere else, and their school systems reflected this other-worldly outlook. The function of the school was chiefly religious; only incidentally was it civic and vocational. Boys in the private Dame schools studied the *a, b, c's*, a benediction, and the Lord's Prayer from their hornbooks. Elementary pupils also read a primer, and a few advanced pupils read the Bible. Those who sought further training in the Latin Grammar Schools, a forerunner of the universities which came later, studied a borrowed classical curriculum and invariably prepared for the ministry. Education for anything else was deemed useless.

Fortunately this state of affairs did not last long, for the American people soon became dissatisfied with their borrowed curriculum and the Latin Grammar Schools. Ideas about what was useful changed fairly rapidly. By Franklin's time new interests were demanding new types of training. Franklin himself made "Proposals Relating to the Education of Youth in Pennsylvania." He wrote:

> As to their studies, it would be well if they could be taught everything that is useful and everything that is ornamental. But art is long and time is short. It is therefore proposed that they learn those things that are likely to be most useful and most ornamental, regard being had to the several professions for which they are intended. . . . All should be taught a fair hand, drawing, arithmetic and accounts and the first principles of geometry and astronomy. The English language might be taught by grammar. . . . Reading should be also taught and pronouncing properly, distinctly and emphatically. . . . History: geography, chronology, ancient customs, morality. . . . And although all should not be compelled to learn Greek and Latin or the modern foreign languages, yet none that have an ardent desire to learn them should be refused. . . .

This interest in diversified and practical training called for institutions of a different type from the classical Latin schools. Franklin drew up plans for a secondary school to be called the Academy; this later became the University of Pennsylvania. Soon academies were growing up all over the country and by 1850 there were more than six thousand of them. Although they were not free, they were much better supported by the people than the Latin schools had been, primarily because they satisfied more pressing needs. Support from land grants, state funds, and tuition was supplemented from time to time by income from lotteries, parish taxes, and endowments. But the academies were doomed, as the Latin schools had been, because they failed after a while to keep up with growing demands. They turned their attention almost entirely to preparing students for college. As the colleges erected more and more stringent entrance requirements, the curriculum of the academies became more and more specialized and consequently less adapted to the general educational requirements of those who did not plan any further formal training. The task of providing wide training for this latter group thus fell, by default, to the high schools. The first of these, as we have said, was established in Boston in 1821. By 1860 there were 40 in the United States; in 1900 there were 6000 and in 1940 approximately 25,000. The growing popularity of high schools can be accounted for partly by their willingness to adapt their curricula to changing conditions. Once the schools became public enterprises, the people saw to it that they provided the kind of instruction that most people needed. They are no longer considered as merely preparatory to college training.

In our own time school curricula have become widely diversified because of the diverse needs of various classes of people. The failure of farmers and housewives to keep abreast of the best knowledge available in these pursuits led the federal government to subsidize college and secondary school courses in agriculture and domestic science. The discovery during the first World War that more than a third of the men drafted for army service were physically unfit led to criticism of the schools for their lack of concern with health problems. Our present-day physical education and health programs are the consequence of this criticism. The increase in the number of extra-curricular activities in our schools is partly an attempt to solve the problems of leisure-time activity — a need made evident by the "flapper era." The collapse of the apprenticeship system following the growth of great industries led to courses in industrial arts and manual training. The depression doubtless evoked greater interest in courses in economics and social science. Even more recently the alarming increase in traffic deaths has led to safety education courses in our public schools. Under pressure of the national defense emergency, courses in aeronautical mechanics will doubtless become increasingly popular.

These constant shifts in school curricula, which have been prompted by the shifting interests of the people of America, indicate that a useful school system can never afford to become completely static. Already new problems are being forced upon the schools and the general educational program. These will affect the curriculum just as past problems have. What are some of them?

One of the greatest problems of the past few years has been youth unemployment. The 1940 census figures showed that more than two million young Americans under the age of twenty-five were vainly seeking employment, and that about a million others had only such employment as was offered by W.P.A. projects and the C.C.C. This constitutes a major social maladjustment, one that has been recognized not only by the schools and the federal government but by various business service clubs throughout the country. If no other solution to the problem is forthcoming, work camps and projects under federal government control, similar to those now under N.Y.A., C.C.C., and W.P.A., are likely to be increased in number and made a permanent part of our social system. Since this is definitely an unhappy prospect, educational leaders feel more and more responsible for providing the sort of training which will permit youth to create opportunities for his own employment.

Other social problems have also become increasingly pressing. Men must learn to live together wisely if they are to keep living together at all. H. G. Wells has said: "Civilization is a race between education and catastrophe." Even the most optimistic people must admit that the outcome is not assured. Physical science and invention have far outrun our ability to apply them to the widest social uses. Consequently education has of necessity turned more and more to the investigation of social maladjustments. Continuous investigation and experimentation are even more necessary in this field than in those other areas where great progress has already been achieved.

Wars, depressions, unemployment problems, and so on are just a few of the things that have led away from the teaching of history as "a chronological account of happenings remote from the environment and lives of the pupils" to more pertinent social problems such as housing, the stock exchange, corporation activity, consumers' needs, investments, post-war reconstruction, international relations, and the like.

The teaching of courses on such controversial subjects is frequently handicapped because the public misunderstands what the schools are trying to do. Often teachers who are patiently trying to investigate such questions are dogmatically classified as "reds," "fascists," or what not simply because they do not consider the issues involved as completely closed. Yet surely all the issues are not closed, or there would be no problem!

In the past the role of education has usually been to conserve the existing social culture practically intact. But failure to be concerned about social, economic, and political problems is thought by many people to be one cause of the social lag which threatens our civilization. It requires a tolerant state and people to have themselves and their favorite dogmas discussed in an impartial way, and this sort of thing could hardly happen outside of a democracy. Danger is involved in it, to be sure, for once one questions beliefs and submits them to reflective analysis there is no guarantee what the final result will be. But not to question them is even more dangerous, for it lulls one into a false sense of security. Honestly facing difficulties is bound to be more productive than treating them with an ostrich-like disdain.

To promote programs of study which can deal effectively with all the new problems that the schools are called upon to face means that teachers must be more thoroughly prepared. It will not be long before every state in the Union will require a year of graduate work or its equivalent as preparation for teaching in the secondary schools. Many teacher-tenure laws have been passed in order to assure the teacher of some freedom from unreasonable assault by opinionated patrons.

Training in citizenship is the newest and most important task of the educational system. As a special Committee of the American Council for Education sums up the problem: "If social chaos is to be avoided, the people of this country must assume the obligation of finding some way of preparing young people for citizenship, in the formation of intelligent social attitudes, and for effective participation in community life."

Methods in American Education

We have seen that the major problems of our society tend to influence *what* is taught. They also influence *how* pupils are taught. Methods have shifted along with subject matter.

In those early days when religion was the most important subject in the curriculum, schoolmasters were rigorous disciplinarians. Children were expected to be little rebels infected with all the wickedness that a very active devil could instill in them. Discipline was repressive. The ferrule, cat-o'-nine-tails, and whipping post were part of the regular school equipment.

The attitude of the typical schoolmaster is well illustrated by the following instructions given to the headmaster of the Dorchester Latin Grammar School in 1645. Between twelve and one o'clock each Monday he was to call his pupils together ". . . to examine them what they have learned, at which time also he shall take notice of any misdemeanor or outrage that any of his scholars shall have committed on the Sabbath, to the end that at some convenient time due admonitions and correction may be administered." The concept of freedom for the child, such as is commonplace today, was conspicuously absent from the thinking of colonial schoolmasters.

With the shift in philosophical mood that came about with the Age of Reason, educational aims and methods changed too. Religion was no longer thought of as the only subject of sufficient importance to warrant man's attention. Man came to be thought of as a rational animal, capable of almost infinite self-improvement through the right use of his intelligence. He was no longer deemed to be merely a sin-stained soul whose one salvation lay in rather narrowly conceived religious disciplines. The well-rounded individual came to be the new ideal, and there was a return to the pagan classics for educational inspiration.

This new "humanistic" outlook led to methods which were believed to secure the greatest self-realization for young students. Their return to the classics, however, still involved a sort of authoritarianism in education, but it was on a broader scale than that which characterized the first schools. Man's wits could be sharpened and his character improved by the mental and moral discipline of coming to understand the great minds of the past. The human being was supposed to possess certain faculties, such as cognition and volition, which through constant discipline could be counted on to lead to the good life.

Education in American Democracy 199

The validity of knowledge was still tested largely in terms of past authority. The typically American method of testing all ideas in terms of consequences was not yet fully realized. This was to be a contribution of pragmatism to educational theory, and it marks the latest tendency in American education. It is intimately related to that other tendency in American educational policy, the tendency toward increased democratization of the schools.

The American school system achieved democratic aims in education long before it achieved democratic methods. The notion that all children should be given equal opportunity to learn was a democratic ideal that was finally realized, at least on the administrative side, by the achievement of free public schools; but democratic techniques for teaching were much slower in developing. School administration was influenced quite early by an underlying desire to provide democratic education.

Pupils were recognized to be of different abilities. Consequently, merely giving each the same instruction was not really giving each the same opportunity to learn. Equal opportunity for all became equal opportunity for each according to his abilities. A boy of sixteen could not profit to his utmost if taught in the same class with a child of six. Nor could a person with musical talent profit as much as possible if given an engineering curriculum. The first administrative device for meeting this type of problem was the simple matter of gradation — segregation of children by grades. Later other devices were conceived, such as freedom to choose certain elective courses, more rapid promotion for the brighter students, gradation by ability rather than age, and so on. These were all administrative devices.

In the classroom children were still filled with knowledge and drilled in skills. Lynd and Lynd, in describing a typical American school classroom in their book *Middletown*, tell of some of the practices in the elementary grades in 1924. Procedure consisted largely in memorizing and reciting facts from textbooks. "Classes visited are occupied with learning facts, and 1890 and 1924 examination questions are interchangeable." Students were frequently taught *about* democracy and other important subjects, but there was little attempt to couple knowing with doing; the result was that the student did not participate fully in the learning process.

In contrast to these authoritarian techniques whereby one simply memorized factual material, other methods were being developed in some of the experimental schools in this country. Educators, philosophers, and psychologists were attempting to work the basic principles of democracy into methods of instruction. These experimentalist schools were broadly divided into two different groups. One was led by John Dewey, as director of the University Elementary School at the University of Chicago in 1896. This branch resulted in what has been called the progressive movement. The other, headed by William T. Harris and Carlton Washburn at Winnetka, and Miss Parkhurst at Dalton, resulted in what has been called the essentialist movement.

The step toward more complete democratization of education taken by this latter group was in the direction of individual instruction. In learning the tool subjects — reading, arithmetic, and spelling — under the guidance of this system, each pupil works by himself to master certain fundamental principles appropriate to his stage of development. To attain a goal of the right level of difficulty for his age he uses specially constructed exercise books. When he thinks he has achieved his goal he gives himself some tests to determine whether he is ready for advanced work. If he satisfies himself that he is ready, further tests are given by the teacher. On passing these, the student is permitted to begin a new project, with a new set of goals to be achieved. This emphasis upon individual achievement is quite in keeping with the democratic ideal that institutions exist for the individual, not vice versa. Two democratic principles are involved in this individualistic approach. Each child is given the opportunity to learn in proportion to his ability, and each learns to take responsibility for his own progress.

One of the most important recent leaders of the essentialist group is Dr. Charles Judd. He believes that all children should be provided an education, and that education should consist of mastering the fundamental principles underlying the major intellectual disciplines. The basic *essentials* to be mastered are language, mathematics, science, and social studies. Dr. Judd is idealist enough to believe that social ends will be best served through having each individual brought to a competent understanding of the fundamental laws of nature and society. This is a rather intellectualistic attitude which does not put much emphasis upon the building of social attitudes as such. The child is expected to develop into an adult who can criticize on a sound basis not only his own writing and oral expression but language itself; not only his own social behavior but social customs; not only his own political action but the various political theories. Schools conducted on such a basis would not be expected to provide social biases one way or another. All this sounds pretty good, but it puts quite a strain upon pure "intellection." Most "fundamental principles" are not readily grasped, and most people who think they can teach without indicating any biases are fooling themselves.

Everyone who reads the current newspapers or magazines is familiar with the controversy that is raging between the "fundamentalists" and the "progressives" in educational circles. The progressives, under the leadership of John Dewey, feel that the essentialists are not essentially democratic in their methods. Despite the latter's emphasis upon individualism, the system remains fundamentally authoritarian according to progressive standards. Preconceived goals are set for the student, whereas the student should participate in setting them. Moreover, much valuable training in self-reliance is lost to the student, the progressives would say, by not giving him a larger place in making plans to realize the goal, once it is set. This tendency to do things for the student, rather than have him do them himself, leads to a kind of "hothouse" education which hardly prepares him for non-school or "life" situations. The world at large does not provide intellectual valets to people in a quandary; and a school which teaches one to depend upon such service is not well calculated to make the best citizens.

The progressives claim to be training students for democratic living better than other groups for still another reason. In the progressive system students are invited to confer with the teachers regarding their readiness to attack advanced problems. One who insisted that he was ready, even if it were evident to the teacher that he was not, might be permitted to go ahead and learn the sad truth for himself. The primary emphasis is always placed upon learning from experience rather than from authority.

It is on this point that the progressives are frequently criticized. It is pointed out that the student is given too much freedom before he is prepared to utilize it. It must be admitted that his training often seems to lack control and direction. Hand in hand with the doctrine of student freedom goes the principle that those who would learn should always be motivated by their own interests. Unless a teacher is skillful enough to lead a student into advanced materials, interest may remain at an unfortunately adolescent stage and ill-disciplined personalities be the only visible result. Some parents who have had experience with "progressive education" doubtless feel the strength of the devastating remark that many people fancy themselves emancipated when in reality they are merely unbuttoned. The new freedom is certainly not fool-proof. Whether its merits outweigh its difficulties is the bone of contention among modern educators.

The philosophy underlying progressive education is pragmatism, a philosophy based upon pure experience. It insists that experience is the only teacher and that experimentation is the only method. It rejects all authoritative approaches to knowledge and provides the basis for the progressive doctrine that the pupil must be given freedom to try his ideas, even if they seem palpably ridiculous to his elders.

Progressives believe that no other value is to be subordinated to democratic living, and they interpret democracy as meaning much more than political democracy. It means a whole way of life — intellectual, aesthetic, religious, economic, social, and political. Education, to be valuable at all, must be integrated with life in general. A divorce between methods of learning and methods of living can only end unsatisfactorily for both, according to the philosophic outlook on which progressivism claims to be based. In a democratic country the schools should be a living example of democracy at work. They should study real life problems in the home, in the local community, in the nation, and in the world at large. They should study them in an active rather than a passive way, realizing all the while that the history of things gone by is not an end in itself, but merely an instrument for reconstructing experience so that new and better values can be realized.

The progressive movement in America represents one of this country's latest contributions to educational theory. John Dewey's influence has spread around the world and has affected educational procedure in many places. But, as we have seen, he has not stood alone in the endless struggle for better schools. Even those who differ most radically from him have contributed invaluably to their development. The conflict of opinions which exists in this country concerning educational aims and methods has proved itself a productive conflict. Future schools are likely to be better instead of worse because freedom of opinion still prevails.

CHAPTER 8

THE SPIRIT OF AMERICAN RELIGION

By Howard B. Jefferson

Freedom of worship is one of the basic freedoms in a democracy. America passes this democratic test with flying colors because every one of her citizens is guaranteed the right to worship God as he sees fit. We have Catholics, Jews, and Protestants of many varieties, all of whom receive equal legal protection. No one religious group has more state support than any other because our American democracy has refused to have an official or established religion. In her religious life America is different from most of the nations in the western world precisely because she does not have one church that is the official American church. One religious group is just as American as any other, and they all live together with an amazing degree of mutual tolerance.

A careful reading of the Constitution of the United States discloses but two brief references to religion. In one place it states that no religious test shall be made a qualification for public office. The second is found in the First Amendment where it is decreed: "Congress shall make no law respecting an establishment of religion or prohibiting the free exercise thereof." These few words mark an epoch in the history of the struggle for religious liberty. They lay down the principle of separation of church and state and the principle of freedom of worship. But these principles were not manufactured by the founding fathers out of whole cloth. They developed gradually from the living experience of the colonial

The Spirit of American Religion

churches. By the time of the Revolution an attitude of mutual tolerance had made notable progress and, so far as New England was concerned, there was deep-seated opposition to having an established church of any kind.

The religion of New England was in the first instance a phase of European Christianity transplanted in the new land. It was derived from English Separatism or Dissent, and from English Puritanism. In England during the reign of Henry VIII, the authority of the pope was rejected and this resulted in the establishment of the Church of England. The chief difference which this made in the religious situation was that a distinctly national church was formed, with England's king replacing the pope as its head. The forms of worship remained essentially Catholic. Many Englishmen among the middle and lower classes wanted to go further than this; they were anxious to have a more thoroughgoing reformation and a genuine purification of the church. Some of them became convinced that it was impossible to reform successfully a church that included the entire English population, and therefore they withdrew from the Established church.

Gradually these Separatists evolved the notion that there should be a separation of church and state, that the church should be a voluntary organization of those who really believe in Christian principles and who make a common pact to follow Christ. Such a church would have among its members only those who have been truly converted. Furthermore, each congregation would be a law unto itself; it would choose its own minister rather than accept a priest assigned to it by the bishop, and it would have no authority other than the Bible.

It is apparent that the principles of democracy were assumed in the thinking of these groups. Because of their "dissent" they were hunted out and persecuted by the Established church. Some of their leaders were hanged as heretics. From this background of Dissent and consequent persecution came the Pilgrims of Plymouth Rock renown. The New World was to them a place of refuge and also an opportunity to build a free church in a free state.

Tolerance, however, is a difficult lesson to learn, and it was by no means an easily won virtue of New England religion. Coupled with the Separatist tradition was a strong ingredient of Puritanism, which acknowledged John Calvin as its spiritual father. Close upon the heels of the Pilgrims came a Puritan company to found the Massachusetts Bay Colony. The original purpose of this group was stated by Higginson, its minister: "We do not go to New England as Separatists from the Church of England, though we cannot but separate from the corruptions in it; but we go to practice the positive part of church reformation, and propagate the gospel in America." It was not long before Congregationalism was the established religion in Massachusetts.

So far as the Puritans were guided by Calvinist principles, their ideal included the building of a community in which God was to be the ruler. This would be a kind of Kingdom of God in the new land, or a "theocracy." Such was the logic of Calvinism. God's rule was universal; it had to do with the whole range of human life. In practice this meant that the interpretation of God's will was in the hands of the church, and that the state was to be the instrument of the church in enforcing divine law. Thus church and state were very closely associated. All residents were taxed to support the church as well as to support the state. On the other hand, membership in the church was restricted so that a comparatively small percentage of the population had a church affiliation. The result was that a religious aristocracy developed, since only church members enjoyed the full rights of citizenship. Neither democracy nor toleration was at first the ideal of the Massachusetts Bay Colony. John Cotton, who defended theocracy in his writings, said bluntly that God did not ordain democracy "as a fit government either for church or commonwealth."

In this situation many acts of intolerance occurred, but there were effective protests. Roger Williams, himself a religious teacher, was banished from Massachusetts and went into the wilderness of Rhode Island to found a new colony. There he purchased land from the Indians, it being one of his convictions that all charters from the king were worthless since the land really belonged to the Indians. Following him to Rhode Island were individualists of all varieties. These people consistently maintained a distinction between religious and civil affairs, and they furthered the practice of extreme democratic freedom in both spheres. Personally, Williams was a dreamer who moved from one religious view to another, but he had a firm grasp of those principles of democracy and freedom which were destined to become the rule in American life. Concerning government he said that "the foundation of all civil power lies in the people," and concerning religion, "God requireth not a uniformity of religion to be enacted and enforced in any civil state; which enforced uniformity is the greatest occasion of civil war, ravishing of conscience, persecution of Christ in his servants, and of the hypocrisy and destruction of millions of souls."

Protests of this sort were among the influences that led to the collapse of the theocratic ideal. It may be that the second and third generations had less religious zeal than the first Puritans and so allowed theocracy to die a natural death. It may be that discouragement resulted from the failure to make it work. Nominally, there was an established church for some time; but the outlook of Separatism, which logically implied the separation of church and state, came to be the strongest influence in New England religious life. Whatever the cause, the political significance of Puritan theocracy came to an end in 1684 when the Massachusetts charter was annulled.

The decline of theocracy and the victory of the Separatist point of view contributed greatly to the spirit of toleration. The conviction that each congregation is its own final authority prevented the development of a central ecclesiastical organization strong enough to enforce particular beliefs and practices. And the doctrine of the separation of church and state meant that the civil power would not be used in the interest of one religious group. Furthermore, every individual was thought capable of arriving at religious truth by reading the Scripture under the guidance of the Holy Spirit. This means that the individual conscience and intelligence are the final court of appeal, and when this principle is clearly understood persecution because of opinion becomes well-nigh impossible.

Another important factor making for tolerance was that there were no vested interests or sacred traditions which men felt called upon to preserve in the new land. The religious attitude of the Separatists was more or less hostile to the past. They felt that a sure foundation for belief and conduct was provided by the Bible and the individual conscience. Such an attitude was reinforced by the actual experience of leaving Europe and engaging in the creative task of building a new country. Their faces were turned away from the past and toward the future. In this new land there were no aged institutions hallowed by the centuries. There were no Gothic cathedrals to remind them of an earlier order of Christian civilization. There were no sacred traditions to shackle them and hinder experimentation. All this contributed to a rather novel principle concerning the limits of toleration. No longer were these limits set by a standard out of the past. It was less important to preserve the past than to build successfully for the future. The new principle which defined the limits of toleration was discovered by asking the question: "What interferes with the building of a good society?" There is no rigid and eternal rule by which we can judge anything to be positively harmful in a creative process. We have to try things out and see how well they work. This principle means, therefore, that a variety of beliefs and practices can be given a chance to meet the test of experience. Minorities as well as majorities have the right to be heard.

Intolerance could not be long effective in such an atmosphere. Lacking were the necessary instruments of a central ecclesiastical authority and of a political power at the service of the church. The chief emphasis was in the opposite direction — groups were eager to establish conditions congenial to their own freedom. But American religious tolerance is not a mere negative thing. It is a positive conviction. American experience has gradually brought about the conviction that the best way of reaching true religious beliefs and valid religious practices is the method of give-and-take. This is quite the opposite of the so-called "church type" of European Christianity in which truth is supposed to reside in a revelation officially interpreted by a priestly class. Americans have come to believe that truth is not so much conformity to past dogma as it is those beliefs that have the power of working out in actual practice and of getting themselves accepted in the market of ideas. This is the same point of view as that expressed in the American philosophy of Pragmatism or Experimentalism which is described in the following chapter. American religious experience has certainly been experimental in character. It is no mystery that the Constitution asserted that the government shall not create an official or established religion. Neither is it a mystery that the Constitution provided for the free exercise of religion. These principles had been fashioned by the actual experience of colonial New England.

True, the religious situation in other colonies — in Virginia, for example — was different from that in New England. In Virginia the religious picture was an attempted transplanting of the Established English church. This colony was an English colony and its official church was the English church. However, religion did not play a particularly significant role in Virginia even though it was placed on a compulsory rather than on a voluntary basis. All citizens were expected to be members of the church, there was provision for church property, and taxes supported the ministers. Still, religion was more or less a perfunctory affair. Few of the settlers were led here by religious motives. Those of relatively high social standing had merely a casual interest in the church; and the rather large number of indentured servants, as well as other laborers, who came to Virginia felt no more kindly disposed toward the Established church after they arrived than they had been while living in England.

Any attempt to make a complete transfer of a religious institution from the old country to the new was bound to fail. Although dependent to a large extent on European culture, the American colonists were intent on working out their own destiny. So long as ministers were sent out from England and tried merely to carry on the English tradition in America, this church could not compete successfully with those groups that were more definitely attuned to the emerging new culture. Hence the English Established church never had a vital hold on Virginia; and if it had tried more conscientiously to make itself felt, it probably would have been firmly, and perhaps violently, resisted because its principles were dangerous to the preservation of the liberties which the settlers were determined to have.

The Revolutionary War was the crucial event in the life of the Established church in Virginia. Most of the ministers fled to England, and the whole position of the church was difficult since it was so closely linked with England and thus opposed to the Revolution. At the end of the war the Established church here found itself badly disorganized and in a state of almost complete collapse. Strangely enough though, it was only after all these events that this religious movement began to have any real influence in American life. This was due to the fact that the church was forced into a reorganization along distinctively American lines.

The Established church of England was transformed into

the Protestant Episcopal church of America. The first thing that happened was the development of a line of American bishops as well as an American clergy. Apparently the Archbishop of London was rigidly opposed to appointing an American bishop, but somehow the Reverend Samuel Seabury of New York managed to get around that difficulty and he was appointed to the office. The prayers offered in this church referred to the government of the United States and not to the king of England. The word "Protestant" in the name of the organization, "Protestant Episcopal Church," suggests an attempt to line up with the dominant religious outlook of America. The church of England had never considered itself "Protestant" in any real sense of the word.

The Episcopal church also moved in a direction not only American but democratic when it recognized the place of laymen in the determination of church policy. Aristocracy in church government is found when a special priestly class is set apart to rule all ecclesiastical affairs. There is democracy in church organization when the laymen as well as the priests have a place in its government.

What happened in the shift from the national church of England to the Protestant Episcopal church of America is more or less the pattern followed by all European national churches in becoming American. Lutheranism, for example, was the state church in Germany and the Scandinavian countries. In these European nations the church had been intimately connected with government in the sense that religious policy was to a great extent determined by the fact that the church was supported by taxation. There it was important to have a carefully worded creed as the basis for offering the state a united church. Where formulation of belief is the primary concern and conduct is secondary, the trained clergy tend to dominate the picture. Laymen cannot compete successfully with educated ministers on matters of technical theology. This situation had always presented the possibility of creating a powerful class of clergymen who would dictate religious policy over the heads of the people and who, since they received government support, might become the instruments of privileged political and economic classes in exploiting the common man.

The great majority of Lutherans who came to this country were from the lower classes. These people welcomed the opportunity which America afforded for democracy in church affairs. They have displayed a particular interest in self-government and they have constantly resisted any tendency to form a powerful ecclesiastical ruling body. The fact that Lutheranism is not an established church in America has compelled these people to learn how to support their churches through voluntary contributions rather than by taxation, and to win membership by offering satisfying services. Democratic tendencies have thereby been furthered. Individual congregations have insisted on local self-government following the pattern of Congregational and Baptist churches. This interest in freedom is probably one of the reasons for the division of American Lutheranism into many religious bodies or synods.

The general line of development followed by those denominations which were established churches in Europe can be seen by reference to the Episcopal and Lutheran churches. They have all become free from political entanglements and have taken their places here as non-political, voluntary sects. We must remember, however, that the denominations with national church backgrounds have retained distinct traces of their origins. In many cases this has been valuable in adding to the richness and variety of American life.

In this connection the Roman Catholic church presents a unique problem. Like the national established churches it is the official state religion in certain countries, but it also has a central organization that is independent of all nations. And, of course, it represents quite the opposite of the Separatist tradition in American Protestantism. Numerous Protestants, and others who have no church affiliation, seem to feel that Roman Catholicism is incapable of becoming a part of the "real" America and that its presence here offers a constant danger to American institutions. Perhaps their attitude is much like that of a man described by George N. Shuster. This man, who had a Protestant background but had become agnostic, made the following remark: "If the Catholic church ever gets the upper hand, numerically, in the United States, I wonder if people like me will not have to stand and fight against her!"

Is such an attitude justifiable? Let us look at some of the facts. As long ago as 1634 a group of Catholic colonists arrived in Maryland and established this colony on the principle of toleration. The governor of the settlement was made to swear that he would protect everyone from persecution for religious beliefs and that he would impose no religious tests in "conferring offices, favors, or rewards." It is true that this principle of toleration not only was readily agreed to by the Maryland Catholics as being of benefit to them in a non-Catholic country, but was also a necessary condition in securing a charter from the Protestant king of England. However, there is reason to believe that there was genuine conviction that mutual tolerance was not merely a matter of temporary expedience but was a positive help in furthering the cause of religion. Lord Baltimore insisted upon the absolute separation of church and state in Maryland long before this principle was firmly established in New England.

The historical facts are that in Maryland the principle of toleration was violated not by Catholics but by Protestants. In 1649 some Puritans were forced to leave Virginia because of conflict with the Established church and they settled in Maryland. Roman Catholic Maryland became a refuge for a Puritan colony. But these Puritans, during Cromwell's regime, gained the upper hand in the Maryland government and then turned upon the Catholics with shameful intolerance. They placed before the Cromwellian Commissioners for Maryland their objection to a situation in which they were obliged to swear "absolute subjection to a government where the ministers of state are bound by oath to countenance and defend the Roman Popish religion." The result was that the Commissioners arrived with armed forces and established a legislature which deprived Catholics of protection under the law.

In spite of these difficulties the work of Jesuit priests continued and many converts were made. By the time of the Revolution the majority of the Catholics in Maryland were individuals who had been converted to Catholicism in the colony. Practically all of them were loyal to the revolutionary cause; among the signers of the Declaration of Independence was the well-known Catholic, Charles Carroll. Two others, Daniel Carroll of Maryland and Thomas Fitzsimmons of Pennsylvania, were among the authors of the Constitution.

There is ample evidence, then, that early American Catholicism was congenial to the spirit of religious toleration and that it played a part in making America an independent nation. Furthermore, an American priesthood has developed and this has actually been encouraged by Rome. These priests have helped to adapt Catholicism to American conditions. American Catholicism is in a genuine sense an American institution.

In view of these facts, why is Catholicism looked upon with suspicion by Protestants and by people with no church connection? And why are there outbursts of persecution in the name of what is "truly American"? The Know-Nothing party of a century ago and the Ku Klux Klan of more recent times have been violently opposed to Catholicism. It is significant that they have looked upon Catholics as "foreigners" even though Catholicism has been part of the American religious scene since early colonial days.

One reason why Catholicism appears foreign is that it is so different from the dominant religious tradition which was derived from the spirit of Separatism or English Dissent and

The Spirit of American Religion

which spread throughout the nation under the leadership of New England. Among the outstanding differences between this outlook and Roman Catholicism are the internal government of the church, the attitude toward religious tradition, and the relation between church and state.

In the Congregational type of church organization there is recognition of the ultimate supremacy of the individual conscience. Each congregation is its own authority; there is no central authority. Whatever national organization exists is democratically controlled. If this is what is meant by democracy in church organization, then it follows that Catholicism at this point is not democratic. It is certainly not built on the authority of individual worshipers. The authority rests in an ordained priesthood and ultimately in the pope, who is endowed with infallibility as regards religious doctrine.

The dependence of Catholicism upon history and tradition marks another fundamental divergence from the dominant Protestant outlook of America. In tracing the religious experiences of early New England we found that the most prevalent notion on this matter was that the Bible and the individual conscience were sufficient bases for determining right conduct and true belief. The whole development of Christian doctrine between the writing of the Bible and the landing of the Pilgrims at Plymouth Rock was ignored. An attitude of this sort blended rather well with experimentalism or the growing American faith that tests of truth are to be found not in past dogmas but in future consequences. The parting counsel of John Robinson, the Pilgrims' pastor in Holland, illustrates this point of view: "He charged us . . . to follow him no further than he followed Christ; and if God should reveal anything to us by any other instrument of his, to be as ready to receive it as ever we were to receive any truth of his ministry; for he was very confident the Lord had more truth and light yet to break forth out of his holy Word." Far different in attitude is the Catholic church. Through the centuries Catholicism has continued to depend upon past tradition for truth. The tension between these two points of view has persisted and is still present.

Perhaps the crucial point of conflict between Catholicism and the individualistic forms of Protestantism is on the question of the relation between church and state and the Catholic attitude toward political democracy. For American Protestantism the democratic faith is part and parcel of Christianity, and the ideal has been the absolute separation of church and state. This ideal has never been realized completely, as we know. Church buildings are exempt from certain types of taxation, the army and navy have their chaplains, and the minister is always a civil servant when he performs a wedding ceremony. But there is nevertheless the deep conviction that the church shall not control government and that government shall not control the church. What is the position of the Catholic church in the United States?

As regards the Catholic position on political democracy, we must remember that the church has lived in many types of state and in many cultures. It made its way in the Roman Empire and yet survived the collapse of Rome. It has lived in monarchies, aristocracies, and democracies. There is no single type of government that is essentially Catholic. It is generally agreed that the Catholic church would prefer a situation in which it might enjoy the status of being the official church, fostered and furthered by state support; thus the American situation is not ideal. But Catholic writers have assured us over and over again that the ideal is not something which they expect to be fully realized. When Archbishop Gibbons went to Rome in 1887 to be made a cardinal, he delivered an address in which he expressed his delight at living in a country where church and state were separate. He positively rejoiced in our situation where "religion and liberty are natural allies."

The traditional policy of Catholicism included the principle

The Spirit of American Religion

of separation of church and state long before the birth of modern democracies. It affirmed the supremacy of the state in political affairs and the supremacy of the church in spiritual affairs. The obvious difficulty here is that it is not always easy to determine what is political and what is spiritual. Should education, for example, be controlled by the state or by the church? In the early years of the American nation, public funds were granted by the government to denominational schools, both Protestant and Catholic. Gradually this arrangement gave way to the policy now in vogue in our public school system. Horace Mann was particularly influential in his insistence that the constitutional principle of the separation of church and state means that the church should not control state-supported schools. During the past century most non-Catholics have come to the conclusion that schools which are supported by public funds should also be subject to public control. Catholicism, on the other hand, believes that the state ought to establish and give financial aid to schools, but that the teaching and educational administration are matters for the church to handle.

Education provides one illustration of the difficulty involved in drawing a line between the spheres of politics and religion. For the religious person there is always a problem of rendering unto the state the things political and unto God the things spiritual. When his government demands of him an activity which he considers contrary to the will of God, the deeply religious person will choose to obey God rather than the state. This is what the Quakers have done in their refusal to bear arms in defense of their country. The chief difference between Protestants and Catholics on this point is the difference in the method of finding the will of God. Protestants feel that Catholics regard the voice of the pope as the voice of God and thus make the choice not between the demands of state and the commands of God, but between the American government on the one hand and the Roman hierarchy on the other. Let us remember, however, that the pope is not free to make any decree he likes. His will is not arbitrary. He too is bound by something beyond himself, namely, the historical accumulation of wisdom in church tradition. Every conscientious Christian, Protestant or Catholic, must search his religious tradition, as well as his own soul, for knowledge of the will of God.

The facts are, then, that Catholicism has made certain adaptations in becoming an American institution, and has been willing to further the ideal of toleration. On the other hand, its own internal organization is not based on popular sovereignty, and it differs from American Protestantism in other ways, especially as regards the relation between church and state. However, so long as both Catholics and Protestants hold that the state should give legal protection and equal favor to all religious groups, the central feature of American religious life will not be disturbed.

Any nation dedicated to the spirit of tolerance is bound to face situations testing whether that nation can remain so dedicated. Crucial tests have been placed before many nations during the past two thousand years by the presence of Jewish minorities. Anti-Semitism is nothing new, but our generation has the misfortune of witnessing one of its crueller manifestations in the theory and practice of Nazi Germany.

Not the least of America's virtues is the fact that the Jews have been as happy or happier here than in any country to which their centuries of wandering have led them. But the situation is far from ideal, and we must not shut our eyes to the anti-Semitic feeling that exists even here. The four million American Jews may serve a useful purpose in fathoming the depth of our belief in toleration.

One charge frequently made against the Jews is that they are excessively clannish and that they seem unable or unwilling to become fully assimilated. They appear to be a compact group in the nation that refuses to become an integral part of American life. The Jews are accused of being "different," both as a race and as a religious group.

The Spirit of American Religion

Their clannish quality is a result of several causes, chief among which is Judaism, the religion of these people. Years before the birth of Christ they pledged their devotion to the universal God, the God of justice and righteousness. The ethical and religious teachings of their early literature are found in the Old Testament of the Christian Bible. The Jews came to believe that their mission on earth was the preservation of these teachings, and this made it necessary for Israel to remain intact. In the absence of a homeland, the Jews have developed their communities within the various nations of the world. One of the most remarkable things in human history is the fact that these people have retained their racial and religious identity in the face of apparently insuperable difficulties.

But it is a mistake to suppose that the Jews have not been altered by their experience of living in America, or that they have made no contributions to our culture. Where but in free America would a Christian minister and a Jewish rabbi exchange pulpits? Jews have cooperated quite as well as Protestants or Catholics in the interfaith program. And their enrichment of our science, literature, and art has been truly great.

For some years an organization called The National Conference of Christians and Jews has been making progress in furthering the cause of mutual understanding. It is quite possible that the religious phase of "the Jewish problem" may be solved. At the present time there appears to be little possibility of conflict between the intelligent, sincere Christian and the conscientious Jew. But, as Rabbi Lazaron has observed, the real difficulty lies in the fact that "many Christians have lost their Jesus, and many Jews have lost their God." It is between these groups that a dangerous tension is found. It seems, therefore, that the spirit of tolerance requires a religious foundation.

Judaism and Catholicism are more inclined to be guided by tradition than is the case with American Protestantism.

Because of the conditions under which the United States was formed, and by virtue of numerical strength, Protestantism remains the most influential religious force in America. We have suggested that Protestant experience here has pointed in the direction of what we have called experimentalism, that is, the belief that truth in matters of religious ideas and conduct is found by reference to future consequences rather than to past dogma. Conduct is good if it contributes positively to the process of building a good society. Beliefs are true if, when acted upon, they lead to desirable consequences. This attitude has made notable contributions to the spirit of tolerance. Its very nature is experimental rather than dogmatic.

In this connection there are many other important factors in the American religious scene, but we shall limit our discussion to two of them. The first has to do with the active participation of laymen in religious leadership, a fact to which casual reference has been made previously. The second is concerned with one of the central beliefs of early Puritanism, or Calvinism, and the manner in which that belief has been modified in the course of our national experience.

It has been suggested that the counterpart of political democracy in church organization is the participation of laymen in the forming of policy. From its very beginning, Protestantism has had a doctrine called the priesthood of believers. This phrase implies that there is no rigid distinction between priest and believer, that every true Christian can be his own priest. The minister functions as the servant of the church and is responsible to the membership. This Protestant doctrine seems to have had a particularly thorough embodiment in America. Not only has it been an overwhelming influence within the churches themselves, but it has also brought about conditions favorable to the growth of organizations controlled exclusively by laymen. The Y.M.C.A. and the Y.W.C.A. are examples of this tendency. The Sunday school, in which religious instruction is given by

The Spirit of American Religion

laymen, is an important part of American church life. There are laymen's organizations among the Jews and Catholics as well as among Protestants.

Those religious movements which had their origin in America, and which were not our own transformation of European institutions, have been lay movements. This illustrates the relative prominence of laymen over clergy in the American religious scene. Mormonism can be understood in this light. The religious beliefs of the Mormons do not differ greatly from those of other Protestant sects. The Mormons rely upon a simple reading of the Bible and merely add to this their special revelation. They differed from other groups chiefly in their early practice of polygamy and their attempt to build a communistic society. The story of Mormonism, or the Church of Jesus Christ of Latter Day Saints, has often been told. Joseph Smith, born in 1805 and brought up in Manchester, New York, claimed to have found a book containing religious teachings and to have translated it before the angel Moroni took it back to heaven. This was the beginning of an adventurous chapter in American history. The group that gathered around him and engaged in unconventional marriage and social practices was forced to move from place to place. Joseph Smith and his brother were murdered by a mob. Much of the history of this movement has been written in blood.

The great vitality in Mormonism defied brutal opposition. Led by Brigham Young, the group finally settled in the desert of Utah Valley in 1847–1848. There a company of five thousand began a process which resulted in a highly commendable community. In no part of the country has the energy of a whole regional population been more effectively directed to the development of natural resources. No one doubts the importance of Mormon leadership in this enterprise. Arid wastes were turned into beautiful gardens. The Mormons delight in telling the story of the visitor to hell who was surprised to find it green and lovely; Satan sadly explained that it used to be a real hell until some Mormons came down and started an irrigation project.

The Mormon movement reflects the lack of a highly organized churchly religion controlled by a priestly class. An ignorant layman was the recipient of a divine revelation. It also is in line with the notion that the Bible and the individual person guided by the Holy Spirit are sufficient foundations for Christianity. This organization, like most Protestant groups, made the Bible the basis of the church, and it had complete faith in the revelation brought to the individual by the Holy Spirit. It was attacked because of its communism and its practice of polygamy, but it has now been modified to such an extent that it is no longer an object of attack.

Another lay movement of great influence was the revival type of Christianity of more than fifty years ago. Dwight L. Moody, its outstanding figure, was not an educated religious leader and yet he became one of the most potent spiritual forces of his generation. To this same general period belong Mrs. Mary Baker Eddy and her Christian Science which appealed to a large number of people. We usually think the distinguishing characteristic of Christian Science to be its emphasis on faith healing, a very ancient religious practice. In reviving this, Christian Science has succeeded in bringing poise and a sense of inner peace to many persons. But we must remember also that this is distinctly a layman's movement, highly individualistic and based on a simple reading of the Bible. What all these movements have in common are the very things that are implicit in the Dissenting tradition, with an exaggerated indifference to an established clergy.

It is by no means true that all features of the prominence of laymen in American religion have been praiseworthy. For one thing, this situation has helped to intrench an uninformed and dogmatic interpretation of the Bible and of Christian doctrine. With the growth of liberalism, therefore, it not infrequently happens that the membership is far more

The Spirit of American Religion

conservative than the minister. Instead of the clergyman trying to call his congregation back to the true faith, the congregation is worried about the orthodoxy of its minister.

On the other hand, when some of the crudities of these lay organizations were replaced by a more enlightened outlook, they tended to reflect the experimental character of American thinking. After all, it is impossible that laymen should have a primary interest in technical theology. Usually they are quite satisfied if they hear the familiar formula or phrase repeated. The primary interest of lay organizations is to put religion to practical service. There is some impatience with abstract theological ideas, but there is great concern for definite social programs. There is interest in general principles only when these can be understood as applying to concrete, particular instances.

In addition to the layman's role in American religion, there is a second development that has moved in the direction of experimentalism. This has to do with a particular theological idea which was present in early American Protestantism and has been progressively modified because it did not square with the living process of America in action.

The Puritans, we have said, were Calvinists. One result of that fact was the attempt to build a theocracy in the new land, an attempt which was doomed to failure. Another feature of Calvinism is the doctrine that men are totally helpless to save themselves, that salvation comes solely through the grace of God. Only a few people — the elect — receive the benefits of the atoning work of Christ; these people are powerless to resist salvation just as all other people are powerless to resist damnation. This theological outlook was given at least nominal credence for many years, but the idea that man is unable to make any contribution to his own salvation could hardly survive in a pioneer civilization where the visible results of human achievement were so obvious.

Jonathan Edwards is usually interpreted as a thoroughgoing Calvinist in his preaching of God's wrath, the doctrine of predestination, and so on. People trembled as they listened to his sermons and held desperately to their seats for fear that they might at that very moment slip into eternal damnation. But it was his preaching in Northampton (1732–1733) that occasioned a religious revival; this was part of a general movement known as the Great Awakening. The revival meeting technique in religion includes an emotional appeal to the individual to be saved. There is the assumption that people have the power within themselves of choosing to take advantage of the saving power of Christ. To this extent, after all, they can do something about their own salvation.

Perhaps the first explicit protest against the notions of total depravity and predestination was the Unitarianism of William Ellery Channing and others. The name Unitarian means that this denomination rejects the traditional view of the Trinity — that God is Father, Son, and Holy Spirit. Unitarianism teaches that Christ is not fully God, but that he is a splendid example for men to follow, and that they have the ability to follow him if they will. Channing, as Unitarian, clearly announced in his famous Baltimore sermon of 1819 a view of man that is the direct opposite of that held by Calvinism. Man, he said, is inherently good because he possesses divine possibilities. He is not totally depraved; he can work out his own salvation by realizing the potentialities that lie within him. Although the Unitarian church has never become large, its view of the nature of man has exerted a wide influence.

Among those who fell under Channing's spell was Ralph Waldo Emerson, whose powerful writing did much to further the idea that man's salvation is in his own hands. He taught the American nation that the most distinctive thing about man is his potential divinity. There are untold possibilities within each of us and salvation means the courageous and nonconformist action in which the possible is made real. Emerson's message was *self-reliance*.

The road away from Calvinism has found its culmination

in what is called religious humanism. This contemporary view of religion contains no trace of the doctrine of total depravity. It teaches that we are equipped with sensitive imaginations which can project those ideals worthy of claiming our loyalty, and that we can apply our intelligence and the methods of science in the progressive improvement of individual and social existence. Salvation, in other words, is in our own hands. The most characteristic thing about us is our ability to adapt the natural environment to human needs.

Religious humanism is the culmination of several lines of development in American religious experience. The experience of many denominations in learning the lesson of mutual tolerance, of give-and-take, and of cooperation in building a better world; the influence of laymen in placing less emphasis on theological ideas and more emphasis on ethical ideals; the developing notion of human self-reliance in bending the forces of nature to human purposes — all these factors have contributed to a distinctive American faith. One expression of that faith is found in humanism. On the negative side this faith is suspicious of an exaggerated loyalty to the past or to a historical tradition. It is convinced that such loyalty prevents men from using their full powers in building a better world. On the positive side this faith defines religion as devotion to ideal ends which are to be realized in the future. It is the future reference that is important, rather than the sanctity of a tradition. Religious ideas which are submitted to this test can claim a vitality and a truth more profound than they could possess within the confines of a single authoritarian church.

At this point it may be well to see how all these elements in the spirit of American religion apply to democracy. In the first place, the typical organization of many American Protestant churches is democratic. Authority rests ultimately with the individual. The local church is self-governing and cooperates voluntarily with the national denomination. In the second place, there is the separation of church and state. No one church has power to force its beliefs on others because no one church has official government support. All religious groups are voluntary organizations and they all have equal legal protection. This situation has taught the democratic lessons of tolerance, cooperation, and the use of persuasion rather than force. Finally, American religion has incorporated a great deal of experimentalism or the pragmatic philosophy, which is the philosophy of American democracy.

There seem to be two stages in the development of a successful democracy. The first is the battle to win recognition of individual rights. This frequently is a long struggle against the hold of tradition and against intrenched classes or institutions having special privileges. We have seen how successful American religion has been in winning that victory. The second stage is reached when we turn around and try to get genuine cooperation on problems that require collective action. Having worked so hard to get freedom for individuals and for the many religious sects, both the individual and the sect may be so jealous of their rights that they are reluctant to join with others in a united enterprise; they are fearful lest they end up with a new regimentation. Yet it is necessary that an attempt be made to overcome some of the difficulties brought about by an extreme individualism.

This need for collective action has several phases. One of them has to do with the religious supervision of morals. In its early days, American religion was so individualistic in its outlook that it conceived of morality as limited to the personal habits of individual men and women. It was concerned with the sins of the senses, with irregular sexual behavior, with drinking, smoking, card-playing, luxury, and laziness. Early American Protestantism used practically all its moral energy in trying to bring the conduct of individuals under religious control. It seemed to have no conception whatever of social morality. This attitude helped to develop the idea that business and politics were without moral significance, and so religion all but emancipated the economic system and the state from its guiding influence. The church insisted that the individual be honest unless he was engaged in a legitimate business enterprise.

Furthermore, the individual virtues admired by religion were such things as sobriety, hard work, shunning of luxuries, thrift, and so on. These are the very virtues that have made possible the growth of American capitalism and are supposed to guarantee financial success to the individual. It was easy, therefore, to ignore the social evils which a growing industrial society brought about, and to dismiss the problem of poverty with a moral condemnation of those who were poor. Their poverty was presumably punishment for their failure to acquire the virtues of hard work and thrift.

Many Christians are realizing that if their religion is to be an effective moral force in the modern world it must overcome the weakness and error of this individualism and enter the arena of social ethics. Recently there has developed a strong religious movement, sometimes referred to as the social gospel, which is primarily concerned with social morality. Its leaders do not deny that a part of religion's task is to persuade individuals to spiritualize their lives, but they are convinced that the most pressing challenge in the modern world is to bring about a radical reform of the social institutions under which people live. It is the democratic principle which should guide all these reforms; that is, the ideal is a society in which opportunity is truly open to all men, the weak as well as the strong.

For example, the social gospel is searchingly critical of some features of capitalism. It is convinced that an uncontrolled profit motive in business life has led to the virtual enslavement of the many workers by a financially powerful minority. Hence it advocates a radical change in the governing principles of economic life. The change should be in the direction of a socialized order in which many business institutions are socially rather than privately owned. This leads to a friendly attitude toward organized labor and collective bargaining. Although the individual worker is helpless in the complex capitalism of the modern world, an organization of workers may be effective in securing the rights of the common man and giving human values a position of precedence over the property rights of the few.

The social gospel joins with other phases of American religion in its moral condemnation of political dictatorship. But it also fights against the suppression of those organizations in our own country which may seem dangerous to conservative citizens. We are not surprised to find that the leaders of the social gospel are particularly active in defending civil liberties.

These men are also concerned with attacking the economic and political evils that lead to international war. They are not content merely to denounce war as an evil or to withdraw into a mystical pacifism. Their interest is rather in changing social institutions in such a way as to lessen the possibility of future wars. They insist that social systems as well as individuals stand in need of Christian salvation. In turning its attention to social problems as one way of overcoming the weakness of individualism, modern religion has brought no threat to democracy. Indeed, every social change which it advocates is to be carried out for the express purpose of making more secure the rights and opportunities of individuals.

Another phase of the reaction against the evils of individualism is found in the tendency toward church unity. Until the recent past the general rule of American religion has been an extreme emphasis on the principle of freedom. This has resulted in a needless multiplication of sects. There have been divisions and subdivisions almost without limit. Obvious evils have resulted from this aspect of individualism, especially where differences are magnified. In small communities more denominations have been represented than

The Spirit of American Religion 229

the populations needed or could afford. Religious groups expended more energy in competing with each other than in doing creative work. Attempts are now being made to overcome this evil at the local, national, and international level. In small communities today new churches are rare. For the most part the tendency is to bring about a federation of two or more groups.

Nationally, some success has been achieved in the union of denominations, and further plans are being made along these lines. Some forty years ago an interchurch conference was attended by delegates from thirty-two denominations. Out of that conference came the definite organization of the Federal Council of Churches of Christ in America. This Council has become a rather important force in American life and on some occasions is able to speak for the greater part of American Protestantism. At the present time there is a remarkable amount of cooperation among Protestants, Catholics, and Jews because of the vitality of the interfaith movement. These accomplishments, although genuine, are still rather meager when compared with the divisions that continue to characterize American religion. However, the intellectual leadership is constantly urging greater unity and no doubt there is a general tendency in that direction.

The urge toward unity goes beyond the borders of our own country. At the international level there is the desire to bring back into a living reality the so-called Church Universal, or a world-wide united Christendom. This was the purpose of the Ecumenical Conference held in Oxford, England, during the summer of 1937. Dr. C. C. Morrison, editor of *The Christian Century,* and other leaders of American Christianity are enthusiastic about this ecumenical movement.

There are crucial factors in the modern world which make imperative the united action of Christianity. Among these are Communism, Nazism, and Fascism. American Christians are coming to understand the threat these offer to genuine religion. Religion teaches that man's one absolute loyalty is to a universal God. Totalitarianism wishes to make the state the object of unconditional loyalty. In other words, it makes a god of the state. Communism and Nazism both see in the Christian church a dangerous rival in claiming the devotion of men and women, and have therefore been hostile toward religion.

This has created a situation in which the Christian churches are sensing the need of overcoming internal division in order to make more effective their common defense against the threatening forces of destruction. There appears to be once again the visible sign of a struggle between Christianity and the non-religious cultures. This is what gives importance to the ecumenical movement. But there is a danger to democracy in all this. Communism and Nazism have achieved unity and efficiency at the cost of individual freedom. There is the danger that religion, in attempting to gain sufficient unity to combat these forces, may sacrifice freedom in favor of efficiency. Complete unity can be brought about only by a return to some sort of authoritarianism. In times of great stress we are tempted to become impatient with the relatively slow processes by which the democratic way seeks to accomplish its results. Our problem is that of preserving freedom, and at the same time finding sufficient unity to make effective the preaching of the essentials of the Christian faith, i.e., the universal fatherhood of God and the universal brotherhood of man.

The hope for a new world-wide unity within Christendom has brought about a revived interest in Christian history and tradition. The basis upon which the various forms of Christianity can get together is their common heritage, and we have been driven to examine that heritage in order to have a better understanding of it. We have said that early American Protestantism ignored the rich tradition of historical Christianity, but today our churches are attempting to reinstate something of the drama and beauty of the older forms of worship, and to restate traditional beliefs in vital form. Modern Christianity has been awakened to a sense of deep attachment to its historical tradition. In so doing it has not abandoned completely the experimental manner of thinking, but it has seen that humanism is not the final word. Many people today are beginning to feel the inadequacy of humanism because their religious lives are so definitely nourished by a historical faith. They are now convinced that our humanitarian ideals, which most of us take for granted, rest ultimately upon a Christian foundation. When such ideals are severed from their historical connection they lose their power.

The new reverence for the past is a desirable corrective of the provincial and barren aspects of American religion, but it also has its dangers so far as democracy is concerned. There is the danger that it may cause us to turn from the experimental approach in finding truth to the dogmatic authority of something already laid down. To be a Christian does, to be sure, involve attachment to the Christian tradition, but it does not involve attachment to a particular or authoritative interpretation of that tradition. The latter is the enemy of the democratic way. Nevertheless, this new historical sense may be compatible with democracy, and may even make a positive contribution to democracy, if we consider the Christian tradition as a continuous and social process. If we can think of ourselves as not only produced by the past but as responsible for improving our heritage, there need be no conflict between reverence for the past and the use of the experimental method.

Although it is necessary to point out the danger inherent in the passionate desire for church unity and in a pious reverence for the past, let us not lose sight of the fact that it was these very interests which resulted in a rediscovery of perhaps the most important element in the religious foundation of democracy. Notice the beginning of the second paragraph in the Declaration of Independence: "We hold these truths to be self-evident, that all men are created equal, that they are endowed *by their Creator* with certain unalienable Rights. . . ." The fundamental basis of democracy is the belief in the sacredness of every human personality and in certain inviolable rights that belong to him. Where do these rights come from? Not from the state, surely, because the state is brought into existence to protect them. Nor is man sacred because of what he is by nature. Thomas Jefferson correctly stated that the individual receives his inviolable rights from his Creator. Human personality is sacred because man is a child of God. It is only as men are God's creatures that they are of infinite worth. And it is only because men are children of a universal God that there can be universal human brotherhood. This is the basic conviction of Christianity, and of prophetic Judaism as well. Without the belief in the value of individual persons there can be no democracy.

CHAPTER 9

THE SPIRIT OF AMERICAN PHILOSOPHY

By Eugene T. Adams

When the sun sets on doomsday perhaps men will agree on a final truth about philosophical problems. Until then there will always be systems which portray better than other systems the distinctive habits and hopes of certain civilizations. Quite apart from the question of *final truth*, it can hardly be doubted that philosophy (which is chiefly a generalized account of our world, ourselves, and our aims) is at once a product of our culture, and a method of criticizing it.

The philosophy which is most distinctively a product of American culture is Pragmatism or, as it is sometimes called, Experimentalism. It is indigenous to the New World in the sense that it was originally put forward by American thinkers, that it amply illustrates the American interest in things practical, that it defends the principle of human freedom, and that it is essentially democratic in its general outlook. The chief promoters of Pragmatism, William James and John Dewey, have been widely influential both here and abroad.

Neither one of these men believed it possible to get *absolutely final* answers to their questions, and they spent a good part of their time in trying to persuade others that tentative answers are good enough. If no one answer is the final one, they argued, it may be the better part of wisdom to recognize that finality is a dream that may better be left to either fools or gods. Men must be content to look ahead with ideas which are subject to change with the accumulation of better evidence; a wise philosophy should reflect this state of affairs.

In this respect Pragmatism reflects the belief of democracy itself. Democracy refuses to foreclose issues, and does not assume that any one man, or group of men, have a stranglehold on truth. Incompetent it sometimes is, but it is always subject to improvement. It is dynamic rather than static, expanding rather than fixed, primarily because it has forsworn a belief in absolute conclusions. Herein lies the reason for its belief in freedom of speech and freedom of action. It is not surprising that a society based upon the principle of tolerance should produce a philosophy of enlightened toleration.

The main purpose of the present chapter is to indicate that America has produced a philosophy which shares the practical, dynamic, tentative, democratic outlook that characterizes her society. But before turning to this most recent and typical development in American thought, let us trace briefly some of the high points in the philosophical thinking that preceded it.

Puritanism

In the beginning America borrowed her philosophy just as she borrowed everything else. Ideas were brought over from the Old World and subjected to whatever changes transplanting to American soil might involve. In general, the changes tended always in the direction of increased individualism, but many of the ideas remained fundamentally alien however much modified by their new environment.

The earliest philosophical thinkers came from a group of people who were known first as Nonconformists and later as Puritans. Their nonconformity had more to do with church forms than with theological opinions, for in this latter respect they were quite orthodox. They debated the same religious issues that had bothered Saint Augustine in the fifth century, and their methods of knowing had not advanced beyond his. Revelation and authority were their avenues to certainty. Just as Augustine had written of the City of God and Calvin had established a theocracy in Geneva, so these early Americans saw no reason why they could not build a City of God in America.

This heavenly city was a strange mixture of democracy and authoritarianism. As the entire movement was based upon religious convictions, the presiding clergyman was a voice of great authority in the community, and government naturally took on a theocratic outlook. Regular town meetings provided an air of democracy but in both the general and the local governments there were religious and property limitations. The prevailing condition of opinion was so distinctly Calvinistic as to breed a very undemocratic type of intolerance. Fortunately minority groups had new territory to inhabit even if they did not have a Bill of Rights on which to rely. Roger Williams was only one of a number of people who found the Indians more hospitable than many of the colonial religious leaders.

Jonathan Edwards ably represented this Puritan or Calvinistic philosophy in America. Keen and analytical of mind, he no doubt would have gained a reputation for originality had he not been committed to an inherited theological outlook. Born in 1703 in a Calvinistic environment, he fully reflected his background and became a most able champion of the faith.

Edwards' general outlook in philosophy was idealistic, and he shared with most idealists the belief that the universe is a perfectly rational system. Philosophies such as this usually assert that visible realities are to be explained in terms of invisible ones, and that the eternal is more real than the temporal. Edwards was not unusual in this respect. Most philosophy before the time of Darwin had a way of minimizing the importance of time and of emerging novelties. The ready acceptance of invisible realities lends itself to religious uses and, one must add, to abuses. To encourage an awareness of unseen realities is to invite one not only to spiritual insight, but to many varieties of superstition. Hobgoblins, witches, and all manner of dreadful things are likely to flourish in such an atmosphere. Persecutions for witchcraft in New England cannot be entirely divorced from the intellectual temper which made belief in such things possible.

On the strictly theological side, Jonathan Edwards was an orthodox Calvinist. He supported Calvin's familiar doctrines of divine providence, human depravity, efficacious grace, divine election, and the perseverance of the saints. Puritanism provided early New England with a rigorous and rather frightening religious and philosophical world view. Its intense emphasis upon the cultivation of such virtues as simplicity, frugality, and hard work adapted it in many ways to the needs of a pioneering society. It was fortunate for an expanding American capitalism that Calvin had broken with the mother church on the question of usury. Puritanism was thus enabled to join hands with capitalism, even in the name of good morals. Hard work begot wealth, so wealth itself came to be looked upon not only as a convenience but as evidence of a good character. There is some evidence that Mammon frequently was confused with the Divine Providence.

While the holy commonwealth of Puritanism was having its day in New England, a rather contrary adventure in community Christian life was being tried in Pennsylvania. The Society of Friends had attempted to establish a society without compulsory religious organizations, one involving a separation of church and state. It was rigorously individualistic and democratic. Although the Friends, or Quakers, ceased to dominate Pennsylvania policies directly after about half a century, their pacifism, charity, and general idealism continued to leaven the spiritual life of the country.

Both the theocratic ideal of New England Calvinism and the democratic ideal of the Society of Friends were realities with which any political philosophy that was to guide our expanding society had to reckon. An interaction of these and many other forces was creating a state of affairs which cried out for a political form sufficiently broad to accommodate conflicting interests. Fortunately, when the time came to settle on a political philosophy, America produced a Thomas Jefferson and England had already provided a John Locke. This introduces us to a new current of American thought.

The Age of Reason

Just as the Puritans had their religion of revelation, some of their contemporaries gloried in a religion of reason. Puritanism had taught that man was completely depraved and never could be saved by his own efforts, but a different intellectual attitude was also brewing in the colonies. Benjamin Franklin, Thomas Jefferson, Ethan Allen, Thomas Paine, and others had a higher regard for human nature than that expressed in the Puritan creed, and they looked with confidence to salvation through human understanding. Reason was considered to be both a necessary and an adequate vehicle for finding all the truths necessary to living a satisfactory life on this earth and to guaranteeing the reality of a life to come. It is hard to think of Jonathan Edwards and Benjamin Franklin as contemporaries, their mental horizons were so completely different. Of the two, it was Franklin who rode the wave of the future. One might almost say of him, "Here was the first American." His versatility, his practical nature, his driving energy — not to mention his humble origin — all marked him as a creature of a young country that was going places. In fact, he was hardly appreciated in America until he was recognized abroad as a great American. His creed consisted of an unlimited faith in reason and industry to solve the problems of the individual or the state. He believed in progress and put his faith to work. His religious ideas were considerably different from the Calvinism which prevailed in New England because he borrowed them from a different source. Like everything else he borrowed, they inevitably became his own and were transformed in the process. In many respects he practiced a philosophy of Pragmatism several centuries before it was elevated to a theory.

The second figure whom we have mentioned as belonging to the Age of Reason was not "officially" a philosopher, but his life was constantly guided by philosophy. This man was Thomas Jefferson, who perhaps more than any other individual deserves to be called the father of American democracy. Jefferson prided himself on being the author of the Declaration of Independence and the Virginia Law for Religious Freedom, and the founder of the University of Virginia. The spirit of tolerance demonstrated by these undertakings is characteristic of the man and of the democracy which he helped to fashion.

The difference between Jefferson's outlook in religious philosophy and that of the New England Calvinists is nicely illustrated by one of his letters to John Adams, in which he wrote: "I can never join Calvin in addressing *his* God. He was indeed an atheist, which I can never be; or rather his religion was daemonism. If ever man worshipped a false god, he did. The being described in his five points is not the God whom you and I acknowledge and adore, the Creator and benevolent governor of the world; but a daemon of malignant spirit." Such a description must make it amply evident that more than one current of thought had been imported into the colonies. A large share of the credit for making it possible for such conflicting notions to live peacefully together must be given to the tolerant opinions of Jefferson himself.

For his political philosophy Jefferson leaned heavily on John Locke. Although champion of the idea that all knowledge must be based upon experience (and so presumably subject to change), Locke propounded a theory of *inalienable rights*, such as the rights to life, liberty, and property. Jefferson borrowed these ideas and incorporated them, with slight modifications, into our Declaration of Independence. Here was a set of borrowed ideas that did more than any other to affect the subsequent history of American thought and institutions. The Age of Reason had found fruitful soil in America and did more than Calvin could to shape our destiny.

Ethan Allen, remembered better today for his military than his intellectual exploits, and Thomas Paine were other influential exponents of the intellectual mood which we have been describing. Paine was the more widely known of the two. His *Age of Reason* became one of the most popular presentations of the claims of reason against revelation, and seemed to many people to be the final funeral oration over the happily buried corpse of superstition. In many respects he was a less careful critic than some of his contemporaries, which may have accounted for his popularity.

In passing on to a brief consideration of some other phases of American thought one word of interpretation of what eighteenth-century writers meant by "reason" might be in point. Too often it meant a kind of inner light, or self-evidence of the truth of propositions. It was not an experimental type of reasoning such as Pragmatism insists upon, and consequently it often tended toward dogmatism. Under the banner of "self-evidence" the most absurd ideas have often paraded themselves as being reasonable. Some of the eighteenth-century rationalists were quite as dogmatic as the Calvinists, their "laws of nature" being the counterpart of the "laws of God." Both were considered to be certainly known and unchanging.

The latter part of the eighteenth century exhibited a growing spirit of individualism, but it was not until the nineteenth century that this spirit came to its fullest expression. It was one of the chief characteristics of an intellectual movement called Transcendentalism.

TRANSCENDENTALISM

This striking movement began in 1836 in Boston, when George Ripley called together a small group of people, including Ralph Waldo Emerson, Bronson Alcott, and others, "to see how far it would be possible for earnest minds to meet." Emerson became the acknowledged leader of the group.

The philosophical ingredients of Transcendentalism came from a number of sources, ranging from Plato to the English and German Romanticists, but it was no mere hodgepodge of ill-assimilated ideas. For Emerson, the important thing about the movement was that it provided a method for viewing life with intense zeal, and he never made it into a rigid philosophical system with a particular body of content. That the individual should develop his own powers for viewing nature was his chief concern, but certain presuppositions about the universe can be gathered from his essays and the writings of other members of the group. These seem to include a belief that the real world is essentially moral, and that consequently values have an absolute status in existence. Moreover, these values are not to be discovered simply through an analysis of experience; they are to be discerned only through intuition. Science might be useful as a means of organizing experience, but it failed miserably to provide the necessary insights into reality itself. Some method beyond science was necessary in order to guarantee certainty rather than mere probability in regard to the moral life.

The Transcendentalists thought of themselves as reformers as well as thinkers, and so carried their ideas into action. There is hardly one of them who did not find himself lined up against established authority at one time or another. It was in connection with the abolition of slavery that most of them found their notions of justice incompatible with the currently fashionable ones. One member of the group was mobbed on several occasions, another imprisoned, still others rebuked for obstructing the Fugitive Slave Law. It is said that Emerson visited Henry David Thoreau when the latter was in jail for refusing to pay taxes to a state which countenanced slavery. "Why are you here, David?" asked Emerson. "Why are you *not* here, Waldo?" was the question asked in reply. There is no doubt that here was a group of people whose moral enthusiasms ran high, and who took seriously the business of plain living and high thinking.

Of special interest to us in tracing the rise of a native American philosophy is Emerson's attitude toward the borrowing of second-hand ideas. *The American Scholar, The Divinity School Address,* and *Self-Reliance* all have independence as their special theme. The first of these three has been referred to as "our intellectual Declaration of Independence." Emerson had said: "We will walk on our own feet; we will work with our own hands; we will speak our own minds." This is the voice of an America that is growing up and developing some self-confidence. Emerson was the prophet of a new day. In literature America had to wait for Walt Whitman, and in philosophy for William James, before her own peculiar history could find authentic expression, but Emerson pointed the way. He brought a powerful individuality to his philosophic task and spoke with utter independence and sincerity; but his own background kept him from straying too far from what Santayana has called the genteel tradition. Emerson himself had a profound intuition of this fact, for in *The Poet* he calls for one to come and do what he himself never did and doubtless felt incapable of doing. It is so typical both of his insight and of America's need that perhaps a rather long quotation is justified. He tells how he looks in vain for the poet he has been describing and says:

We have yet had no genius in America, with tyrannous eye, which knew the value of our incomparable materials, and saw, in the barbarism and materialism of the times, another carnival of the same gods whose picture he so much admires in Homer; then in the middle age; then in Calvinism. Banks and tariffs, the newspaper and caucus, methodism and unitarianism, are flat and dull to dull people, but rest on the same foundations of wonder as the town of Troy, and the temple of Delphos, and are as swiftly passing away. Our logrolling, our stumps and their politics, our fisheries, our Negroes and Indians, our boats, and our repudiations, the wrath of rogues, and the pusillanimity of honest men, the northern trade, the southern planting, the western clearing, Oregon and Texas, are yet unsung. Yet America is a poem in our eyes; its ample geography dazzles the imagination, and it will not wait long for metres.

Surely this was invitation to Walt Whitman and those like him who could find the voice to say things of America and could have the courage to know that it was still poetry. But it was also an invitation to philosophy to reckon with the same things. Emerson could sense the need but could not master it. Carlyle, who admired him greatly, had been forced to write to the editors of the *Dial:* "You seem to me in danger of dividing yourselves from the fact of this present universe, in which alone, ugly as it is, can I find any anchorage, and soaring away after these Ideas, Beliefs, Revelations, and such like, — into perilous altitudes as I think. . . . It is the whole Past and the whole Future, this same cotton-spinning, dollar-hunting, canting and shrieking, very generation of ours. Come back into it, I tell you." Emerson was not quite as tough-minded as William James thought a philosopher should be, or he might have made James unnecessary. Perhaps the best explanation of their differences might be that Emerson wrote before Darwin and James after. Distrust of time and love of the eternal made Emerson neglect the things he saw in favor of the things he could not see. James could swallow the paradox that time was of the "essence."

The story is told that shortly after James' birth Emerson was invited to "admire and give his blessing to the little philosopher-to-be." The blessing must have worked wonders, for in at least one respect James carried on the torch of Transcendentalism — he never ceased to be an individual!

Later Developments

So far we have mentioned three main currents in the philosophical history of our country. Calvinism, rationalism, and Transcendentalism were all distinctly influential but no one of them was genuinely indigenous. Other experiments with borrowed material were tried in the nineteenth century. It was in the latter part of the century that science imposed a new influence on philosophy with the rise of the doctrine of organic evolution. Biology seemed at last to have joined hands with physics in pointing the way toward a purely mechanical explanation of nature. To Emerson and other religiously-minded philosophers, nature was divine, and the aspects of nature which were open to science were but symbols of a meaning that ran much deeper than the scientific mind could ever penetrate. Now science appeared to lay bare the inner mechanism of life itself. Worst of all, the theory that evolution proceeded by natural selection seemed to run completely counter to the much-favored theological doctrine of intelligent design in nature. Hence it was vigorously opposed by theologians and intellectual leaders from all quarters. This theory still worried many religiously-minded people long after most philosophers had learned to live with it. Most of us can still remember the Scopes trial, which represents about the last public attempt at refutation of the theory.

Although evolution added fuel to the "warfare between science and theology," its influence was by no means limited to the field of religious thinking. Herbert Spencer made it the basis of a whole theory of reality. No field of thought was left untouched by its influence; sociology, anthropology, psychology, and philosophy were all destined to be reoriented because of it. Its most radical influence on philosophy was exerted only after James and Dewey developed a theory of mind in the light of it, as we shall see presently; but "evolutionary naturalism" became a popular outlook in philosophy. There was a tendency to explain all nature in terms of pure mechanism. Herbert Spencer was widely read in this country, and evolution was thought of as the key to all mysteries.

In American philosophy men like John Fiske did much to make the evolutionary theory more palatable than it might otherwise have been, by declaring that it was not incompatible with a religious interpretation of things since the continued creativity of God was merely made manifest thereby.

At the other pole from the materialistic naturalism which received a stimulus from the evolutionary theory was the philosophy of absolute idealism. To mention this philosophy is to be reminded again of the fact that Americans leaned heavily on outside influences for their intellectual diet. Of all the systems imported into American philosophy, idealism sank its roots deepest into the academic tradition and became what might be called the orthodox philosophy of the universities. The rise of Pragmatism can be partly accounted for as a reaction against the idealism which had assumed a tremendous influence by the beginning of the present century. By the latter part of the nineteenth century the American intellectual horizon was still so limited that hardly any serious scholar felt qualified to begin his work without spending several years in leading German universities. The prevailing philosophy was absolute idealism and it was naturally brought into the American academic tradition. It is interesting to note that in the hands of men like Josiah Royce idealism took on a much more individualistic tone than it had before. The American temperament was making itself felt, even if it had to do it simply by modifying alien material.

The borrowing of a German philosophy was made easy not only because our scholars studied in German universities, but because the constant stream of immigration to this country washed in ideas as well as people. In 1866 a group of German intellectuals found themselves living together in St. Louis, and there founded the St. Louis Philosophical Society.

A Connecticut school teacher, William T. Harris, who had moved to St. Louis to teach the newly devised method of Pitman shorthand, joined the group and soon became its recognized leader. The study of Kant and Hegel was a primary aim of the society, and in order to "make Hegel talk English" Harris launched the *Journal of Speculative Philosophy*. The group worked with definite missionary zeal and soon had representatives in most of the major cities in the Midwest and New England, to which place Harris returned to head a group of idealistic philosophers at Concord.

In launching the *Journal of Speculative Philosophy* Harris seems to have been motivated by more than just the inclination to tell people about the philosophy of a German named George Hegel. He sincerely believed that he was providing America with an intellectual basis for her religious and political institutions. In the first issue of the *Journal* he wrote as follows: "There is no need, it is presumed, to speak of the immense religious movements now going on in this country and in England. The tendency to break with the traditional and to accept only what bears for the soul its own justification, is widely active and can end only in the demand that Reason shall find and establish a philosophical basis for all those great ideas which are taught as religious dogmas." This illustrates the interest of idealism in matters of religion and is typical of the idealistic philosophy. But Harris had political interests too.

The same issue of the journal that explained why a speculative philosophy was necessary to our religious aspirations also dealt with our political needs. To quote again: "Likewise it will be acknowledged that the national consciousness has moved forward on a new platform during the past few years [Civil War years]. The idea underlying our form of government had hitherto developed only one of its essential phases — that of brittle individualism — in which national unity seemed an external mechanism, soon to be entirely dispensed with, and the enterprise of the common man or the corporation substituted for it. Now we have arrived at the consciousness of the other essential phase, and each individual recognizes his *substantial* (italics mine) side to be the State as such. The freedom of the citizen does not consist in the mere Arbitrary, but in the realization of the rational conviction which finds expression in established law."

There can be no doubt that Harris was calling attention to a growing deficiency in our political life. *Pure* individualism issues in a haphazard society. But in attempting to find the "substantial side" of the individual in the state he was swinging the pendulum too far in the opposite direction. At any rate, Pragmatism, in its reaction to this sort of absolutism, whether it says that the "substantial side" is individualistic or nationalistic, attempts to do justice to both sides of the issue without accepting the deficiencies of either. It is for this as well as other reasons that we are willing to accept it as the most authentic voice of the American spirit. Hegelianism as a philosophy did full justice to the Prussian state, but did not express the American temperament or genius.

Since all this may sound a bit abstract, perhaps it is time to indicate what the philosophy of absolute idealism is. In its purest form it holds to the notion that all particular things are only *apparently* particular because their real essence is understood only when they are related to the whole of which they are a part. This Whole is an Absolute Mind, or God; this is the sole reality, apart from which neither understanding nor existence is possible. This phase of idealism is illustrated nicely by the following story.

On a cruise to Australia Royce wrote to his great friend but philosophical enemy, James, as follows:

> My companionships aboard the ship have been highly agreeable. The Captain . . . is contemplative. . . . He grows more and more meditative over the vast stellar distances, and the rest, and at last observes: "Well now, what do you teach your classes at Harvard about all this?" Thus called upon to explain amid the trade-winds, and under the softly flapping canvas, the mysteries of absolute

idealism, I put the thing thus: "There was once a countryman," I say, "from Cape Cod, who went to Boston to hear Mark Twain lecture, and to delight his soul with the most mirth-compelling of our humorists. But, as I have heard, when he was in Boston, he was misdirected, so that he heard not Mark Twain, but one of Joseph Cook's Monday lectures. But he steadfastly believed that he was hearing Mark. So when he went home to Cape Cod, they asked him of Mark Twain's lecture. 'Was it *very* funny?' 'Oh, it was *funny*, yes, — it was *funny*,' replies the countryman cautiously, 'but then, you see, it wasn't so *damned* funny.' Even so, Captain," says I, "I teach at Harvard that the world and the heavens, and the stars are all *real*, but not so *damned* real, you see."

James and Dewey could never quite swallow the doctrine that the particulars of experience were not real — in fact, damned real. Once one begins to put more stock in the *whole* of things than in the particular aspects that meet the eye, he always tends to solve problems at the theoretical rather than the practical level. Evil can be dismissed as merely "appearance," "partial good," or what not. Meantime the experienced evils of life continue to thrive upon a philosophical theory that disdains to notice them.

Although absolute idealism was the prevailing philosophy, there were many other points of view being presented. The attempt had been made to establish "common-sense realism," which had been imported from Scotland and which relied on a benevolent intuition to guarantee that things were much as they appeared to be. Its influence was fairly short-lived. At the other extreme from idealism there was of course a variety of realistic naturalisms. Like idealism, these systems were "speculative" in that they pretended to grasp the inner essence of reality. It was in reaction to these "certainties" that Pragmatism developed a wholly different outlook.

Lest we seem to be emphasizing Pragmatism out of all proportion to its membership in the philosophical community, perhaps we had better indicate again that we do not mean that Pragmatism is either the "true" philosophy or the one with the largest following in the academic tradition. We mean merely that it is the philosophy which is most indigenous and which reflects the American temperament better than any other one. Evidence for this must wait a little longer. Meantime, a word more about the history of American philosophy in the present century.

For the past forty years an almost incredible amount of philosophical energy has been spent upon theories of knowledge, or epistemology. John Dewey has called this a "form of intellectual lockjaw." Philosophy appeared to be concerned almost exclusively with questions of knowledge — whether truth really means the correspondence of an idea with a fact (the common-sense, dualistic theory) or the coherence of ideas as they might be conceived by an omniscient being. The absolute idealists hold to this latter theory; the former has been held by realists of various types. When Pragmatism came on the scene it offered a theory of knowledge that differed from both of these and made it truly radical.

An American Voice

Not long after Jesse James had ceased to terrorize the Southwest with his wild and woolly ways, William James (no relative) began to do a similar service for New England. Since Jesse's only weapon was a gun his influence was limited to a relatively short range. William went about armed with revolutionary ideas and so could never be confined to one place. Indeed, his influence extended around the world, and abroad he became one of our best-known citizens.

William James (1842–1910) first achieved a reputation in psychology but, characteristically enough, soon felt the call to wider spaces and gave up the "nasty little subject" to devote the rest of his life to philosophy. Even here he found the traditional ideas too confining and would have nothing to do with any system of ideas that talked about the universe

The Spirit of American Philosophy

as if it were a static and finished thing. (Both idealism and materialism had concerned themselves with a fixed order of existence.) He felt that philosophy "like life must keep the doors and windows open." In short, he seemed to suffer from a sort of intellectual claustrophobia, and his insistence upon an "open universe" where real novelty could occur became the background of his most characteristic theories.

Philosophy for James was no spare-time academic luxury, but a practical necessity. He felt that a man's philosophy was the most important thing about him. That more people did not recognize this was probably due, he might have said, to the fact that classical philosophy had divorced itself from the living facts of experience in its quest for eternal and changeless truths. Let philosophy come back to experience for its inspiration, and be content with describing *its* characteristics. Too many philosophies, in attempting to tell the truth about some ideal world, ended up by lying about the actual world of human experience. James liked to describe his outlook as one of *radical empiricism*, meaning thereby that he would stick resolutely to the standpoint of experience. From this point of view how do things look?

In the first place, experience shows that this is a changing world, and that emerging novelties must be accepted as real. From the point of view of experience nothing is eternal. We talk about the *everlasting* hills, but they are not really *everlasting*; they merely last a little longer than the squirrel who makes his home there. Reality is not outside of time, as many philosophies contend, but is itself temporal. It is a place where things happen. James had only to appeal to evolution to demonstrate this fact.

Reflecting upon the ceaseless variety and change in things, he was led to one of his most radical theories. If reality is ever-changing, the truths about it can hardly be general and eternal; they must be particular and temporal. They must keep up with the novel experiences themselves. Truth then would not be a mere static correspondence of an idea with a preexistent fact, it would be much more dynamic. In fact, truth emerges along with experience, and man actively helps to *create* it rather than merely discover it. The test for truth is always in the future rather than the past. An idea that leads one to a satisfactory conclusion is called true. In short, truth is that which works when put to the test. This idea is really the radical part of James' theory, and the one most open to criticism. His failure to define exactly what kind of satisfaction could count toward establishing the truth of an idea led many people to assume that any emotional satisfaction they derived was good enough evidence. Dewey, who has developed a similar theory of truth, is much more careful in this respect.

The general intention of James' theory was that truth and verification are the same thing (in this respect he was like Dewey) but he was not careful enough to describe the verifying process accurately. To say that truth and verification are the same seems scandalous to many people because truth ought to refer to whatever is the case, whereas verification merely refers to whatever we take to be the case after careful investigation. Conceivably we might be wrong about what we take to be the case and so have to change our minds afterward. Not many people would agree that when we change our minds we also automatically change the truth of things. Theoretically the pragmatist seems to be wrong on this issue; and yet one can hardly deny that the truths by which we govern our lives are simply the verifications or anticipated verifications that we experience. *Practically*, we live *as if* truth and verification were the same thing. Pragmatism merely elevates this practice of ours into a theory. As James might put it, truth is the "cash value" of an idea — an assessment of its working value. It was his emphasis upon the practical that led people to call his system "Pragmatism."

Often the evidence for an idea and the evidence against it seem to cancel each other, and yet in many such cases a decision one way or the other is a practical necessity. In all such instances James recommends that the *will* be entitled to cast the deciding ballot, and that we assume that side of the controversial question to be true that will work to our best advantage. Often our action will help to make one or the other idea true. For example, act *as if* someone loves you and you may bring that state of affairs to pass, even if it would not have happened otherwise. James expressed this idea in a famous essay called *The Will to Believe,* and showed the possibility of its application to moral and religious questions. So many people interpreted him as suggesting that "wishing will make it so" — even in spite of evidence — that he wished later that he had called it "The Right to Believe." His whole point was that we do have a right to believe — not against the evidence, but when evidence is lacking and when there is still a real option for belief. It was an intellectual justification for faith and, within certain limits, it was sound enough and definitely practical.

Another aspect of James' thought which comes from taking experience seriously is his attitude toward traditional solutions of the problem of evil. Idealistic philosophies usually end up by calling evil either "mere appearance" or "partial good" because they first commit themselves to the idea that the universe is reasonable through and through, and being reasonable must also be good. Hence their major problem turns out to be "explaining evil away." Materialism, on the other hand, assumes that the universe is merely an unmeaningful accident; consequently such a philosophy is hard-pressed to account for the apparent order and goodness that life can display. James felt that both sides were wrong because each neglected some aspect of experience. Stick to the facts as you find them in experience and you will discover that good and bad are both honest-to-goodness things; the only real problem of evil is how to get rid of it. He called his position *meliorism,* meaning that we might as well admit that good and evil are both real, but that the amount of good can be increased, and the evil decreased, if men will join in the fight and throw the full weight of their power on the side of good. Again we see his practical interest dictating his theory.

There are many sides to philosophy and James touched on almost all of them in a most interesting fashion. There was a freshness to his point of view that made him an authentic American voice, unafraid to defend experience as he found it. His brother Henry had fled to England to become a *littérateur* of the "genteel tradition," but William, as one of Henry's characters might have said, was "incorrigible." Two other ideas which will help to show that he was distinctly within the American tradition must be referred to briefly. The first deals with the problem of human freedom. Philosophically this is the question of whether or not people can help doing what they do. All of us have had hopelessly fatalistic moments so the question should not appear too academic. Countless arguments have been advanced for each side. James belongs to the free-will crowd. How he came to feel certain of human freedom brings us another reminder of his practical approach to problems. After worrying about the question for several years and finding no theoretical solution, he decided to act for one year *as if* he were free. The consequences proved so satisfactory that he felt his faith to be justified. To a pragmatist of his type this meant that the idea was verified; hence he found one more piece of evidence to prove that philosophy was essentially practical.

The other idea for which he fought has to do with the relation of individuals to the groups of which they are a part. Although often called the problem of the "one and the many," it really is not as far removed from practical affairs as that abstract way of putting it may sound. Today we hear a good deal about democracy *versus* totalitarianism; any discussion of the two is sure to raise the question of the relationship of individuals to their state. Is the state a reality in its own right, and the individuals merely its creatures? All forms of totalitarian government proceed on this

The Spirit of American Philosophy 253

assumption. Translated into the language of philosophy, this means that they take the *one* reality (the state) to be superior to the *many* (the people). People are said to be instruments of the state instead of vice versa. Democracy, on the other hand, proceeds in exactly the opposite way; the only excuse for the state is that it serves the interest of the people who constitute it. On this problem, as on so many others, James' philosophy was on the side of the democratic outlook. For him individual things are the primary reality, and while they act together in all sorts of interconnections, the uniqueness of the individual as such is never overlooked. Things have just as much interconnection as experience shows them to have, but experience indicates that they are never completely subservient to any one unity; the individual cannot be wholly subservient to the state.

In all the points we have been discussing we can see that James' philosophy reflects American traditions and habits of thought. It provides intellectual support for a belief in the value of the individual, it emphasizes the practical character of experience, it provides a meaning for individual freedom, and it is elastic enough to find a place in which all kinds of opposing tendencies can live peacefully together. Furthermore, it insists that experience is the only teacher and so reinforces the American habit of looking forward to things new, rather than measuring the value of everything in terms of past standards.

James influenced people through his writings and through the power of his dynamic personality. One of his great friends was Justice Holmes, whose Supreme Court decisions were illuminated by a pragmatic leaning in philosophy. His liberalism was the product of a seasoned philosophical outlook. The pragmatic spirit which James was promoting in philosophy was also being furthered by the energetic work of John Dewey. Dewey quite self-consciously went about the task of providing a philosophical defense for the democratic way of life. James never concerned himself greatly with political philosophy as such, whereas Dewey makes his interest in social problems the very center of his philosophical system.

EXPERIMENTALISM

Like James, Dewey holds always to the standpoint of experience, and invites all philosophers to do likewise. He is less individualistic than James, being always mindful that men live in a social context. Too great an emphasis upon the individual is likely to create false problems, he feels, for too often it issues in a sort of dualism between the individual and his society — as if they were (or could be) two alien things. In most other respects he shares James' outlook.

He accepts the theory of truth that James had developed and improves it by being more critical than his predecessor in stating just what is implied in it. He has been more systematic than James in developing his philosophy; there is hardly an area of philosophical discourse which he has not interpreted anew. Since academic philosophy in America had become almost exclusively concerned with the problem of knowledge, it had, so Dewey felt, alienated itself from almost everything that was real and important. He believed that in cutting itself off from the ordinary affairs of men philosophy not only was making itself a social liability instead of an asset, but was generating utterly meaningless, as well as useless, problems. He wrote of the need for a recovery of philosophy as follows:

"Philosophy recovers itself when it ceases to be a device for dealing with the problems of philosophers, and becomes a method, cultivated by philosophers, for dealing with the problems of men." Again, in the same work he says: "I believe that philosophy in America will be lost between chewing a historic cud long since reduced to woody fiber, or an apologetics for lost causes (lost to natural science), or a scholastic, schematic formalism, unless it can somehow bring to consciousness America's own needs and its own implicit principle of successful action."

The need and principle to which he referred is "the necessity of a deliberate control of policies by the method of intelligence. . . ." By intelligence Dewey always means purposeful activity, not some esoteric inner light that can discover truths apart from activity. Let us sketch briefly some of the main features of his philosophy.

As early as 1904 Dewey and some of his associates at the University of Chicago declared their philosophical faith in a book entitled *Studies in Logical Theory*. The point of view defended there has remained essentially unchanged, although its implications have been traced out in a dozen different fields in the meantime. Ethics, aesthetics, logic, psychology, education, metaphysics, social philosophy — all these and more have received book-length consideration from this untiring worker. It is not our intention to indicate his particular outlook in each of these fields, but if we can catch his general view and get the temper of his approach to things, we shall readily see why he has been influential in nearly every one.

Darwin's theory of evolution played an important role in shaping Dewey's philosophy. The principle of continuity with nature which that theory suggests provided the basis for a theory of mind and of ideas that is basic to the experimental outlook. Just as hands, legs, and other organs of the body are instruments of adaptation to our environment, so "mind" is simply the instrument *par excellence* for adapting us to the world in which we live. Better still, it is an instrument for adapting the world to our needs, for the world is sufficiently plastic to be molded somewhat by intelligence. For Dewey mind is no special "entity" with a special faculty for seeing truths. It is merely a way of referring to the psychophysical organism when it is engaged in purposive behavior. Classical philosophy had too often, he would say, looked upon mind as a special entity endowed with the ability to reflect eternal truths which the universe contained. The job was made difficult because nature spoke to men only through experience which would hardly stand still long enough to be photographed in any eternal mood. In bringing mind down from its Olympian heights, Dewey sought to make intelligence available for action. The tendency to divorce reason from action has had vicious consequences, according to his analysis. Activity goes on in any case; what the world needs is intelligent activity instead of activity *and* intelligence, each going its separate way to the utter disadvantage of both. Reason's preoccupation with the world of eternal truths has left the world of experienced change too often at the mercy of chance instead of design. Men have to live in a changing world, and if human intelligence is to do any good it must be put to work here and now.

Dewey's theory of mind gives him a theory of ideas, which in turn leads to his doctrine of truth. Ideas are best understood as plans of action. In so far as they are meaningful and useful they are not merely idle imaginings, but specific plans for doing something. If the plan of action (idea) succeeds, it is called true; if it fails, it is false — this is the whole meaning of truth and falsity. You will notice that Dewey avoids one error that James courted. Dewey insists that the only consequences which shall count toward the verification of an idea are those which the idea, as a plan of action, intended. No accidental goods which come from acceptance of the idea have any verifying force. This precludes the possibility of saying that a thing is true simply because it is pleasant.

Bertrand Russell has listed Pragmatism along with Nietzsche's theories as a philosophy of power wherein might makes right. Dewey would agree with him that it is a philosophy of power in one sense, namely, that it provides for making intelligence effective and so gives man better control of his destiny, but he would surely disagree that it implies that might makes right. What is "right" is simply an-

The Spirit of American Philosophy 257

other question for intelligence to solve and it can be solved only in terms of weighing all the evidence available. To release intelligence from its servitude to a realm of the eternal and return it to the battlefield of ideas in which men spend their lives is, Dewey would say, the first step toward making "right" meaningful, and values secure.

The theory that ideas are not a mere reflection of things as they are, but plans of action for things that can be, has wide implications. In the first place, as everyone knows, if one interprets ideas as merely plans of future operations no one will be tempted to become too dogmatic about them. Plans are always subject both to change in view of circumstances and to the test of consequences. The spirit of tentativeness which such an outlook produces is admirable in many ways. It is a philosophy of progress for it is an invitation to experiment. Past ideas that have become hardened into absolute certainties are always an invitation to violent revolt when they have lived too long to fit the times; but if they were continually looked upon as hypotheses still subject to the test of consequences, intelligent shifts might be made instead of violent ones. Insistence upon the hypothetical character of all ideas has earned this philosophy the name of "experimentalism." What it amounts to is putting the spirit of science (modern science) into philosophical discussion. Dewey feels that one reason why our social advances lag so far behind those made in some of the sciences is our unwillingness to employ the methods that have been so conspicuously successful in these other fields. The methods of custom and authority still largely prevail when problems of society are concerned.

Applying his experimentalist theory to the field of ethics naturally led Dewey to abandon all forms of authoritarianism in this field. The *best* can never be discovered so long as some past *good* has been taken to be absolute and normative. This is simply one more instance of the idea that intelligence is our best method for solving problems, and that the only kind of intelligence that can be effective is the one illustrated in experimental types of inquiry.

In education Dewey has been tremendously influential, as another chapter in the present volume shows. One of the chief scandals of American education, he thinks, has been an implicit contradiction between its aims and its methods. Democratic America should supposedly be educating for democracy, and yet her methods have been traditionally autocratic. The old school master who crammed "larnin'" down the throats of unwilling pupils by strong-arm methods was hardly imbued with the spirit of real democracy. Only that kind of education can be an effective instrument for democracy which provides for a sharing of interest between the individual and his group, and equips the individual with habits of mind that will secure necessary social change without introducing disorder. In short, schools must practice democracy if they hope to teach it effectively.

In speaking of his interest in social philosophy we mentioned his insistence upon experimental modes of thinking and the spirit of tentativeness which such a method should induce. Another important aspect of this method is its concern with *specific* problems rather than with generalities. Once engage in a discussion about totalitarianism and democracy as purely abstract questions, and thought becomes entangled in a maze of irrelevancies. Not only are the words shot full of emotional overtones which have no pragmatic meaning and lead only to distraction, but they are concepts of such generality as to forbid their translation into plans of action. Hence they are incapable alike of being tested by consequences and of being treated with the sort of tentativeness which hypotheses demand. Fear of losing sight of specific meanings and specific plans of action has led Dewey to fear labels of nearly every kind. That society must be made more socialistic, in the primary meaning of the term, is a truism; but it does not lead him into becoming a *So-*

cialist — or any other "ist." He is fond of pointing out that physical science solves its problems not *in general,* but only in specific situations which obtain here and now. Social science must learn the same technique.

The tendency to solve problems at too general a level has been one of the major sins of philosophy, because it inevitably leads to a false sense of security. As we pointed out in discussing James and the problem of evil, a philosophy which proves that the universe is *really* good is hardly calculated to help make the experienced world better. Its energy has been wasted on the problem of achieving theoretical certainty at the cost of practical security. Dewey dealt with this point at length in his famous book, *The Quest for Certainty.* When that quest leads one to the realm of the eternal, where all is as it should be, the realm of the temporal, where things are often as they should not be, is left to the mercy of chance rather than intelligence. Only by developing the attitude that things are not certain, values not secure unless intelligence steps in to *make* them so, can philosophers do the one thing to which they are adapted. Intelligence must be released from its fruitless quest after imaginary security, and pressed into the service of making things secure in human experience.

There are aspects of Dewey's theory of knowledge that are open to criticism, but we shall not concern ourselves with them here. It is enough that we grasp the major emphases of his outlook. We have seen that he emphasizes the practical in the best meaning of the term. It is a gross distortion of his view to assert that it is "practical" merely in the sense of leading to a "bread and butter" materialism. To secure bread and butter is surely a necessary and practical undertaking, one that is primary to all other undertakings; but to say that such interests exhaust the meaning of his philosophy is to misunderstand its primary concern. All values — physical, spiritual, personal, social — are more likely to be achieved by a method which employs intelligence in the search for them, than by one which leaves them to accident or blind power.

One other phase of Dewey's work that needs to be mentioned is his attitude toward the problem of freedom, about which we spoke in connection with James. Here again Dewey's habit of being specific in his attack upon problems is an outstanding characteristic. He would say that people are not much concerned about the sort of metaphysical freedom which philosophers discuss. Their interest is directed to specific freedoms in political and economic life. Is this man free from political intimidation, or that one free from economic tyranny? Let philosophy ponder these problems and use the right method to make such freedoms factual instead of purely academic realities.

We have called Dewey's philosophy distinctively American. Before summarizing our reasons for this, perhaps a word of caution is necessary. Philosophy, like science, can never be completely nationalistic. Experimental philosophy, such as Dewey advocates, is always subject to trial and verification wherever there are people. Ideas cannot be quarantined; they are public property. However, they do have origins and emphases that are connected with the culture in which they had their origin. Dewey's philosophy bears the stamp of an American and democratic background.

In the first place, it is original with him, although it has close affiliations with the work of James, another American. It exhibits the American talent for getting things done. More especially, it shows a break with the older tradition in philosophy. Such a break was easier in America than elsewhere because this country had no tradition except imported academic ones. Dewey's insistence on human freedom and on the plastic aspect of experience is another indication of his American heritage. Custom counts less than results, both in our country and in his philosophy. Class distinctions, with their implication of the fixity of human nature and custom, are not wholly absent from the American scene, but our history has made us free enough in this respect to make new horizons possible. Our background was more congenial to the breaking of old habits of thought than any European one could have been. Finally, Dewey's philosophy is focused around a completely democratic scheme of things. Truth, beauty, and goodness are not the prerogatives of any special class in a democratic society. They are open to all who have the intelligence to join in their pursuit. A philosophy which turns its back upon custom and authority as special keepers of truth, beauty, and goodness, is the articulate voice of such a society.

The implications of Dewey's philosophy for our democratic way of life must be fairly clear. Education must be open to all, and democratically constructed. Particular injustices which appear because some individual or group of individuals uses power (political, economic, or what not) to constrain the freedom of other groups must be righted. This entails an alertness and a willingness to subscribe to the method of intelligence.

Democracy will survive just so long as it works for the widest interests of those who constitute it. To keep working, it must be constantly alert to the movements within it which make it democratic in name only, rather than in fact. Concentration of power which does not result in more freedom than it usurps, unholy reliance on custom and habit, and indifference to these and other abuses are the constant dangers threatening the democratic way of life. Eternal vigilance and reliance on effective methods of control are both necessary to the continuance of human freedom.

POSTSCRIPT

ON SOME ENEMIES OF DEMOCRACY

By Eugene T. Adams

In the long march of civilization men have bound themselves together, or have been bound together, under various forms of government. Some of these have reduced the individual to a state of slavery. Some have tolerated freedom of the individual within limits. Democracy alone has encouraged the individual to establish and safeguard his own freedom. It alone provides for free criticism of its policies and their periodic ratification by the people, who thus remain masters rather than servants of the state. It alone makes full use of the gift of individuality, the ultimate source of all novelty and progress.

Our American democracy has proved its value in terms of its achievements. Some of these have been recorded and acknowledged here. We Americans are proud of all of them and are eager to defend the way of life which makes them possible. That we shall defend it adequately against the external aggression of any tyrannous autocracy is certain. The call to heroic deeds is usually sufficiently dramatic to insure action, once the foe is recognized. But there are other less obvious enemies of the democratic spirit, against which we must fight not only periodically but incessantly. They lie within our own borders and thrive on our indifference to them. We tolerate them because they are not wholly bad and often wear a countenance of plausibility.

The first of these insidious foes to human freedom is a

stubborn conservatism which refuses to change things even when they stand most patently in need of change. It is a self-defeating conservatism, for it invariably leads to the destruction of those very values which it would conserve. History should teach us once and for all that change will come as surely as tomorrow, and that ours is the task of directing it to profitable ends — not the impossible task of avoiding it altogether. It is a simple truth that democracy will be maintained so long, and just so long, as it serves our common needs. The needs of today are different from those of yesterday, and techniques for dealing with them must shift accordingly. Because we can maintain our democratic processes only by maintaining their effectiveness to meet new situations, blind resistance to change is as dangerous as an irresponsible changing of things to no purpose. Either procedure is unrealistic to the point of self-destruction.

Perhaps the greatest foe of democracy is our own indifference to abuses which arise within it. The growth of monopolistic power is one of these abuses. Such power has always been the foe of freedom, even while presenting itself as a doer of good deeds. When it grows too strong in the economic realm it must be controlled by government. When it grows too strong in the political realm it must be controlled by an alert electorate. The instruments which are used to overcome one tyranny can themselves become tyrannous unless kept from it by a vigilant people jealous of their freedom. Indifference is an open invitation to the abuse of power.

The undemocratic use of power does not always take such striking forms as the word monopoly suggests, but indifference to any expression of power is a costly habit. No violation of our liberties is too slight to warrant our attention and, except in most unusual circumstances, our quick repudiation. No vote was ever coerced, no legitimate idea ever suppressed, no legal behavior ever thwarted, that did not weaken the foundations of democracy itself.

A sterile conservatism and a paralyzing indifference join hands with a third foe of democracy — intolerance. That the will of the majority should find expression is the very essence of democracy, yet our forefathers wisely provided for the protection of minority rights so far as they can be protected by law. But the spirit of democracy must transcend all legalism if it is to remain a positive force. We must become enthusiastic not only about democratic values, but about the means of preserving them. Among the greatest of these values is respect for the rights of others, even when they represent a small minority. The tyranny of great crowds can be quite as malicious as the tyranny of a few people.

It is sometimes said that democracy is weak precisely because of its tolerance. Because it cradles contradictory ideas, some think that it can engender no positive faith. Of our educational system it has been said that the schools are divided against themselves. Progressives hold one point of view, essentialists another. Of government it has been said that we need more centralization of power and that we need less. Of business it has been said that we need more government regulation and that we already have too much. In the midst of such cross currents of opinion, where shall any individual pin his faith?

This brings us to the very heart of the democratic principle. *The supreme faith of democracy is that the strife of ideas is a productive strife,* and that when all individuals actively defend that course which upon investigation seems best to them, the resultant compromise is not weaker but stronger than any alternative decision could be. It is stronger not only because the chaff has been winnowed out in the public forum, but because it gains strength by representing the common will. This is the faith that America has grown strong upon. It is the faith of all those who shun autocracy. It is a positive faith.

Freedom from tyranny is never guaranteed, for there is not one tyranny but many. The very weapons which subdue one tyrannous foe may in their turn prove tyrant, needing themselves to be subdued by weapons fashioned for the hour. Thus freedom is not a gift, but an achievement constantly won anew. We in America speak of our heritage of freedom, and sing our songs of gratitude and praise to those who forged our liberties. But neither gratitude nor praise nor ardent hope can save that heritage unless we ourselves fight the same battles that our fathers fought. The fronts of battle shift and change, new problems ever requiring new techniques; but only the same indomitable spirit and jealous care that first secured our liberties for us can make our liberties secure.

APPENDIX OF SELECTED READINGS

For those who wish to read further on various phases of our American Democracy. Titles marked with an asterisk are more exhaustive studies.

Chapter 1. ON AMERICAN HISTORY

Adams, James T. *The Epic of America.* Boston: Little, Brown and Company, 1931.
Schlesinger, A. M. *New Viewpoints in American History.* New York: The Macmillan Company, 1922.
*Beard, Charles A. and Mary. *The Rise of American Civilization* (2 vols.). New York: The Macmillan Company, 1930.
*Morison, S. E., and Commager, H. S. *The Growth of the American Republic.* London: Oxford University Press, 1930.
*McLaughlin, A. C. *Steps in the Development of American Democracy.* New York: Abingdon Press, 1920.
*Becker, Carl. *The Declaration of Independence.* New York: Harcourt, Brace and Company, 1922.
Smith, Bernard (editor). *The Democratic Spirit.* (A source book.) New York: Alfred A. Knopf, 1941.

Chapter 2. AMERICAN DEMOCRACY AND AMERICAN GOVERNMENT

Merriam, Charles E. *The New Democracy and the New Despotism.* New York: McGraw-Hill Book Company, Inc., 1939.
Sait, Edward M. *Democracy.* New York: D. Appleton-Century Company, 1929.
*Tead, Ordway. *New Adventures in Democracy.* New York: McGraw-Hill Book Company, Inc., 1939.
*Friedreck, C. J. *Constitutional Government and Politics.* New York: Harper & Brothers, 1937.
*Griffith, Ernest S. *The Impasse of Democracy.* New York: Harrison-Hilton Books, Inc., 1939.
*Lippmann, Walter. *The Good Society.* Boston: Little, Brown and Company, 1939.

Chapter 3. DEMOCRACY IN THE AMERICAN ECONOMY

Arnold, Thurman. *The Folklore of Capitalism.* New Haven: Yale University Press, 1938.

Kallett, Arthur, and Schlink, F. J. *100,000,000 Guinea Pigs.* New York: Grosset and Dunlap, 1933.

Ware, Caroline F., and Means, Gardiner C. *The Modern Economy in Action.* New York: Harcourt, Brace and Company, 1936.

*Burns, Arthur E. *Decline of Competition.* New York: McGraw-Hill Book Company, Inc., 1936.

*Koontz, Harold D. *Government Control of Business.* Boston: Houghton Mifflin Company, 1941.

*Robbins, Lionel. *Economic Planning and International Order.* London: Macmillan and Company, Limited, 1937.

Chapter 4. THE SPIRIT OF AMERICAN SCIENCE

Barnal, J. D. *The Social Function of Science.* New York: The Macmillan Company, 1941.

Davis, Watson (editor). *The Advance of Science.* New York: Doubleday, Doran and Company, 1934.

Crowther, J. G. *The Social Relations of Science.* New York: The Macmillan Company, 1941.

Crowther, J. G. *Famous American Men of Science.* New York: W. W. Norton and Co., Inc., 1937.

French, S. J. *Torch and Crucible.* Princeton: Princeton University Press, 1941.

Chapter 5. THE SPIRIT OF AMERICAN ART

Watson, Forbes. *American Painting Today.* Washington, D. C.: American Federation of Arts, 1941.

Cahill, Hoger, and Barr, Alfred, Jr. (editors). *Art in America in Modern Times.* New York: Reynal and Hitchcock, 1934.

LaFollette, Suzanne. *Art in America.* New York: Harper & Brothers, 1929.

Neuhaus, Eugen. *The History and Ideals of American Art.* Palo Alto, California: Stanford University Press, 1931.

Isham, Samuel, and Cortissoz, Royal. *The History of American Painting.* New York: The Macmillan Company, 1936.

Boswell, Peyton, Jr. *Modern American Painting.* New York: Dodd, Mead & Company, 1939.

Chapter 6. DEMOCRACY IN MODERN AMERICAN LITERATURE

Anthologies, Collections, Series: Harper, Oxford University Press, Houghton Mifflin, American Book Company, and other publishers have anthologies of American literature available at reasonable cost.

The reader who wishes to probe more deeply into the life and writings of a major American author will find *The American Writers Series,* H. H. Clark, general editor, one of the most satisfactory of several series.

History and Criticism—
Blankenship, Russell. *American Literature.* New York: Henry Holt and Company, 1931.
Brooks, Van Wyck. *The Flowering of New England.* New York: E. P. Dutton and Company, 1936; *New England: Indian Summer.* New York: E. P. Dutton and Company, 1940.
Hicks, G. *The Great Tradition.* New York: The Macmillan Company, 1933.
Lewisohn, L. *The Story of American Literature.* New York: The Modern Library, 1939.
*Parrington, V. L. *Main Currents in American Thought.* New York: Harcourt, Brace and Company, 1930. (Revised edition.)
Taylor, W. F. *A History of American Letters.* New York: American Book Company, 1936.

Chapter 7. THE SPIRIT OF AMERICAN EDUCATION

The Educational Policies Commission. *The Purpose of Education in American Democracy.* 1201 Sixteenth St., N. W., Washington, D. C.
*Ulrich, Robert. *Fundamentals of Democratic Education: an Introduction to Educational Philosophy.* New York: American Book Company, 1940.
*Washburn, Carleton. *A Living Philosophy of Education.* New York: John Day & Company, 1940.
*Dewey, John. *Education Today.* Edited by Joseph Ratner. New York: G. P. Putnam's Sons, 1940.

Chapter 8. THE SPIRIT OF AMERICAN RELIGION

Brown, William Adams. *Church and State in Contemporary America.* New York: Charles Scribner's Sons, 1936.

Hall, Thomas Cuming. *The Religious Background of American Culture.* Boston: Little, Brown and Company, 1930.

Holt, Arthur Erastus. *Christian Roots of Democracy in America.* New York: Missionary Education Movement, 1941.

Niebuhr, Helmut Richard. *The Kingdom of God in America.* Chicago: Willett, Clark and Company, 1937.

Finkelstein, Louis; Ross, J. Elliot, and Brown, William Adams. *Religions of Democracy; Judaism, Catholicism and Protestantism in Creed and Life.* New York: Devin-Adair, 1941.

Chapter 9. THE SPIRIT OF AMERICAN PHILOSOPHY

Smith, Thomas V. *Democratic Way of Life.* Chicago: University of Chicago Press, 1939.

Feibleman, James K. *Positive Democracy.* Chapel Hill, N. C.: University of North Carolina Press, 1940.

*Dewey, John. *Philosophy and Civilization.* New York: Minton, Balch and Company, 1931.

*Muelder, Walter G., and Sears, Laurence (editors). *The Development of American Philosophy.* Boston: Houghton Mifflin Company, 1940.

INDEX

Acts of Trade, 22
Adams, John, 35, 97, 238
Adams, Samuel, 32
Adamson Act, 42
Age of Reason, 239
Age of Reason, the, in education, 185, 198; in philosophy, 237–239
Agricultural Adjustment Administration, 58
Alcott, Bronson, 157, 239
Alcott, Louisa, 165
Allen, Ethan, 25, 237, 239
American democracy, historical background of, 8 ff.; basic assumption of, 10, 47, 264; principles of, 10–11, 264; principles vs. form of, 12; steps in development of, 15 ff.; restrictions of, 19, 20, 29, 80; Jeffersonian, 34–35; and the West, 35, 36; Jacksonian, 36–37; and American government, 46 ff.; and American economy, 64 ff.; and American science, 94 ff.; and American art, 120 ff.; and American literature, 153 ff.; and education, 181 ff.; and religion, 204 ff.; and philosophy, 233 ff.; enemies of, 262 ff.
American Gothic, 140
American Revolution, 12, 13, 21, 25, 39, 40, 51, 98, 189, 205, 210, 214
American Scholar, The, 241
American Tragedy, An, 171, 175
Anderson, Maxwell, 168, 177
Anderson, Sherwood, 170
Anna Christie, 176
Anti-Semitism, 218
Arrowsmith, 168
Art, and the Calvinistic spirit, 120, 128; realists in, 120–134, 136 ff.; and the American character, 121 ff.; European influence, 125, 145; and the academic tradition, 127; journalism in, 131, 132; humor in, 134, 151; imaginative, 147, 148, 149; women in, 150, 151
Articles of Confederation, 26, 27, 30
Astronomy, 105
Atlantic Monthly, 162, 167
Augustine, 234–235
Authoritarianism, 62, 63, 66; and the economic system, 69; and education, 197, 198; and philosophy, 261

Babbitt, 168
Bacon, Peggy, 150
Baeyer, Adolph von, 101
Baker, George Pierce, 175
Baltimore, Lord, 213
Baptist Church, 212
Beard, Charles A., 39
Becker, Carl, 21
Becquerel, Henri, 106
Bell, Alexander Graham, 99
Bellows, George, 129, 130, 131, 132
Benton, Thomas, 140, 142
Bernal, J. D., 116
Between Rounds, 131
Beyond the Horizon, 175
Bill of Rights, 54, 55, 204
Bingham, Caleb, 120, 121, 122, 123, 124, 125, 130, 150
Bohrod, Aaron, 147
Boothe, Clare, 177, 178
Boston, 168
Boston Tea Party, 23
Bound East for Cardiff, 174
Boyle, Robert, 100, 101
Brass Check, The, 168
British, see England.
Brook, Alexander, 147
Brooklyn Daily Eagle, 154
Bryan, William Jennings, 41, 158

Burbank, Luther, 99
Burchfield, Charles, 136, 137, 138, 150
Business enterprise, 69, 71, 72, 86

Cadmus, Paul, 143, 144, 145
Caldwell, Erskine, 171
California, 169, 178, 179
Calvin, Calvinism, in art, 120 ff.; and literature, 173; in religion, 206, 220, 223, 235, 236, 237, 238, 239, 241, 243; and philosophy, 234–237
Canada, 57, 59, 64
Capital goods, 78, 79
Capitalism and Calvinism, 227, 236
Carlyle, 242
Carnegie, 105
Carolinas, 17
Carroll, Charles, 214
Carroll, Daniel, 214
Catholics, 204, 205, 212–218, 220, 229; and education, 185, 186
C.C.C., 192, 195
Chamberlain, T. C., 112
Channing, W. E., 224
Chekov, 173
Chemistry, 102, 103, 104, 106, 111
Chicago, 160
Christian Century, The, 229
Christian Science, 222
Church, and state, 204, 207, 216, 217; of England, 205, 209–210; Congregational, 206, 212, 215; separate view of, 207; Protestant Episcopal, 211; Lutheran, 211–212; Baptist, 212; Catholic, 212–218; and education, 217; Unitarian, 224
Civil liberties, 54, 55, 56, 57, 204, 234, 238
Civil service, 53
Civil War, 39, 61, 156, 170, 179, 245
Clayton Anti-Trust Act, 42
Coercive Acts, 23
Coleman, Samuel, 124
Colonies, 16 ff.
Communism and religion, 220
Congregationalism, 206, 212, 215
Congress, 14, 28, 29, 31, 50, 51, 52, 53, 62, 189
Connecticut, 17, 23, 187, 188

Connecticut Yankee, The, 165
Conrad, Joseph, 175
Conservatism, 263, 264
Constitution, the, 9, 10, 11, 30, 31, 32, 33, 34, 48, 50, 61; and the courts, 51, 52, 54, 57, 58, 62; and science, 91, 113; and education, 185; and religion, 204, 209
Constitutions, written, 12, 13, 15; revolutionary, 25
Cook, Joseph, 247
Coolidge, Calvin, 43
Corn Is Green, The, 174
Corporations, as political prototypes, 17; in the economic system, 82, 85
Cotton, John, 206
Crane, Ichabod, 187
Crane, Stephen, 167, 169, 170, 175, 177
Crawford, Broderick, 178
Crawford, F. Marion, 166
Criticism and fiction, 166
Cromwell, 213
Crowther, J. G., 102
Cullom Interstate Commerce Act, 41–42
Curie, Marie, 100, 106
Curry, John S., 140, 141, 142

Dalton, John, 100
Darwin, Charles, 98, 100, 103, 235, 242, 255
Daughters of the Revolution, 141
Davy, Sir Humphry, 100
Declaration of Independence, 10, 23, 24, 30, 31, 61, 214, 231, 238
Democracy, see American democracy.
Democratic Vistas, 153, 156
Dempsey, Jack, 131
Desire Under the Elms, 176
Dewey, John, 200, 201, 203, 233–234, 243, 247, 248, 249, 250, 253–261
Dial, 242
Dictatorship, see Authoritarianism.
Dissent, see Separatists.
Divinity School Address, 241
Division of power, 14, 15, 57
Dodsworth, 168, 169
Dos Passos, 153, 169
Dostoevski, 166

Index

Dreiser, Theodore, 153, 159, 170, 171, 175
Due process, 57
Dun and Bradstreet, 84
DuPont, Eleuthère Irénée, 98

Eakins, Thomas, 120, 121, 125–129, 130, 131, 132, 138, 140, 148, 150
Economics, 64 ff.; and American wealth, 64; and democracy, 65, 66; and scarcity, 67; and price system, 69 ff.; and politics, 73, 74; and distribution of wealth, 76, 77; and capital goods, 78, 79, 80; and consumer, 80; and labor, 83, 86, 87; and government, 88 ff.
Ecumenical movement, 229
Eddy, Mary Baker, 222
Edison, Thomas A., 95, 99, 107, 110
Education, 181 ff.; equal opportunity for, 181, 189–191; diversity in, 182; democracy in, 182; early schools, 183, 184; and religion, 183 ff.; secularization of, 184–187; centralization of control of, 187–189; function of, 192–197; methods of, 197 ff.; and essentialists, 200 ff.; and progressivism, 200 ff.; and philosophy, 258
Edwards, Jonathan, 224, 235–236, 237
Einstein, Albert, 96, 103, 115
Elections, 13, 14, 47, 48
Emerson, Ralph Waldo, 1, 5, 126, 146, 155, 162, 163, 224, 239–243
Emperor Jones, The, 176
England, and American colonies, 12 ff.; and American government, 50 ff.; and American economy, 66; and scientific research, 116; and American art, 122, 123; and American political philosophy, 237, 238
Epistemology, 248
Ethics, 256–258
Europe, and American history, 12 ff.; and American government, 50 ff.; and American economy, 66, 69, 70; and American science, 97 ff.; and American art, 122, 123, 124, 128, 131, 135, 141, 145, 146, 147, 149; and American literature, 164, 166,

169, 173, 174; and American education, 193; and American religion, 205 ff.; and American philosophy, 234, 240, 244, 245
Evangeline, 163
Evolution and philosophy, 242–244, 255–257
Experimentalism, in education, 200 ff.; in religion, 209, 220, 226; in philosophy, 233, 247 ff., 254–261

Famous American Men of Science, 102
Faraday, Michael, 95, 98, 100, 101, 102, 103, 106
Faulkner, William, 171
Federal Council of Churches of Christ in America, 229
Federal Farm Loan Act, 42
Federal Reserve Act, 42
Federal Trade Commission Act, 42
Federalism, 57–59; beginnings of, in America, 18, 21; Articles of Confederation, 26, 27; perfected form of, 30
Federalist party, 32, 33, 38
Feudalism, 19
Fields, W. C., 165
Firpo, Luis, 131
Fiske, John, 244
Fitzsimmons, Thomas, 214
Flaubert, 169
Fog, 160
For Whom the Bell Tolls, 171
Ford, Henry, 107, 108, 109
Forty-Two Kids, 132
France, 166, 169
Franklin, Benjamin, 94–96, 153, 154, 183, 189, 193, 194, 237
Free private enterprise, 69, 72, 75, 91, 92
Freedom, of speech, 56, 234; political, 62, 63; individual, 65, 238, 260, 262, 263, 265; and the economic system, 67, 68, 69; limitations, 80, 81, 82, 83, 84; and American Science, 98, 115, 116; and art, 151, 152; and literature, 180; and education, 200–203; of religious expression, 204 ff.; as essential to democracy, 262 ff.

274 Index

Freedom of the will, 252, 260
Frontier, political, 20; and the growth of individualism, 66; and art, 122 ff.; in literature, 161, 164
Frost, Robert, 153, 160, 161
Fulton, Robert, 99

Garland, Hamlin, 167, 168, 169
George, Henry, 164, 167
George III, 95, 101
Georgia, 20
Germany, 55, 69, 100, 101, 102, 103, 104, 106, 107, 109, 110, 115, 116, 119, 244, 245
Gibbons, Archbishop, 215
Gibbs, J. Willard, 103–104
Goodrich, Samuel G., 188
Gould, Jay, 164
Government, Jeffersonian conception of, 34, 35; machinery of, 47, 52; claims upon, 49; and the individual, 54, 57, 60, 62; and economic regulation, 87–91; and education, 191, 192, 195; as a monopoly, 263
Grapes of Wrath, 169, 178
Green, Paul, 177
Guggenheim, 105

Hamilton, Alexander, 30, 32, 34, 35, 41
Hancock, John, 32
Harding, Warren G., 43
Harper's Weekly, 123
Harris, William T., 200, 245, 246
Harte, Bret, 157, 179
Hauptmann, 173
Hay, John, 157
Hegel, George, 245, 246
Heisenberg, Werner, 115
Hemingway, Ernest, 170, 171
Henry, Patrick, 32
Henry VIII, 205
Hiawatha, 161
Higginson, 206
High school, 194 ff.
Hitler, Adolf, 55, 115, 116
Holmes, Oliver Wendell, 162
Holmes, Justice Oliver Wendell, 253
Homer, 241
Homer, Winslow, 120, 121, 123, 125, 130, 131, 140, 151
Hoover, Herbert, 43

Hopper, Edward, 136, 137, 138, 140, 150
Howard, Sidney, 177
Howells, William Dean, 154, 162, 163, 164, 166, 167
Huckleberry Finn, 165
Humanism, and education, 198; and religion, 225

Ibsen, 173, 179
Idealism, 244–247
Imagism, 159
Imperialism, British, 25, 26, 51; in literature, 158
Individualism, 34, 40, 122, 163, 246
Innocents Abroad, 164
Institute of Higher Learning, 109
Interior, 174
Interstate Commerce Commission, 53
Intuition, 240, 241
Invention in America, 99, 105
Italy, 69

Jackson, Andrew, 36, 37, 157, 160
James, Henry, 167, 252
James, Jesse, 248
James, William, 233–234, 241, 242, 243, 246, 247, 248–254, 256, 260
Japan, 64
Jefferson, Thomas, 10, 20, 29, 32, 33, 34, 35, 37, 41, 61, 97, 154, 185, 232, 237, 238
Jerome, William Travers, III, 1
Jews, 185, 204, 218–219, 220, 229
Jim Bludso of the Prairie Belle, 157
Joan of Arc, 165
Journal of Speculative Philosophy, 245
Judaism, 218, 219
Judd, Dr. Charles, 201
Judicial review, 51, 52, 62
Jumping Frog of Calaveras, The, 164
Jungle, The, 168

Kalamazoo Decision, 191
Kansas-Nebraska Act, 39
Kant, 245
Kaufman, George, 178
Kekulé, August, 101
Know-Nothing Party, 214
Ku Klux Klan, 214

Labor unions, 85, 86, 87
Langmuir, Irving, 112
Lanier, Sidney, 157, 158, 161
Laplace, P. S., 104, 112
Lardner, Ring, 121
Latin Grammar Schools, 183, 193, 198
Lavoisier, Antoine, 98, 100, 101
Lawrence, Ernest, 112
Lazaron, Rabbi, 219
League of Nations, 27
Leaves of Grass, 154, 157, 161
Lee, Doris, 150
Lee, Richard Henry, 32
Lewis, Gilbert, 111
Lewis, Sinclair, 141, 168, 169
Liberty, see Freedom.
Liebig, Justus, 100, 101
Lincoln, Abraham, 39, 155, 160, 189
Lindsay, Vachel, 159
Lobbies, 49
Locke, John, 10, 22, 97, 237, 238
Longfellow, Henry Wadsworth, 157, 161, 162, 163
Look Homeward Angel, 172
Lowell, Amy, 153, 159
Lowell, James Russell, 154, 157
Lucioni, Luigi, 146, 147
Luks, George, 131, 132, 133, 134, 135, 150
Lusitania, 173
Lutherans, Lutheranism, 211–212
Lynd and Lynd, 199, 200

Maeterlinck, 174
Maggie, 170
Main Street, 168
Main-Travelled Roads, 167
Maine, 123
Man That Corrupted Hadleyburg, The, 166
Man with the Hoe, The, 158, 167
Mann, Horace, 185, 217
Markham, Edwin, 158, 167
Marsh, Reginal, 143, 144, 147
Marshall, John, 37, 52
Marshes of Glynn, The, 157
Maryland, 17, 24, 213–214
Massachusetts, 17, 19, 20, 23, 32, 185, 206, 207
Massachusetts Bay Company, 17, 206
Masters, Edgar Lee, 159

Maxwell, Clerk, 100, 103
McCormick, Cyrus, 99
McKinley, William, 42, 43
Mein Kampf, 115
Meliorism, 251
Melville, Herman, 153, 171
Mencken, H. L., 177
Mending Wall, 160
Michelson, A. A., 111
Middletown, 199
Midwest, in art, 139 ff.; in literature, 159, 160
Millikan, Robert, 111
Miniver Cheevy, 159
Monopoly, 263; political, 56; economic, 84, 87; as enemy of democracy, 263
Monroe, Harriet, 158
Monroe, James, 36
Monte Cristo, 175
Montesquieu, 50
Moody, Dwight L., 222
Moody, William Vaughn, 158
Mormons, Mormonism, 221–222
Morrison, C. C., 229
Morse, Samuel F., 99
Moulton, Forest R., 112
Mourning Becomes Electra, 176
Mussolini, Benito, 116
Mysterious Stranger, The, 166

Napoleon, 116
Nathan, George Jean, 174
National Conference of Christians and Jews, 219
National income, 64; distribution of, 77
National Relations Board, 53
Natural rights, 55, 232, 238
New Deal, the, 43–45
New England, in art, 146; in literature, 160, 161; in education, 183 ff.; religion of, 205–209, 215; in philosophy, 234 ff.
New Freedom, the, 42
New Hampshire, 16, 23, 32, 159
New Nationalism, the, 42
New York, 32, 51, 133, 134
New York City, 15, 143, 185
Newton, Sir Isaac, 97, 98, 100, 101, 102, 103
Nietzsche, 256

Index

Nobel, Alfred, 114
Nobel Prize in literature, 168
Norris, Frank, 167
North, the, 38, 39, 48
North Carolina, 32, 171, 177
Northeast, the, 36, 38, 39, 41
Northwest Ordinance, 27, 28, 29
N.Y.A., 192, 195

Ode in Time of Hesitation, An, 158
Odets, Clifford, 177
Oenslager, 178
Of Mice and Men, 178
Of Time and the River, 172
Ohio, 29
Old Times on the Mississippi, 165
On a Soldier Fallen in the Philippines, 158
One and the many, 26; in philosophy, 252–253
O'Neill, Eugene, 174–177, 179
Ostwald, Wilhelm, 101
Our Town, 178

Paine, Thomas, 155, 237, 239
Pal Joey, 174
Parkhurst, Helen, 200
Pasteur, Louis, 100
Pauper schools, 189, 190
Pennsylvania, 17, 24, 25, 189, 193, 194, 236
Philosophy, and American culture, 233 ff.; and religion, 234–237; and politics, 238–239, 252, 253; and science, 240, 243, 255; and the academic tradition, 244–246; and experience, 249 ff.; and education, 258
Physics, 106, 108, 111
Pilgrims, 206, 215
Poe, Edgar Allan, 148
Poet, The, 241
Poetry: A Magazine of Verse, 158
Political parties, 48, 49, 55
Populist party, 40, 41
Portrait painting, 129
Pragmatism, *see* Experimentalism.
Prairie Folks, 167
Price system, 70, 71, 72, 73; compared to political system, 73, 74; and the consumer, 75
Priestley, Joseph, 96, 100

Prince and the Pauper, The, 165
Princeton University, 175
Problem of evil, 247, 251, 259
Progressive party, 42
Propaganda, and art, 151, 152; and literature, 168
Proposals Relating to Education of Youth in Pennsylvania, 193
Protestant Episcopal Church, 211
Protestants, Protestantism, 204, 214, 217, 218, 220, 225, 229
Pulitzer Prize, 179
Pupin, Michael, 96
Puritanism, in art, 120, 128, 139 ff.; in literature, 173; and religion, 205, 206, 213, 220, 223–224; and philosophy, 234–237

Quakers, 217, 236
Quest for Certainty, The, 259

Radical empiricism, 249
Ramsay, Sir Andrew, 106
Real Thing, The, 167
Realism, in art, 120 ff.; in literature, 170 ff.; in philosophy, 247
Red Badge of Courage, The, 170
Religion, 204 ff.; freedom of, 204; European influence on, 205 ff., 210; tolerance in, 206, 208–209; theocratic form, 206, 207; Revolutionary War, 210; and denominationalism, 211 ff.; Catholic form of, 213 ff.; Judaistic form of, 218, 219; laymen in, 220–223; and social gospel, 226, 227, 228; and totalitarianism, 229, 230
Remington, Frederic, 124, 125, 130
Republican party, 39; and rugged individualism, 40
Revolution, right of, 11, 23; second American, 40; literary, 153 ff.
  See also American Revolution.
Rhode Island, 17, 23, 32, 207
Rice, Elmer, 177
Rights, human vs. property, 10; property, 79, 80, 81
  See also Natural rights.
Ripley, George, 239
Roberts, Justice Owen, 58
Robinson, E. A., 153, 159, 160, 161
Robinson, John, 215

Index

Rockefeller, John D., 105, 164
Romains, Jules, 170
Roosevelt, Franklin D., 43, 44
Roosevelt, Theodore, 42, 43, 125
Roughing It, 164
Royce, 246
Russell, Bertrand, 256
Russia, 69, 116, 117
Ryder, Albert Pinkham, 148, 149

Sacco-Vanzetti case, 168
San Francisco Examiner, 158
Sandburg, Carl, 153, 160, 161
Sandys, Sir Edwin, 16
Santayana, George, 138, 241
Sargent, John Singer, 128, 129
Saroyan, William, 177, 179
Scarcity, the problem of, 67
Scheele, Carl W., 100
Schnitzler, 173
Schopenhauer, 177
Schroedinger, Erwin, 115
Science, American contributions to, 94 ff.; and democracy, 94; and war, 110, 115; and German politics, 115, 116; and philosophy, 257
Scott, Walter, 157
Seabury, Samuel, 211
Self-Reliance, 241
Separation of powers, 14, 50, 52
Separatists, Separatism, 205, 207
Seward, Gov. William, 186
Shahn, Ben, 143, 145
Shakespeare, 148, 179
Shaw, Bernard, 173
Sherman Anti-Trust Act, 42
Sherwood, Robert, 179
Short History of Chemistry, A, 106
Shuster, George N., 213
Sim Burns' Wife, 167
Sinclair, Upton, 168
Sister Carrie, 171
Sloan, John, 131, 132, 133, 134, 135, 150
Smith, Adam, 90
Smith, Joseph, 221
Social Function of Science, The, 116
Social gospel, 227–228
Social security, 59
Soddy, F., 106
Sommerfield, Arnold F., 115
Song of Myself, 155

South, the, 18, 36, 37, 38, 48; and the Civil War, 39; in literature, 157, 158; and education, 190
South Carolina, 24
Soyer, Raphael, 146, 147
Spencer, Herbert, 243, 244
Spielers, The, 134
Spoon River, 159
Stag at Sharkey's, A, 131
Steenbrook, Harry, 112
Steinbeck, John, 168, 169, 177, 178, 179
Steinmetz, Charles P., 96
Strindberg, 173
Stuart, Gilbert, 121
Studies in Logical Theory, 255
Sullivan, John L., 160
Sundermann, 173
Supreme Court, 14, 253; and the Constitution, 51; powers of, 52
Suzzalo, Henry, 182
Swimming Hole, The, 127
Swinburne, 157
Synge, 173

Taking the Count, 131
Tarkington, Booth, 167
Taxation, 20, 22
Tempest, 179
Theocracy, 206, 207, 235, 236, 237
There Shall Be No Night, 179
They Knew What They Wanted, 177
Thomas Aquinas, 186
Thomson, Sir Joseph, 106
Thoreau, Henry David, 153, 157, 240
Time of Your Life, The, 179
Tolerance, in New England religion, 206, 208–209; and experimentalism, 220, 225, 234, 264
Tom Sawyer, 149, 162, 165
Torch and Crucible, 98
Tories, 21
Tornado Over Kansas, 141
Totalitarianism, 9; and the economic system, 69, 70; and science, 115, 116; and art, 151, 152; and religion, 230; and philosophy, 252–253
Transcendentalism, 239–243
Truth, 55, 233, 250, 251, 253, 256

Twain, Mark, 122, 149, 154, 162, 166–167, 172, 247
Two-party system, 48
Tyranny, 264, 265

Underwood Tariff Act, 42
Unitarianism, 224
University of Chicago, 158, 200
Untermeyer, Louis, 160
Urey, Harold, 112
Utah, 221

Vanderbilt, Cornelius, 163
Venable, F. R., 106
Verdict of the People, A, 124
Verdun, 170
Vermont, 25; in art, 146; in literature, 160, 161
Victorian Age in art, 136
Villon, François, 174
Virginia, 16, 18, 32, 36, 37, 209–211
Virginia Company, 16
Voters, 28, 29, 30, 55, 56, 264

Warner, Charles Dudley, 164
Washburn, Carlton, 200
Washington, George, 32, 141
Watt, James, 99
Wealth of Nations, The, 90
Welles, Orson, 177
Wells, H. G., 196
West, Benjamin, 121

West, the, 20, 25, 27, 33, 35, 36, 38; in art, 124; in literature, 157, 158, 162, 169
What Is Man? 166
What Price Glory, 177
Whistler, James McNeil, 128, 162
Whitman, Walt, 126, 153–157, 158, 159, 160, 169, 242
Whitney, Eli, 99
Whittier, John G., 157, 162, 166
Wilder, Thornton, 177, 178
Will to Believe, The, 251
Williams, Roger, 207, 235
Willkie, Wendell, 68
Wilson, Woodrow, 42, 43
Winterset, 168, 177
Wöhler, 101
Wolfe, Thomas, 138, 171, 172
Women, The, 178
Women painters, 150, 151
Wood, Grant, 139, 140, 141, 150
World War I, 110, 171, 194
W.P.A, 192, 195
Wright Brothers, the, 114
Wurtz, A., 101

Y.M.C.A., 220
You Can't Go Home Again, 172
Young, Brigham, 221
Y.W.C.A., 220

Zola, 169